NEW YORK
Yankees
FIRSTS

NEW YORK
Yankees
FIRSTS

The PLAYERS MOMENTS and RECORDS
That Were FIRST in TEAM HISTORY

HOWIE KARPIN

LYONS
PRESS

Essex, Connecticut

An imprint of Globe Pequot, the trade division of
The Rowman & Littlefield Publishing Group, Inc.
4501 Forbes Blvd., Ste. 200
Lanham, MD 20706
www.rowman.com

Distributed by NATIONAL BOOK NETWORK

British Library Cataloguing in Publication Information available

Library of Congress Cataloging-in-Publication Data available
Names: Karpin, Howie, 1954– author.
Title: New York Yankees firsts : the players, moments, and records that
  were first in team history / Howie Karpin.
Description: Essex, Connecticut : Lyons Press, [2023] | Includes
  bibliographical references.
Identifiers: LCCN 2022046148 (print) | LCCN 2022046149 (ebook) | ISBN
  9781493068456 (trade paperback) | ISBN 9781493075478 (epub)
Subjects: LCSH: New York Yankees (Baseball team)—History. |
  Baseball—Records—New York (State)—New York.
Classification: LCC GV875.N4 K374 2023 (print) | LCC GV875.N4 (ebook) |
  DDC 796.357/64097471—dc23/eng/20220929
LC record available at https://lccn.loc.gov/2022046148
LC ebook record available at https://lccn.loc.gov/2022046149

♾™ The paper used in this publication meets the minimum requirements of American National
Standard for Information Sciences—Permanence of Paper for Printed Library Materials, ANSI/
NISO Z39.48-1992.

CONTENTS

INTRODUCTION

A FIRST OF SOMETHING IS ALWAYS SPECIAL. A FIRST CAN BE A MEMORA-ble experience like a first car, a first job, or maybe a first date. If you're fortunate to become a parent, having a child is a special moment, but the first one is really special.

As a baseball fan, you remember your first game. We can recall the first time we walked in a ballpark or witnessed something special, especially if you shared those first moments with family.

One thing we know for sure: A first of something can only happen once. In baseball, for the players, a first game, first hit, or first home run will be forever etched in their memories. For a pitcher, a first team, first batter faced, first strikeout, first win, or first save will be a memorable experience.

There are many fascinating firsts littered throughout the glorious history of the Yankees. Derek Jeter was the first Yankee to get 3,000 hits, but what other first in Yankee history has his name on it? Babe Ruth was the first to hit a home run at the original Yankee Stadium, but what other first in Yankee history is he responsible for?

New York Yankees Firsts is sorted into four chapters: First Award Winners, Stadium Firsts, Postseason Firsts, and Other Notable Firsts.

First Award Winners goes deeper than just the MVP or Cy Young. Stadium Firsts encompasses the three versions of Yankee Stadium, along with Shea Stadium, where the Yankees played their home games in 1974 and 1975. Other Notable Firsts accounts for the unusual, record-setting, and memorable first events in Yankee franchise history.

Who was the first Yankee pitcher to throw an immaculate inning? Who was the first Yankee to win the World Series MVP Award without

1

hitting a home run? Can you name the first Yankee to win the Home Run Derby?

There are many Yankee firsts for each of the three versions of Yankee Stadium, including, the first Yankee hit, first Yankee home run at Stadiums II and III, and the first Yankee winning pitcher.

Did you ever wonder who pitched the first no-hitter by a Yankee in the original Yankee Stadium, who was the first Yankee to hit for the cycle at Yankee Stadium II, or who was the first Yankee winning pitcher at the current Stadium?

New York Yankees Firsts has questions about Yankee firsts in postseason play, along with award winners.

Most fans, young and old, know that Don Larsen pitched a perfect game in the World Series, but who had the Yankees' first hit in that game? A walkoff home run, much less a walkoff hit, doesn't happen often in World Series play. The first Yankee to have a walkoff home run to win a World Series game had a very special moment because it had never been done before.

The first Yankee to win the American League Rookie of the Year Award can always say he was the first in that category. The first Yankee to win back-to-back American League Most Valuable Player awards may be one of the Yankees' all-time greats; then again, he may not be.

New York Yankees Firsts will not only feature the all-time greats, but also the less heralded Yankees who played important roles in franchise history. For every Mariano Rivera and Mickey Mantle, there is a Ray Keating or Shane Spencer.

Whether you are a longtime devotee of the Bronx Bombers or a young fan just getting to know the men in pinstripes, this book will lead you on a journey through some great and not-so-great moments in New York Yankees history.

FIRST AWARD WINNERS

Baseball has a number of prestigious awards for both pitchers and hitters. There haven't been many, if any, awards that a Yankee has not won. Let's see how well you know your Yankee first award winners.

Who was the first Yankee to win the American League Most Valuable Player Award? Bonus: Name the first Yankee second baseman to win the award.

In 1923, the immortal Babe Ruth was the first Yankee to win the American League's Most Valuable Player Award.

Ruth's numbers were typically off the charts in 1923. The Bambino had a slash line of .393/.545/.764 with 41 home runs, 130 RBIs, and 151 runs scored as the Yankees cruised to the American League pennant. Ruth also walked 170 times and finished with a 14.2 WAR.

Some of Ruth's highlights during his 1923 MVP season included hitting the first home run to christen Yankee Stadium when it opened on April 18, and a late September game at Fenway Park in which he had five hits including a home run and drove in three to lead the Yankees to a 24–4 win over the Boston Red Sox.

Ruth came to the Yankees from the Red Sox in a controversial transaction. Red Sox owner Harry Frazee needed money and sold Ruth's contract to Yankees owner Jacob Ruppert for $100,000.

Ruth played 15 of his 22 major-league seasons with the Yankees. The "Sultan of Swat" hit 714 career home runs, a record that stood until 1974 when it was broken by Hall of Famer Hank Aaron.

Babe Ruth in 1922
WIKIMEDIA COMMONS

In 1927, Ruth became the first player in major-league history to hit 60 home runs. The Babe reached the milestone on September 30 against the Washington Senators at Yankee Stadium.

In the bottom of the eighth inning, the game was tied at 2 and Ruth faced Senators pitcher Tom Zachary. Before a reported crowd of 8,000 fans, the Bambino hit a 1-1 pitch into the right field seats for the milestone home run.

Ruth still holds Major League Baseball's all-time career records with a .690 slugging percentage, a 1.164 OPS, and 206 OPS+.

The Yankees retired Ruth's #3 in 1948. In 1949, the Yankees honored their all-time great with a monument in center field to join the ones already there for Miller Huggins and Lou Gehrig.

In 1942, Hall of Famer Joe Gordon became the first Yankee second baseman to win the AL MVP Award. Gordon hit .322 with 18 home runs and 103 runs batted in to beat out Boston's Ted Williams, who had a Triple Crown season with a .356 average, 36 home runs, and 137 RBIs. The Yankees finished nine games ahead of the Red Sox in the standings.

The Sacramento, California, native signed with the Yankees in 1936 and reported to the Oakland Oaks of the Pacific Coast League, where he hit .300 in 143 games.

In 1937, Gordon reported to spring training with the Yankees in St. Petersburg. Tony Lazzeri, the incumbent second baseman, knew the Yankees were grooming Gordon to take his place. Nonetheless, the classy Hall of Famer did his best to help the youngster. Lazzeri was released after the 1937 season and Gordon became the starting second baseman in 1938.

Gordon consistently put up good numbers with the Yankees that culminated with his MVP season of 1942. He played seven of his 11 major-league seasons with the Yankees from 1938 to 1945. He was a six-time All-Star with the Yankees and won four World Series championships.

In his first season, Gordon hit 25 home runs and had 97 RBIs. One of Gordon's highlights in his first season was a two-run, inside the park home run on June 20 against the St. Louis Browns at Sportsman's Park. In a game at Detroit's Briggs Stadium in August, Gordon hit a two-run home run in the top of the 11th inning as the Yankees beat the Tigers, 10–7.

The 23-year-old rookie shined in his first World Series appearance. In the four-game sweep of the Chicago Cubs, Gordon batted .400 with a home run and six runs batted in.

Gordon was even better in his sophomore season of 1939. The Yankees' second baseman raised his batting average from .255 in 1938 to .284 in 1939. He hit 28 home runs and had 111 RBIs, his best total as a Yankee, and was named an All-Star for the first time.

In the 1941 World Series win against the Brooklyn Dodgers, Gordon hit .500 in the five-game series with a home run and seven runs batted in. He also had seven walks and did not strike out in 14 at-bats.

In the fateful ninth inning of Game 4, Gordon's two-run double gave the Yankees a 7–4 cushion. Gordon may never have come to bat, if not for Dodgers catcher Mickey Owen's famous gaffe.

With two out and no one on, Tommy Henrich appeared to strike out swinging to end the game, but Owen missed the ball and the Yankees right fielder was allowed to reach to keep the game alive. After the Yankees, took the lead, Gordon's clutch hit later in the inning made it a three-run margin, and the Yankees went on to win Game 4 and the Series in five.

After the 1941 season, the United States entered World War II and many players were pressed into military service.

Gordon had a tough time in the 1942 World Series loss to the St. Louis Cardinals. The Yankee second baseman hit .095 as the Yankees lost in five games. The Yankees rebounded to beat the Cardinals in the 1943 World Series. Gordon had at least one hit in each of the first four games.

Gordon missed the 1944 and 1945 seasons due to military service, but he returned to the Yankees in 1946 and his numbers took a drastic turn downward.

In 1946, Gordon had a rough start to the season as he suffered a hand injury in spring training that required surgery. A torn leg muscle and a fractured hand really limited Gordon's production as he batted a career low .210. After the season, the Yankees traded Gordon to the Cleveland Indians in exchange for pitcher Allie Reynolds. The trade worked out well for both teams.

In 1948, Gordon hit 32 home runs and had a career-high 124 RBIs to help Cleveland win the World Series. Reynolds helped the Yankees win six World Series championships.

The Yankees have had nine Rookie of the Year Award winners in their history. Who was the first Yankee to be named Rookie of the Year?

In 1951, infielder Gil McDougald became the first Yankee to win the Rookie of the Year Award. The 22-year-old posted a slash line of .306/.396/.488 with an OPS of .884, all top-10 numbers in the American League. His batting average led the Yankees, and he became a key member of the team that won their third consecutive World Series championship.

McDougald played his entire 10-year career with the Yankees. The San Francisco native played on eight American League pennant winners and five world championship teams in New York and was a six-time All-Star.

McDougald was invited to spring training in 1951 and impressed Yankee manager Casey Stengel with his versatility. There was some question about McDougald's batting stance, which was unorthodox, but effective. Stengel told the *New York Times*, "There ain't anything wrong with the way he swings it."

In the first nine games of the 1951 season, McDougald got only one at-bat. The Yankees already had Jerry Coleman at second base and Bobby Brown at third base. The Korean War was on so some of the players were subject to military service. Second baseman Billy Martin was drafted, but he was discharged and was returning to the team, fueling speculation that McDougald would be sent down to the Yankees' Triple-A affiliate in Kansas City. Stengel stuck with his young infielder, and the loyalty began to pay off because McDougald started to justify his manager's faith in him.

McDougald was the starting third baseman in 1952 and made the All-Star team for the first time. He appeared in 152 games, mostly at third, and his numbers dropped off from his first season, but he helped the Yankees to their fourth consecutive World Series championship. In Game 7 of the 1952 World Series, McDougald had two hits and scored a run in the Yanks' win over the Brooklyn Dodgers at Ebbets Field.

McDougald experienced two traumatic incidents that, in all likelihood, cut short his career.

In 1955, McDougald was struck by a batted ball during batting practice just behind his left ear off the bat off Bob Cerv. McDougald was initially diagnosed with a concussion, but he began to lose hearing in his left ear. Later on, he lost his hearing in the right ear as well (40 years later, McDougald had a revolutionary cochlear implant that restored some of his hearing).

Two years later, McDougald's career nearly came to an end. On May 7, 1957, the Yankees were playing the Cleveland Indians at Cleveland Stadium. In the top of the first inning, McDougald hit a line drive that struck Indians starting pitcher Herb Score in his right eye. The ball bounded to Indians third baseman Al Smith, who threw to first for the out. McDougald was so distraught, he never ran all the way to first.

Score's face was bloodied, and he was eventually transported to a local hospital with numerous facial fractures. There was some concern that Score might lose the sight in his eye. After the game, McDougald was quoted as saying, "If Herb loses the sight in his eye, I am going to quit the game."

Score, who was the 1955 American League Rookie of the Year and a promising 24-year-old pitcher on the rise, was really never the same after the incident. According to multiple reports, Score's mother phoned McDougald to assure him that the family did not blame him and that he should continue playing.

The accident haunted McDougald for the remainder of his career because he never stopped blaming himself. "I guess I didn't pray hard enough," McDougald, a devout Catholic, would say after he learned that Score was sent back to the minors in 1961 when he was attempting to resurrect his career with the Chicago White Sox.

McDougald continued playing as the Yankees' starting shortstop in 1957, but he was being pushed by a highly regarded prospect named Tony Kubek. The 22-year-old Kubek played most of his games in the outfield and won the 1957 American League Rookie of the Year Award, but he was being pegged to take over at shortstop in 1958.

McDougald moved to second base in 1958, but Bobby Richardson was the heir apparent and became the starter in 1959. McDougald saw the writing on the wall as the Yankees were transitioning to a younger infield.

Despite his diminishing role, McDougald continued to make subtle contributions as the Yankees continued to win with him in the lineup.

After the Yankees lost the 1957 World Series in seven games to the Milwaukee Braves, McDougald played a big role in the rematch in 1958. Yankee pitcher Bob Turley was named the Series MVP but it easily could have gone to McDougald.

The Yankees trailed the Series three games to two with Games 6 and 7 scheduled for Milwaukee. With Game 6 tied at 2 in the top of the 10th, McDougald led off with a home run off of Braves pitcher and Hall of Famer Warren Spahn to give the Yankees a 3–2 lead. The Yankees added a run and won the game, 4–3 in 10 innings, to force Game 7.

In Game 7, McDougald had two more hits but he was also superb in the field. McDougald handled nine chances (three putouts, six assists, one double play) flawlessly at second base to back Turley's relief effort (one run in 6.2 IP), as the Yankees became the second team and the first American League club to rally from a three games to one deficit to win the Series.

In McDougald's final season of 1960, his opportunities lessened even further as he played in a career-low 119 games and had a career low of 337 at-bats.

McDougald appeared in six of the seven World Series games against the Pittsburgh Pirates in 1960. In Game 7, McDougald entered the game in the ninth inning as a pinch-runner and scored the tying run on Yogi Berra's groundout. Bill Mazeroski's famous home run ended the game in the bottom of the ninth in what turned out to be McDougald's final game.

Baseball was expanding in 1961 and McDougald was left off the Yankees' protected list for the upcoming expansion draft. McDougald was not chosen by either the New York Mets or the Houston Colt .45s, and he decided to retire in December 1960. McDougald said he had his mind made up during the World Series, and that being left unprotected was not the reason that he decided to retire.

Three Yankees have won back-to-back Most Valuable Player awards. Who was the first Yankee to be a back-to-back winner?

In 1954 and 1955, Hall of Famer Yogi Berra was voted the American League's Most Valuable Player, making him the first Yankee to win the prestigious award in back-to-back seasons. Berra had previously won the award in 1951.

Berra caught 149 games in 1954 and produced a slash line of .307/.367/.488, with an OPS of .855, 22 home runs, and a career-high 125 RBIs. The Yankees finished in second place, three games behind the Cleveland Indians, but Berra still copped the award in a close vote over Hall of Famer and Cleveland Indians outfielder Larry Doby.

Berra's overall numbers dipped slightly in 1955 (.272/.349/.470, OPS .819), but he edged out Hall of Famer and Detroit Tigers outfielder Al Kaline in the voting.

Berra is the greatest catcher in franchise history and is widely regarded to be the second-best catcher in baseball history, behind Hall of Famer Johnny Bench. Berra could always hit, but, in his early years, he had to work on his defense behind the plate and eventually put it all together to become a leader on the field.

The St. Louis native played 18 seasons with the Yankees and played in a record 14 World Series while winning a record 10 world championships. Berra was an 18-time All-Star, and, to this day, he still holds a number of World Series records including most games (75), most hits (71), and most wins with 10.

Berra signed with the Yankees, who assigned him to Norfolk in the Piedmont League for the 1943 season. After serving two years in World War II, where he saw action at Normandy on D-Day, June 6, 1944, Berra

Yogi Berra with backup catcher Gus Niarhos
COURTESY OF THE BOSTON PUBLIC LIBRARY, LESLIE JONES COLLECTION

was assigned to the Newark Bears, the Yankees' Triple-A affiliate in the International League.

Berra was a September callup and made his major-league debut on September 22, 1946, against the Philadelphia Athletics in the first game of a doubleheader at Yankee Stadium. In his second major-league at-bat, Berra hit his first major-league home run, a two-run shot off of Athletics pitcher Jason Flores in the fourth inning.

Berra's career really took off when the Yankees hired manager Casey Stengel in 1949. Berra was taking criticism in his first few years, not only for his defensive play, but, at 5'7" and 185 pounds, he wasn't exactly an athletic-looking player. Berra also had what was described as an awkward-looking swing and he would swing at balls out of the zone, but Stengel would not be deterred. It was not a coincidence that Berra's emergence as a star catcher combined with Stengel's hiring coincided with an unprecedented five straight World Series titles.

Berra had established himself as a clutch hitter, but he really broke out in the 1953 World Series win over the Brooklyn Dodgers. Berra batted .429/.538/.619 for an OPS of 1.158 with a home run and four runs batted in.

In the seventh and deciding game of the 1956 World Series against the Dodgers at Ebbets Field, Berra hit two home runs off of Brooklyn pitcher Don Newcombe to power a 9–0 win. Berra had three home runs and 10 runs batted in during the seven games. Obviously, winning the Series was most important to the greatest winner in baseball history, but he always felt the highlight for him was catching Don Larsen's perfect game in Game 5 at Yankee Stadium.

In the latter years of his career, Berra began to see more time in the outfield. In those years, there was no designated hitter rule and Elston Howard had taken over the starting catcher's job, so in order to keep an aging Berra in the lineup, he played in the outfield.

After the Yankees lost the 1963 World Series to the Los Angeles Dodgers, Berra retired as a player and was named the manager for the 1964 season when the previous manager, Ralph Houk, moved up to the front office as the general manager.

Berra led the Yankees to the 1964 World Series, where they lost to the St. Louis Cardinals in seven games. Berra's fate had already been decided by management before the World Series began, and the Yankees fired him after the loss. Houk later admitted that the decision had been made in August.

Berra went on to join the New York Mets as a coach in 1965. He also played in four more games, catching in two of them as a 40-year-old, and was in uniform when the Mets won the World Series in 1969 (and in 1973 when he managed the team to the National League pennant).

Berra's success labeled him a good-luck charm. He returned to the Yankees as a coach in 1976, and they went on to win three straight American League pennants and two world championships.

Berra returned for a second stint as Yankee manager in 1984 and was fired by owner George Steinbrenner only 16 games into the 1985 season. Berra felt so insulted that Steinbrenner sent a member of his staff to give him the news, instead of telling him face-to-face, that he was estranged from the Yankees until 1999. Steinbrenner, who admitted later on that firing Berra was one of his worst mistakes, apologized and made amends with Yogi.

The Yankees held a Yogi Berra Day on July 18, 1999 and invited Don Larsen to be one of the guests, asking him to throw out the ceremonial first pitch to Berra so that they would re-create the final pitch of the perfect game. It was also the day that David Cone pitched a perfect game against the Montreal Expos.

Berra became well known for his malapropisms, or "Yogisms." Some of his tautologies somehow made sense. Quotes like, "It ain't over 'til it's over," and "It's getting late, early," have made their way into the American lexicon.

Berra was inducted into the Baseball Hall of Fame in 1972 and his #8 was retired (also for Bill Dickey) on July 22, 1972.

Mickey Mantle was the Yankees' second back-to-back winner in 1956 and 1957.

In 1956, Mantle won the Triple Crown by leading the league in batting average (.353), home runs (52), and runs batted in (130). The switch-hitter beat out Ted Williams for the award in 1957, despite the

Boston Hall of Famer leading the American League with a .388 batting average, along with a .526 on-base percentage and a .731 slugging percentage for an OPS of 1.257.

Roger Maris was the third Yankee who won back-to-back MVP awards, in 1960 and 1961.

Who am I? I was the first Yankee manager to be a two-time winner of the Manager of the Year Award. Bonus: Name the only other Yankee manager to win the award.

Hall of Fame manager Joe Torre was the first Yankee manager to be a two-time winner of the Manager of the Year Award.

Torre won the award in 1996 when he led the Yankees to their first American League Eastern Division title in 15 years, and 1998, when the Yankees set an American League record (since broken) with 114 regular-season wins. In both years, the Yankees went on to win the World Series.

Torre is a baseball lifer who had an outstanding playing career and a Hall of Fame managerial career. He's the only person to have 2,000 hits as a player and 2,000 wins as a manager. Most of that Hall of Fame managerial resumé was a result of his success with the Yankees, where he managed for 12 years from 1996 to 2007 and never missed the playoffs.

After three previous stints as a manager with the New York Mets, Atlanta Braves, and St. Louis Cardinals, Torre was hired by Yankee owner George Steinbrenner following the 1995 season. The Yankees had just been eliminated in a heartbreaking five-game series against the Seattle Mariners, so Steinbrenner fired manager Buck Showalter and replaced him with Torre. Many felt Showalter should not have been fired, so the hire was met with some controversy including a famous headline that adorned the back page of the *New York Daily News*, "Clueless Joe."

Torre dispelled any doubts as he led the Yankees to their first World Series championship in 18 years. The Yankees won the division and then, after not having a playoff win as a manager, Torre beat the Texas Rangers and Baltimore Orioles to reach the World Series for the first time in his baseball career.

Joe Torre
WIKIMEDIA COMMONS

In the 1996 World Series against Torre's former team, the Atlanta Braves, the Yankees lost the first two games at Yankee Stadium but rebounded to win the next four and claim the championship.

In 1997, the Yankees were eliminated by the Cleveland Indians in five games in the American League Divisional Series, but they rebounded in 1998 at a record-setting pace. Winning a record 114 games set the Yankees up as the heavy favorites to win the World Series. After sweeping the Texas Rangers in the divisional series, the Yankees found themselves trailing the Indians two games to one in the American League Championship Series, but they rallied to win in six games. The Yankees went on to win their second World Series in three seasons as they swept the National League champion San Diego Padres in four straight.

The Yankees repeated in 1999 and capped it off by beating the Braves for a second time in four seasons. This time, the Yankees swept the Braves in four straight, but it wasn't an easy season for Torre, who was diagnosed with prostate cancer before the season began and missed the first 36 games. Bench coach Don Zimmer served as the interim manager

(21-15) before Torre returned on May 18 in the first of a three-game series against the Red Sox at Fenway Park. The classy Boston fans gave the Yankee manager a two-minute standing ovation when he came out to exchange the lineup card.

In 2000, Torre would win a third straight American League pennant and face another one of his old teams in the World Series, but this time it was the crosstown New York Mets. The first "Subway Series" in 44 years would pit the Yankees against the Mets, but with an impetuous owner who did not like losing to the Mets, there was enormous pressure on Torre and the team.

The Yankees beat the Mets in five games to win their third straight World Series, and fourth in the last five seasons. Torre would take the Yankees to two more World Series appearances, but they would lose to the Arizona Diamondbacks and Florida Marlins in 2001 and 2003, respectively. The Yankees would also make the playoffs in each of Torre's final four seasons as the manager, but they would come up short each time.

Torre's 1,173 wins with the Yankees is second in franchise history behind Joe McCarthy's 1,460. Torre won 10 division titles, six American League pennants, and is second to McCarthy and Casey Stengel with four World Series championships.

On July 27, 2014, Torre was inducted into the Baseball Hall of Fame as a manager. A little less than a month later, the Yankees retired Torre's #6 on Joe Torre Day.

The only other Yankee manager to win the award was Buck Showalter in 1994.

Showalter managed in the Yankees farm system in the late 1980s. He was promoted to the Yankees as a coach in 1990 and 1991 and then was named manager in 1992.

In Showalter's first season, the Yankees finished under .500. It was the fourth straight season that the Yankees posted a losing record, but that streak ended in 1993 when the Yankees won 88 games under Showalter.

In 1994, Showalter had the Yankees in first place in the American League East in August, but the baseball strike ended any hopes of making a postseason run.

Five Yankees have won a Silver Slugger and Gold Glove Award in the same season. Who was the first Yankee to win both awards in the same year?

One of the most accomplished athletes to ever wear the Yankee pinstripes, Hall of Famer Dave Winfield became the first Yankee to win the Silver Slugger and Gold Glove Award in the same season in 1982. During parts of nine seasons with the Yankees, Winfield won five Silver Sluggers and five Gold Glove awards.

Winfield grew up in St. Paul, Minnesota, and was a two-sport (baseball and basketball) star at St. Paul Central High School. After being drafted as a 17-year-old by the Baltimore Orioles in the 40th round of the 1969 MLB June Amateur Draft, Winfield did not sign and made a decision to attend the University of Minnesota on a half baseball scholarship.

In his junior and senior seasons, Winfield played for the basketball team on a full scholarship. Following his senior season, Winfield was chosen by four different teams in four different leagues in three sports. The Atlanta Hawks chose Winfield in the fifth round of the National Basketball Association Draft while the Utah Stars selected him with their fourth round pick of the American Basketball Association Draft. Winfield's hometown Minnesota Vikings also chose him in the 17th round of the NFL Draft. Winfield ended up signing with the San Diego Padres, who made him the fourth overall pick of the 1973 MLB June Amateur Draft.

The 6'6" Winfield played eight seasons in San Diego and was a four-time All-Star, but the Padres had only one winning season. After the 1980 season, Winfield became a free agent and signed what was then a record 10-year, $123 million contract to join the Yankees for the 1981 season.

Winfield played parts of nine seasons with the Yankees and made eight All-Star teams, but he was at odds with Yankee owner George Steinbrenner over a contract dispute. A compromise was reached, but Winfield continued to play under a cloud of controversy.

Winfield had a pretty good first season with the Yankees in 1981, posting a slash line of .294/.360/.464 with an OPS of .824, despite a strike-shortened season that limited him to 105 games played.

16

The Yankees beat the Milwaukee Brewers in five games in the 1981 American League Division Series. Winfield slashed .350/.381/.550 with an OPS of .931, but he had a tough time for the rest of his first postseason, including the six-game loss to the Los Angeles Dodgers in the 1981 World Series.

The 29-year-old Winfield was 1-for-22 in the Series, which did not sit well with the owner. Steinbrenner signed Winfield to be the heir apparent to 35-year-old Reggie Jackson, who was an impending free agent and was injured during the Series and only played in three games. What irked Steinbrenner even more was when Winfield finally got a hit in the fifth game to snap a 0-for-16 skid, he sarcastically asked for the ball. The Yankees would have only one losing record during Winfield's tenure, but 1981 would be the only time that the talented outfielder would play in the postseason.

In 1984, Winfield and teammate Don Mattingly were locked in a tight battle for the American League batting title. The Yankees were out of the race for the division title, so the pursuit of the batting title became the focus of the media and the fans down the stretch. It turned into a bitter pursuit for Winfield because some teammates and Yankee brass were openly rooting for Mattingly. Winfield led Mattingly on the final day by two percentage points (.341 to .339), but he went 1-for-4 to finish at .340 while the Yankee first baseman had four hits to end up at .343.

After Mattingly singled in his final at-bat in the eighth inning, he was forced out at second on Winfield's grounder to third. Scott Bradley pinch-ran for Winfield, so he was able to leave the field with Mattingly in a show of support for each other, as the fans gave them both a standing ovation. Winfield was upset with the unfair treatment he had received during the season and was not available after the game.

In the next few years, Steinbrenner tried to trade Winfield, but his contract featured a no-trade clause for the first five years so he had veto power over any potential deal. In 1987, Steinbrenner tried to send Winfield to the Detroit Tigers for outfielder Kirk Gibson, but by that time, the Yankee outfielder had a right to veto because he had accumulated 10 years in the majors and had five with the same team.

Despite the distractions, Winfield continued to play well. In 1988, he batted .322 with 25 home runs and 107 runs batted in, while finishing fourth in the voting for the American League's Most Valuable Player Award.

Winfield missed the entire 1989 season due to a herniated disc in his back. He returned to start the 1990 season but got off to a slow start. In May, the Yankees traded Winfield to the California Angels for pitcher Mike Witt, but he refused the deal claiming the right to veto because of the 10 and 5 rule. The Angels stepped in and offered a three-year contract extension and Winfield accepted the trade, ending a tumultuous time in New York.

Winfield retired in 1996 and was elected to the Baseball Hall of Fame in 2001.

The other four Yankees who won Silver Slugger and Gold Glove awards in the same season include Mattingly, Wade Boggs, Derek Jeter, and Robinson Canó.

Name the first Yankee to win the All-Star MVP award.

Hall of Famer Derek Jeter was the first Yankee to win the All-Star Most Valuable Player Award.

Jeter went 3-for-3 with two runs batted in and a run scored in the American League's 6–3 win over the National League in the 2000 All-Star Game at Atlanta's Turner Field. The game also marked the first time that Jeter started the game.

Among his many accomplishments, Jeter was a 14-time All-Star and always played well in the All-Star Game.

In the 2001 game at Seattle's Safeco Field, Jeter hit his first All-Star home run. The Yankee shortstop led off the sixth inning with a solo shot on a 3-0 pitch from Chicago Cubs pitcher Jon Lieber.

In 2004, at Houston's Minute Maid Park, Jeter had his second three-hit game in an All-Star Game. Ironically, Jeter lost out on a second All-Star MVP Award to his former teammate, Alfonso Soriano (two hits, HR, three RBI), who had been traded to Texas in the previous offseason for Alex Rodriguez.

Jeter played in his final All-Star Game in 2014 at Minnesota's Target Field and went 2-for-2. Jeter had announced that 2014 was going to be his last season, so the crowd of 41,886 roared and his fellow All-Stars applauded when he was introduced as the leadoff batter in the American League lineup.

The first batter of the game was Pittsburgh Pirates center fielder Andrew McCutchen, and he lined one toward the middle that Jeter dove for, got up, and threw a little late to first. McCutchen respectfully smiled as Jeter nearly made a tremendous defensive play to start the game.

When he came to bat in the bottom of the first, the familiar voice of the late Bob Sheppard's recorded introduction that featured his melodic "number two" played at Target Field. Jeter tipped his hat to the crowd who were giving him a standing ovation.

Derek Jeter
CLARE AND BEN VIA WIKIMEDIA COMMONS

In the top of the fourth, Jeter came out to his position to be saluted by the crowd one more time. He left the field before the inning began, hugged his replacement at shortstop, Alexei Ramírez of the Chicago White Sox, and headed toward the dugout as the crowd again came to their feet. The game was paused for a few moments as Jeter was being congratulated and getting hugs from his AL All-Star teammates and coaches, and finally, there was a curtain call before the game resumed.

From the "flip play" in the 2001 American League Division Series to his walkoff home run to end Game 4 of the 2001 World Series, Jeter has provided numerous highlights and thrills throughout the 20 years that he played for the Yankees.

In 1996, Jeter was the American League's Rookie of the Year. He was a 14-time All-Star, five-time Gold Glove winner, and five-time Silver Slugger Award winner. Jeter is the Yankees' all-time leader in games played (2,747), hits (3,465), and stolen bases (358).

On July 9, 2011, at Yankee Stadium, Jeter became the first Yankee to reach 3,000 hits when he homered off of Tampa Bay pitcher David Price in the third inning. Jeter went 5-for-5 in that game and his final hit, an RBI single in the eighth inning, drove in what proved to be the winning run in a 5–4 win against the Rays.

In his final home game on September 25, 2014, Jeter hit a walkoff RBI single in the bottom of the ninth to give the Yankees a 6–5 win. It was also Jeter's final game at shortstop.

Jeter played two more games against the Boston Red Sox at Fenway Park as a designated hitter. In his final at-bat, Jeter had an infield single that drove in a run. Brian McCann pinch-ran for Jeter, who got a huge ovation from the respectful Red Sox fans as he left the field for the final time.

Hall of Fame closer Mariano Rivera and Giancarlo Stanton are the only other Yankees to win the award. Rivera was named All-Star MVP in the 2013 game at Citi Field. Stanton hit a mammoth home run in the 2022 All-Star Game at Dodger Stadium and was named the MVP.

Rivera is deemed the greatest closer in the history of baseball. The native of Panama holds the major-league record with 652 saves and was a 13-time All-Star and five-time World Series champion.

Rivera was at his best in the postseason. The Hall of Famer pitched in 96 postseason games and recorded 42 saves with an ERA of 0.70.

Who was the first Yankee catcher to win a Gold Glove Award?

In 1963, Elston Howard became the first Yankee catcher to win the Gold Glove Award. More importantly, the classy Howard was the first African-American player to don a Yankee uniform.

As a 19-year-old, Howard played outfield and first base with the famed Kansas City Monarchs of the Negro American League in 1948. Hall of Famer Buck O'Neil, who was Howard's manager, tipped off Yankee scout Tom Greenwade (who was famous for signing Mickey Mantle) about his young phenom.

The Yankees signed Howard and assigned him to the Class A affiliate at Muskegon, Michigan. Howard had a solid season, but he would spend the next two years in the military and two more years in the minors before the Yankees would promote him.

Howard made his major-league debut in April 1955 and was accepted by the players from the start. Yogi Berra and Phil Rizzuto invited the 26-year-old rookie to dine and socialize with the team.

Hank Bauer, an ex-Marine, took Howard under his wing and deflected some of the ignorant and racist remarks that were being directed toward the young player from the stands. Bauer would be the first to answer those remarks in his own way. When he was asked why he was sticking up for his teammate, Bauer made it a point to say it was because Howard was his friend.

In his first few seasons, Howard was not a regular player. Yogi Berra, who was in his prime, was the starting catcher and the outfield spots were taken by Bauer, Mickey Mantle, and Irv Noren. Some felt manager Casey Stengel was shunning Howard because he was Black. It didn't help that Stengel made racially insensitive remarks to Howard in front of the team.

In the 1955 World Series against the Brooklyn Dodgers, Howard hit a home run in his first World Series at-bat. Unfortunately, he also made the final out of that series.

The next season, Stengel started Enos Slaughter in the first six games of the World Series against the Dodgers, but he played a hunch

Elston Howard, center, with Jim Gentile and Norm Cash at Fenway Park for the 1961 All-Star Game
COURTESY OF THE BOSTON PUBLIC LIBRARY, LESLIE JONES COLLECTION

and started Howard in Game 7 at Ebbets Field. It was Howard's only appearance in the Series, and he probably won some points with Stengel. Howard had two big hits, including a solo home run to lead off the fourth inning against Dodgers pitcher Don Newcombe, as the Yanks captured the Series.

Howard started to get more playing time in 1957 and was named by Stengel, who was the American League manager, to his first All-Star team.

Howard's skills were on full display in the 1958 World Series. The Yankees were trailing the Milwaukee Braves, three games to one. In Game 5 at Yankee Stadium, the Yankees led the Braves 1–0 in the sixth inning, but Milwaukee had the tying run on first with no one out. Milwaukee's Red Schoendienst hit a sinking liner to left field. Howard dove forward and made a great play to catch the ball. He then got up and threw to first to double up the Braves' Bill Bruton in what many called a turning point in the Series. The Yankees won Games 5 and 6 and for the second straight year, the clubs were headed to a seventh game.

The game was tied at 2 in the top of the eighth, when Howard singled to score Berra with the go-ahead run as the Yankees went on to win the game and the Series. Howard's performance earned him the New York Baseball Writers Chapter's Babe Ruth Award as the outstanding player in the Series.

From 1957 to 1965, Howard made the All-Star team every year and played in 12 All-Star Games. (From 1959 to 1962, there were two All-Star Games played in each season.)

After the Yankees lost to the Pittsburgh Pirates in the 1960 World Series, manager Casey Stengel was fired and replaced by Ralph Houk. With the new manager on board for the 1961 season, Howard caught 111 games, while Houk began using Berra a little more in left field.

The native of St. Louis, Missouri, had a great year in 1961 but was overshadowed by Roger Maris and Mickey Mantle's pursuit of Babe Ruth's 60-home-run mark. Howard's slash line was a career-best .348/.387/.549 with an OPS of .936. Howard had 21 home runs with 77 RBI while he finished 10th in the MVP voting.

After the 1961 season, the Yankees were being pressured to segregate, so they changed their spring training home from St. Petersburg to Fort Lauderdale, Florida, for the 1962 season. The team's headquarters hotel in St. Pete would not house African-American players, so the decision was made to leave after 31 years.

In 1962, Howard compiled a career-high 91 runs batted in. That included the greatest single game in Howard's career. On August 19, 1962, Howard had four hits, four runs scored, two home runs, and a career-high eight runs batted in as the Yankees smashed the Kansas City Athletics, 21–7, at Municipal Stadium.

In 1963, Howard became the first African-American player to win the American League's Most Valuable Player Award. The Yankee catcher batted .287 with a career-high 28 home runs while winning his first of two Gold Glove awards. Howard garnered 15 of 20 first-place votes to beat out Detroit Tigers outfielder Al Kaline.

Howard was the only Yankee who did anything in the 1963 World Series against the Los Angeles Dodgers' formidable pitching led by Hall of Famers Sandy Koufax and Don Drysdale. In the four-game loss, Howard had a team-leading five hits and drove in one of the four runs that the Yankees scored all series.

Howard had one more big season in 1964 when he hit .313 with 15 home runs and 84 RBIs. During the offseason, the Yankees made a managerial change after they lost the 1964 World Series to the St. Louis Cardinals. Johnny Keane, who was the Cardinals manager, replaced Yogi Berra as the manager.

In the first spring training under Keane, Howard injured his elbow and didn't return until mid-June. Howard's numbers steadily declined in 1965, 1966, and 1967.

On August 3, 1967, the Yankees traded the 38-year-old Howard to the rival Boston Red Sox for a player to be named later that turned out to be pitcher Ron Klimkowski. Howard helped Boston win the American League pennant and retired after the 1968 season.

Howard returned to the Yankees as a first base coach from 1969 to 1979. His #32 was retired by the Yankees in 1984.

A number of Yankees have won the American League Pitcher of the Month Award since its inception in 1979. Who was the first Yankee pitcher to be named AL Pitcher of the Month?

Tommy John was the first Yankee pitcher to be named AL Pitcher of the Month.

John captured the award in April 1979 at the age of 36 when he posted a 4-0 record with a 1.12 ERA in five starts. John got off to a 9-0 start and finished with a sparkling 21-9 record and a 2.96 ERA. He finished second in the American League Cy Young Award voting to Baltimore Orioles pitcher Mike Flanagan, who won 23 games with a 3.08 ERA.

John is famous for being the first to undergo a revolutionary procedure that saved his baseball career and became known as "Tommy John surgery."

In 1974, the 31-year-old John, who was with the Dodgers, was in his 12th season and was 13-3 in mid-July when he hurt a ligament in his throwing elbow. His career seemed to be over until Dr. Frank Jobe performed an operation and replaced the ligament with a tendon from John's right forearm.

John missed all of the 1975 season and returned to the mound in April 1976 and made 31 starts. The crafty left-hander won 20 games in 1977 and pitched against the Yankees in the 1977 and 1978 World Series.

After the 1978 season, the 36-year-old John signed with the Yankees as a free agent for the first of two stints. In his first two seasons with the Yankees in 1979 and 1980, John made 73 starts and was a combined 43-18.

John did not blow away hitters with a 95-mph fastball, but he had good stuff and was able to use his experience and guile to get hitters out over a 26-year major-league career.

A near tragedy in August 1981 put the Yankee pitcher into the headlines. John's two-year-old son, Travis, fell out of a window and plummeted three stories and was in a coma for about two weeks. John received an enormous amount of support from all around the country, including a get well card to Travis from President Ronald Reagan.

The Yankees gave John permission to be with his son, so he only pitched in home games for a short time. Travis recovered and John resumed his normal routine with the Yankees.

In the 1981 World Series, the Yankees faced John's former team, the Dodgers. The left-hander started Game 2 and pitched seven shutout innings against his former team as the Yankees took a 2–0 series lead.

The Yankees lost the next three, but they had John on the mound for Game 6 at Yankee Stadium. He pitched one-run ball over the first four innings, but in a controversial move, Yankee manager Bob Lemon pinch-hit for John in the bottom of the fourth with the game tied at 1.

There were runners on first and second with two out, so Lemon went to Bobby Murcer who flied out to end the inning. The Dodgers went on to score seven runs over the next two innings against an ineffective

Yankee bullpen to put the game and the Series away. Lemon was widely criticized for taking John out so early in a tie game.

John was 39 years old when he had an up and down season in 1982. By the end of August, John was 10-10 with a 3.66 ERA, but he was also involved in a contract dispute with the Yankees. At the trade deadline on August 31, the Yankees traded John to the California Angels in exchange for 23-year-old, 6'7" left-handed pitcher Dennis Rasmussen.

After parts of four seasons with the Angels and a half season with the Oakland Athletics in 1985, John was unsigned for the 1986 season. Believing he could still pitch at the age of 43, John went to spring training with the Yankees but did not make the team. Injuries plagued the Yankee rotation so John was signed in May, but the veteran missed two months due to an Achilles tendon injury.

When he returned in August, John put together back-to-back outings of shutout ball, totaling 15 innings. In early September, John injured his left thumb in a fall and was done for the season. John would go on to pitch in three more seasons for the Yankees.

In his final major-league season of 1989, the 45-year-old John was the Yankees' Opening Day starter against the Minnesota Twins and reigning American League Cy Young Award winner Frank Viola at the Metrodome. John outpitched Viola as he gave up two runs in seven innings in a 4–2 win. John had one more solid outing but struggled mightily in May and was released by the Yankees at the end of the month.

Ron Guidry won the American League Player of the Month Award in June and September 1978. There was no AL Pitcher of the Month Award in existence yet.

Name the first Yankee second baseman to win the Gold Glove Award.
In 1961, Bobby Richardson became the first Yankee second baseman to win a Gold Glove Award. For five straight seasons, from 1961 to 1965, Richardson was deemed the best-fielding second baseman in the American League.

Richardson played parts of 12 seasons with the Yankees from 1955 to 1966 and established himself as one of the best second basemen in franchise history. Besides being a five-time Gold Glove winner, Richardson was an eight-time All-Star and played in seven World Series, winning three.

Richardson made his professional debut as a 17-year-old in 1953. Two years later, Richardson was promoted to the Yankees. Gil McDougald was injured, so the young second baseman made his major-league debut on August 5, 1955, against the Detroit Tigers at Yankee Stadium.

Richardson batted second, behind Hank Bauer and in front of Hall of Famer Mickey Mantle. In the fourth inning, Richardson walked and scored on Yogi Berra's three-run home run as the Yankees beat the Tigers, 3–0. Richardson got his first big-league hit in the seventh inning when he singled off Tigers rookie pitcher and Hall of Famer Jim Bunning.

In his first two seasons of 1955 and 1956, Richardson played in a total of 16 games. In 1957, the Sumter, South Carolina, native began to get more playing time and was an All-Star for the first time.

Richardson's breakout season came in 1959 when he hit .301 and was the only Yankee to hit over .300 that season. Richardson, who was an All-Star for the second time, came into the final day at .298, but he had two hits in the final game of the season to finish at .301.

In the 1960 World Series loss to the Pittsburgh Pirates, Richardson began to make his mark as a player who thrived in the Fall Classic.

In Game 2 at Pittsburgh's Forbes Field, Richardson had three hits, two RBIs, and three runs scored. In the top of the sixth, Richardson had two hits in one inning to tie a World Series record as the Yankees evened the Series with a 16–3 win.

In the first inning of Game 3 at Yankee Stadium, Richardson, who had hit three major-league home runs before that at-bat, hit a 3-2 pitch from Pirates pitcher Clem Labine into the left field bleachers for a grand slam.

Richardson added a two-run single in the fourth to finish the game with six runs batted in, a World Series record that has since been tied (Yankee DH Hideki Matsui, Game 6, 2009, and St. Louis Cardinals first baseman Albert Pujols, Game 3, 2011).

Despite the Yankees losing in seven games on Bill Mazeroski's home run, Richardson was named the Series MVP, becoming the first and only member of the losing team to win the award. Richardson hit .367 (11 for 30) with a home run and a World Series record 12 runs batted in.

After the Series, the Yankees fired manager Casey Stengel and replaced him with Ralph Houk, who had more faith in Richardson than the former skipper. There were times that Stengel would pinch-hit for Richardson in the early innings of a game and sometimes he would bat him ninth, behind the pitcher. Houk did not use a platoon system as much as Stengel, and that helped Richardson become a more consistent player.

Houk used Richardson at the top of the lineup for most of the 1961 season, and he scored 80 runs hitting in front of Roger Maris and Mickey Mantle, who were chasing Babe Ruth's single-season home-run record. Richardson slashed .391/.391/.435 with an OPS of .826 in the 1961 World Series win against the Cincinnati Reds. Richardson had at least one hit in all five games, and had three hits in Games 1 and 4.

In 1962, Richardson had the best season of his career. The Yankee second baseman slashed .302/.337/.406 with a career-best OPS of .743 and was named to both All-Star Games (there were two All-Star Games in 1962). Richardson won his second consecutive Gold Glove and was the runner-up to teammate Mickey Mantle for the 1962 American League Most Valuable Player Award.

Richardson went on to play four more seasons with the Yankees and was an All-Star in each of those years. Richardson retired after the 1966 season at the age of 30. He batted .251 in his final campaign as the Yankees wound up in last place.

The Yankees have played in 40 World Series and have won 27 times. Who was the first Yankee to be named World Series Most Valuable Player?

The World Series Most Valuable Player Award was first presented in 1955 when Brooklyn Dodgers pitcher Johnny Podres was named the initial winner.

In 1956, Yankee pitcher Don Larsen was the first Yankee to be named World Series MVP. Larsen won the award based on his performance in

Game 5 of the 1956 World Series when he tossed the first perfect game in World Series history against the Brooklyn Dodgers.

Larsen was a journeyman pitcher who marched to the beat of his own drum. He notoriously missed curfew and was described by teammate Bob Turley as a "fun loving guy who liked to go out and have a beer or two and talk to people in bars."

The 6'4" gangly right-hander, who was nicknamed "Gooney Bird" for his tall, thin frame, was acquired by the Yankees in what became a 17-player trade with the Baltimore Orioles in November 1954. Larsen had just come off a season where he lost 21 games, but he beat the Yankees twice and that impressed manager Casey Stengel.

Larsen was 45-24 as a Yankee. His best season in New York was 1956 when he was 11-5 with a 3.26 ERA. He won 10 games in 1957, but only 15 over his final two seasons.

Larsen was hammered in his only appearance in the 1955 World Series loss to the Dodgers. The Yankee right-hander started Game 4 and gave up five runs in four innings in the 8–5 loss to Brooklyn.

Before he pitched his perfect game in Game 5 of the 1956 World Series, Larsen started and lost Game 2. Larsen failed to get out of the second inning as he walked four batters and gave up one hit and four unearned runs. It was a surprise that Larsen got the starting nod in Game 5, but Stengel still had faith in him.

Stengel had a ritual to name his starting pitcher. He would have coach Frank Crosetti place a baseball in one of the starter's shoes before they arrived at the clubhouse. Larsen went out drinking the night before Game 5, but when he got to the ballpark, he saw a baseball in one of his shoes and knew he was the starting pitcher.

The rest is history. After pinch-hitter Dale Long struck out to end the game, Larsen had etched his name into the record books.

In Game 3 of the 1957 World Series against the Milwaukee Braves, Larsen tossed 7⅓ innings in relief of Bob Turley, but he started and lost Game 7.

In the rematch against Milwaukee in the 1958 World Series, Larsen started Game 3 with the Yankees already down two games to none and pitched seven scoreless innings in a 4–0 win. Larsen started Game 7 but was relieved by Turley and got a no decision as the Yankees beat the Braves, 6–2.

Larsen was 6-7 with a 4.33 ERA in his final Yankee season of 1959. After the season, the Yankees traded Larsen to the Kansas City Athletics as part of a seven-player deal that brought Roger Maris to New York.

Name the first Yankee pitcher to win the Gold Glove Award.

The Gold Glove Award was introduced in 1957. Bobby Shantz won the award in its first year of existence. He was also the first Yankee in franchise history to claim the honor and won the award in every season of his four-year tenure with the Yankees.

Shantz was a left-handed pitcher who defied the odds and epitomized the term *crafty left-hander*. The Pottstown, Pennsylvania, native was listed as 5'6" tall, yet was able to forge a 16-year career in the major leagues and was regarded as one of the best-fielding pitchers of his era.

Bobby Shantz, right, with Athletics coach Albert Bender in 1951 before being traded to the Yankees
COURTESY OF THE BOSTON PUBLIC LIBRARY, LESLIE JONES COLLECTION

Before coming to the Yankees, Shantz won the 1952 American League Most Valuable Player Award. He was 24-7 with a 2.48 ERA for the Philadelphia Athletics and got more votes than Yankees pitcher Allie Reynolds and future teammates Mickey Mantle and Yogi Berra.

Shantz came to the Yankees before the 1957 season as part of a 13-player trade with the Kansas City Athletics. In his first season with the Yankees, Shantz was 11-5 and led the major leagues with a 2.45 ERA. Shantz got off to a 9-1 start and was named to the All-Star Game. He also had nine complete games, one shutout, and five saves.

For the final three years of his Yankee career, manager Casey Stengel transitioned Shantz from being a starting pitcher to working out of the bullpen. In 1958 and 1959, Shantz appeared in 66 games but made only 17 starts. Shantz worked strictly out of the bullpen in the 1960 season and had a career-high 11 saves. Shantz played a role in the famous Game 7 of the 1960 World Series loss to the Pittsburgh Pirates.

After two innings, the Yankees were down 4–0. Shantz was brought on to start the third inning, and he kept the Pirates off the board until the Yankees were able to take a 7–4 lead in the eighth.

In the bottom of the eighth, the Pirates had a man on first with no one out against Shantz when Bill Virdon hit what appeared to be a sure double-play ball to shortstop. The ball took a bad hop and hit Yankees shortstop Tony Kubek in the adam's apple for an infield single that turned the game.

The next batter, Dick Groat, singled to drive in a run and Shantz was removed from the game—and the rest is history. The Pirates upset the heavily favored Yankees on Bill Mazeroski's ninth-inning, walkoff home run.

After the season, Shantz was left unprotected in the expansion draft and was selected by the expansion Washington Senators. Two days later, he was traded to the Pirates.

Who was the first Yankee to be named the winning pitcher in three All-Star Games?

Hall of Fame pitcher Vernon "Lefty" Gomez is the first Yankee to be named the winning pitcher in three All-Star Games.

In 1933, Gomez was the winning pitcher in the inaugural All-Star Game at Chicago's Comiskey Park. The left-hander started and gave up two hits over three scoreless innings as the American League All-Stars beat the National League All-Stars, 4–2.

In the 1935 game at Cleveland Stadium, Gomez gave up a run in six innings pitched. In his final inning of work, Gomez walked Hall of Famer Arky Vaughan, but he retired Hall of Famers Mel Ott, Joe Medwick, and Bill Terry in order to complete his outing. The American League won, 4–1.

Gomez got his third All-Star win in the 1937 game at Griffith Stadium in Washington, DC, tossing three more scoreless innings in the American League's 8–3 win.

Gomez played 13 of his 14 years with the Yankees. The Hall of Famer was a seven-time All-Star and six-time World Series winner.

In 1929, Gomez was pitching for the San Francisco Seals in the Pacific Coast League, where he finished 18-11 with a 3.44 ERA. In one stretch of the season, Gomez won 11 in a row, and the Yankees paid $35,000 to sign him and allowed him to finish the season with the Seals.

Gomez made his major-league debut on April 29, 1930 against the Washington Senators and gave up two runs in four innings pitched. Six days later, he won his first major-league game, giving up one run in a complete-game, 4–1 win over the Chicago White Sox at Yankee Stadium. He gave up five hits, including a home run to Chicago's Willie Kamm, did not walk a batter, and struck out six.

Gomez began to struggle and was sent back to the minors in July. Gomez pitched well for the St. Paul Saints of the American Association and convinced the Yankees that he could be a contributor with the big club.

Gomez began the 1931 season in the bullpen, but as the season wore on and he got a few more chances to start, he finished with 21 wins and a 2.67 ERA. He gave up 206 hits in 243 innings pitched with 150 strikeouts as he began a streak of durability and success that would last for the next nine seasons.

Gomez was a stalwart in World Series play. In five World Series, all wins, Gomez was 6-0 with a 2.86 ERA. He got his first taste of World

Series play in 1932 against the Chicago Cubs. In Game 2 at Yankee Stadium, Gomez pitched a complete game in beating the Cubs, 5–2.

Gomez's best season was 1934. If the American League Cy Young Award had been in existence, Gomez would have won it. He led the league with 26 wins, a 2.33 ERA, and 25 complete games, while he tied for the league lead with six shutouts.

The Yankees finished second in 1934 and 1935, but they returned to the World Series in 1936 against the New York Giants. The Yankees ran away with the pennant. Gomez dealt with a sore arm yet still won 13 games.

Gomez got the nod in Game 2 at the Polo Grounds and cruised to a complete-game victory as the Yankees pounded the Giants 18–4 to even the Series at a game apiece. Gomez got into the box score with a run-scoring single that gave him two RBIs in the rout.

In Game 6, Gomez again got plenty of run support as the Yankees won the Series with a 13–5 win at the Polo Grounds. Gomez pitched into the seventh and gave up four runs, but he was the winning pitcher and also had a run-scoring single in the game.

Gomez won 21 games in 1937 and led the American League with a 2.33 ERA. He also led the major leagues with 194 strikeouts. The Yankees once again beat the Giants in the World Series to repeat as champions. Gomez duplicated his performance from the year before with two wins, including Game 1 at Yankee Stadium and the Game 5 clincher at the Polo Grounds.

Gomez was part of a Yankee team that won four consecutive World Series from 1936 to 1939. In the 1938 World Series four-game sweep against the Chicago Cubs, Gomez pitched Game 2 at Wrigley Field. The southpaw tossed seven innings in beating the Cubs, 6–3.

After missing the World Series in 1940, the Yankees rebounded to win the 1941 American League pennant and faced the Brooklyn Dodgers. Gomez won 15 games to tie for the team lead, but manager Joe McCarthy did not use him at all in the Series as the Yankees won in five games. It was something that bothered Gomez, even after he retired.

In 1942, Gomez was 33 years old and the amount of innings that he had thrown over the years began to take their toll. He made 13 starts, but only one after July, and his career with the Yankees was over.

The Boston Braves purchased Gomez's contract for the 1943 season, but he never appeared in a game. He was released in May and picked up by the Washington Senators, where he made one start before calling it a career.

The Silver Slugger, emblematic of the best offensive player at each position, was first awarded in 1980. Who was the first Yankee catcher to win a Silver Slugger?

Mike Stanley was the first Yankee catcher to win a Silver Slugger Award in 1993. Stanley earned the award by slashing .305/.389/.534, with an OPS of .923 and 26 home runs and a career-high 84 RBIs. He was behind the plate for 122 of his 130 games played as the Yankees finished over .500 for the first time in five seasons.

Stanley was signed as a free agent in January 1992 to back up Matt Nokes, who was the starting catcher. The right-handed-hitting catcher appeared in 68 games and had eight home runs.

Stanley became the starter in 1993 and was involved in one of the most unusual plays of the season.

The Yankees were three games behind the first-place Toronto Blue Jays in the AL East when they hosted the Boston Red Sox at Yankee Stadium in mid-September.

The Yankees trailed 3–1 in the bottom of the ninth and were down to their final out, but Dion James was hit by a pitch to bring the tying run to the plate, and Stanley was sent up to pinch-hit against Red Sox pitcher Greg Harris.

Stanley hit a flyball that was caught by Red Sox left fielder Mike Greenwell and the game appeared to be over. However, a fan darted onto the field and time was called by third base umpire Tim Welke before the pitch was thrown.

Stanley got another chance and singled to left to put two runners on. The Yankees eventually rallied to win the game 4–3 on Don Mattingly's walkoff RBI single to score Gerald Williams, who ran for Stanley.

The Fort Lauderdale, Florida, native hit .300 with a .929 OPS in the strike-shortened season of 1994, and in 1995, he was named an All-Star for the only time in his career. In the 1995 American League Division

Series against Seattle, Stanley hit .313 (5-for-16) with a home run and three RBIs in five games.

After the season, the veteran catcher did not re-sign with the Yankees, but in August 1997, Stanley was traded from the Red Sox back to the Yankees in a rare in-season deal between the rivals.

Stanley had one more moment in his final game as a Yankee. In the deciding Game 5 of the 1997 American League Division Series against the Cleveland Indians, Stanley was 3-for-4, but the Yankees lost 4–3.

Who was the first Yankee pitcher to win the American League Rookie of the Year Award?

Bob Grim was the first Yankee pitcher to win the American League Rookie of the Year Award in 1954. Grim was 20-6 with a 3.26 ERA and captured 15 of 24 votes to beat out Philadelphia Athletics infielder Jim Finigan and Detroit Tigers outfielder and Hall of Famer Al Kaline for the honor.

Grim lost his first two starts and did not win his first major-league game until May 14 when he pitched five innings of one-run ball in relief in the Yankees' 6–4 win over the Tigers at Briggs Stadium. The 24-year-old went on to win five straight decisions capped off by a complete-game win over the Washington Senators at Yankee Stadium.

After suffering a loss to Baltimore, Grim won five more decisions and was 10-3 at the All-Star break, but he was not named to the American League team. The young right-hander went 10-3 in the second half and won his 20th game on September 21, a complete-game win over the Senators at Yankee Stadium.

The Yankees used Grim as both a starter and reliever in 1955 and 1956. He got his first taste of World Series play in Game 1 of the 1955 World Series against the Brooklyn Dodgers at Yankee Stadium. Grim was brought on in the ninth inning to protect a one-run lead and faced three Hall of Famers en route to his first postseason save.

Grim caught Pee Wee Reese looking at a called third strike. After Duke Snider singled, Roy Campanella hit one to deep right field that was caught by Hank Bauer in front of the 344-foot sign. The 24-year-old got Carl Furillo swinging as the Yankees held on for a 6–5 win in

Game 1. Grim started Game 5 and was roughed up for four runs in six innings pitched.

Grim was used totally in relief in 1957, and he led the major leagues in saves with 19. At one point of the season, Grim had a streak where he went 12 straight appearances and did not give up a run. During that stretch, Grim had eight saves and two wins.

In Game 4 of the 1957 World Series against the Milwaukee Braves at County Stadium, Grim was called upon to pitch the bottom of the 10th with a man on first and no one out and the Yankees leading 5–4. Following a sacrifice bunt that moved the runner to second, Grim gave up a game-tying double to Braves shortstop Johnny Logan and a game-winning, two-run home run to Hall of Famer Eddie Mathews. Milwaukee evened the Series at two games apiece and went on to beat the Yankees by winning the seventh game at Yankee Stadium.

In 1958, Yankee manager Casey Stengel had relegated Grim to the back of the bullpen and was using him in low-leverage situations. In June, the Yankees traded Grim to the Kansas City Athletics.

The Home Run Derby debuted in 1985. Who was the first Yankee to win the Derby?

Tino Martinez was the first Yankee to win the Home Run Derby.

In 1997 at Cleveland's Jacobs Field, Martinez topped Colorado outfielder and Hall of Famer Larry Walker in the final round to capture the honor.

Martinez got off to a rocky start in his Yankee career but, once he established himself, he became a fan favorite. The left-handed-hitting first baseman played seven seasons with the Yankees. He was an All-Star, Silver Slugger Award winner, and won four World Series with the Yankees.

In December 1995, Martinez was acquired in a five-player trade with the Seattle Mariners. Just two months before, Martinez had been part of the Seattle team that eliminated the Yankees in the American League Division Series. Now, along with pitcher Jeff Nelson and Jim Mecir, Martinez was headed to New York.

The Yankees sent third baseman Russ Davis and pitcher Sterling Hitchcock to the Mariners, but the acquisition of Martinez (and Nelson, who became a key piece of the bullpen) became one of the pivotal moves that jumpstarted the Yankee dynasty that won four World Series championships in five seasons.

After the loss to Seattle, first baseman Don Mattingly retired, so Martinez was handed the unenviable task of replacing a legend. Martinez got off to a 3-for-34 (.088) start and he was hearing it from the fans, but his season began to turn around. Martinez got a hit in 20 of his next 23 games to raise his average to .254 by mid-May, but it was one hit that became the turning point of his season.

On May 1, the Yankees were playing the Baltimore Orioles at Camden Yards and the score was tied at 6 in the top of the 15th inning. The Yankees had bases loaded and one out with Martinez facing Orioles pitcher Jimmy Myers. The Yankee first baseman drove a first pitch changeup into the left field stands for a grand slam as the Yankees went on to an 11–6 win.

Martinez went on to have a terrific first season with the Yankees. In 155 games, Martinez batted .292 with 25 home runs and 117 runs batted in as he earned the first of four championship rings with the Yankees.

Martinez had the best season of his career in 1997. The Tampa, Florida, native hit .296 with 44 home runs and 141 runs batted in, all career highs. He won the only Silver Slugger Award of his career and finished second in the AL MVP vote to Seattle outfielder and Hall of Famer Ken Griffey Jr.

The Yankees came up short in 1997, but a record-setting 1998 season put Martinez in position for a memorable postseason moment. The Yankees were back in the World Series and were facing the National League champion San Diego Padres in Game 1 at Yankee Stadium.

The Yankees were trailing 5–2 in the bottom of the seventh, but Yankees second baseman Chuck Knoblauch tied the game with a three-run home run off of Padres pitcher Donne Wall. Padres left-hander Mark Langston relieved Wall and faced Martinez with the bases loaded and two out.

With the count at 2-2, Martinez looked at Langston's pitch that appeared to be a strike but was called a ball by home plate umpire Rich Garcia. Martinez took advantage of the break and drove Langston's next pitch into the upper deck in right field for a grand slam and a 9–5 lead. The Yankees took Game 1 and swept the Series in four games.

Martinez continued to put up consistent power numbers during his first six years with the Yankees and gradually became known as a clutch performer. Martinez played seven seasons with the Yankees in two separate stints.

The Yankee first baseman had his best overall postseason in 2000 when the Yankees won their third consecutive World Series championship. In 16 games against the Oakland A's, Seattle Mariners, and New York Mets in the World Series, Martinez hit a combined .338 (24-for-71) with a home run, five doubles, and seven runs batted in.

Martinez would have one more, big postseason moment in the 2001 World Series loss to the Arizona Diamondbacks.

The Yankees trailed in the Series, two games to one, and were trailing 3–1 in the ninth inning of Game 4 at Yankee Stadium. With Paul O'Neill on first base and two out, Martinez hit the first pitch from Arizona closer Byung-Hyun Kim over the right-center field wall for a game-tying home run as the Stadium literally shook from the fan eruption.

The Yankees went on to win Game 4 in 10 innings on Derek Jeter's walkoff home run in the 10th inning. The Yankees lost the Series in seven games, and Martinez was not re-signed after the season as he became a free agent. After three seasons with the St. Louis Cardinals and Tampa Bay Devil Rays, Martinez signed as a free agent and returned to the Yankees for his final major-league season in 2005.

In 2002, Jason Giambi beat out the Cubs Sammy Sosa to win the event at Milwaukee's Miller Park.

Robinson Canó had his father, Jose, pitch to him, and he beat out Boston's Adrián González to win the Derby in 2011 at Chase Field in Arizona.

Aaron Judge won the Derby in his rookie season of 2017 at Marlins Park in Miami, Florida. Judge defeated Minnesota's Miguel Sanó in the final round.

In 1974, the Player of the Month Award debuted. Graig Nettles was the first Yankee to win in April 1974. Who was the first Yankee designated hitter to win the award?

Glenallen Hill was the first Yankee designated hitter to win the American League Player of the Month Award.

Hill was acquired in a trade with the Chicago Cubs on July 21, 2000. The Yankees were looking for a right-handed bat and the Santa Cruz, California, native always had good numbers against left-handed pitching.

Hill slashed .411/.456/.877 with an OPS of 1.332 in August and was named American League Player of the Month. He slammed 10 home runs with 19 RBIs and also had a 13-game hitting streak and scored 14 runs in August.

Hill played 40 games for the Yankees in 2000 and finished with 16 home runs and 29 RBI's in 132 at-bats. A few days after his acquisition, Hill made an immediate impact. The Yankees trailed the Minnesota Twins 5–4 in the top of the ninth inning at the Hubert H. Humphrey Metrodome, a place that had not been kind over the years.

After Jorge Posada tied the game at 5 with an RBI single, Hill came up with the bases loaded and hit a grand slam home run off of Twins' right-handed pitcher Bob Wells to give the Yankees an important 9–5 win.

Hill was not a big contributor in the postseason, but he earned a championship ring with the Yankees. In March 2001, Hill was traded to the Anaheim Angels.

Five pitchers in Yankee history have won the Cy Young Award. Who was the first Yankee reliever to win the award?

In 1977, left-hander Sparky Lyle was the first Yankee reliever to win the American League Cy Young Award. Lyle relied on a devastating slider to beat out Hall of Famers Jim Palmer and Nolan Ryan.

During his award-winning season, Lyle led the American League by appearing in 72 games, while finishing 60 games, saving 26, and posting a 2.17 ERA.

In March 1972, the Yankees acquired Lyle in a trade with the Boston Red Sox for Danny Cater. The acquisition became one of the best in franchise history as Lyle helped the Yankees win three American League pennants and two World Series championships. In his first season, Lyle was 9-5 in relief with a 1.92 ERA and an American League leading 35 saves, at the time, a record for left-handed relievers.

Lyle, who became a fan favorite, would enter the game in a car that drove him in from the bullpen. "Pomp and Circumstance," a theme that is traditionally played at graduations, was Lyle's entry theme.

In 1976, the Du Bois, Pennsylvania, native led the American League with 23 saves as the Yankees won their first ever American League Eastern Division title. Lyle's first postseason save came in Game 3 of the 1976 American League Championship Series against Kansas City. Lyle tossed a scoreless ninth inning in the Yankees' 5–3 win at Yankee Stadium.

In the 1977 ALCS rematch against the Royals, Lyle had his signature Yankee moment. The Yankees were trailing the best of five series, two games to one, with Games 4 and 5 in Kansas City. In the bottom of the fourth inning of Game 4, the Royals had scored two runs to cut the Yankees' lead to 5–4 and had two on and two out with Hall of Famer and Yankee nemesis George Brett due up.

Yankee manager Billy Martin was pulling out all the stops, so he brought in Lyle to replace Dick Tidrow, who had given up a run-scoring hit to Frank White. Lyle retired Brett on a line drive to left field to preserve the one-run lead. The Yankee closer tossed 5⅓ scoreless innings as the Yankees went on to tie the Series with a 6–4 win.

The very next day in Game 5, Lyle closed the game with 1⅓ innings of scoreless ball as the Yankees rallied to beat the Royals 5–3 to win the pennant for a second consecutive season.

Lyle did not get a save in the 1977 World Series against the Los Angeles Dodgers. He blew the save in Game 1 when he gave up a game-tying single to Dusty Baker, but he pitched 3⅔ innings and got the win when the Yankees won 4–3 in 12 innings.

After the season, Yankee owner George Steinbrenner signed free agent reliever and Hall of Famer Rich "Goose" Gossage, making it a precarious situation, as far as Lyle's status with the team. Gossage became the closer while Lyle had nine saves, his second lowest total as a Yankee.

After the 1978 season, Lyle was traded to the Texas Rangers as part of a 10-player deal. In that trade, the Yankees received young left-hander Dave Righetti, who went on to become the 1981 American League Rookie of the Year.

Other Yankees who have won the Cy Young Award:

- Bob Turley (1958)
- Hall of Famer Whitey Ford (1961)
- Ron Guidry (1978)
- Roger Clemens (2001)

STADIUM FIRSTS

The original Yankee Stadium opened in 1923 and was in existence through the 1973 season. The Stadium was being refurbished in 1974 and 1975, so the Yankees played their home games during that time at Shea Stadium. The Stadium's second opening was in 1976 and ran through the 2008 season. In 2009, the Yankees christened Yankee Stadium III. See how many firsts you can answer from the places that the Yankees called home.

On April 16, 2009, the Yankees hosted the Cleveland Indians in their first game at their new home, the current Yankee Stadium. Who hit the first Yankee home run at the "new" ballpark?

Yankees catcher Jorge Posada hit the first Yankee home run and the very first home run in the first game at the current Yankee Stadium.

The Yanks trailed the Cleveland Indians 1–0 in the bottom of the fifth when Posada tied the game with a solo home run to left-center field off of Indians pitcher Cliff Lee to become the first player to round the bases in the current Stadium's history.

A switch-hitting catcher who played 17 years for the Yankees, Posada was a five-time All-Star and five-time Silver Slugger Award winner. In 2003, Posada hit 30 home runs to become only the second Yankee catcher (after Hall of Famer Yogi Berra) to reach that milestone.

Posada was chosen by the Yankees in the 43rd round of the 1990 MLB June Amateur Draft. He began his professional career as a second baseman, but the Yankees felt he didn't profile as an infielder so he began to learn the catching position in 1992.

Jorge Posada
KEITH ALLISON VIA WIKIMEDIA COMMONS

Posada made his major-league debut in September of 1995. The Puerto Rico–born catcher was on the postseason roster for the American League Division Series vs. Seattle. In Game 2, he entered the game as a pinch-runner for Wade Boggs and scored a run.

After an eight-game stint in 1996, Posada backed up starting catcher Joe Girardi in 1997 and gradually got into more games in 1998 and 1999. On May 17, 1998, Posada caught David Wells's perfect game. Girardi left the Yankees as a free agent after the 1999 season and Posada was officially anointed the starting catcher.

In 2000, Posada appeared in a career-high 151 games and posted a slash line of .287/.417/.527 with 28 home runs and 86 RBIs. Posada was named an All-Star for the first time, and he also won his first Silver Slugger Award.

Posada was an integral part of four World Series championship teams. In Game 3 of the 2001 American League Divisional Series against the Oakland A's, Posada was on the receiving end of Derek Jeter's famous "flip play." He also homered to account for the only run of the game in a 1–0 win that began the Yanks' comeback from a 2–0 series deficit to win in five games.

Posada's best season was in 2003 when he batted .281 with career highs of 30 home runs and 101 runs batted in, finishing third in the voting for the American League Most Valuable Player Award and winning his fourth consecutive Silver Slugger Award.

In Game 7 of the 2003 American League Championship Series against the Boston Red Sox, Posada's two-run double off of Boston's Pedro Martínez in the bottom of the eighth inning tied the game at 5. The Yankees went on to beat Boston for their 39th American League pennant. Posada had a postseason career high of six runs batted in during the seven-game series.

Posada had already established himself as a key cog in the Yankees' championship success that began in the late 20th century and continued into the early 21st century when he had the best playoff series of his career. In the 2006 American League Division Series loss to the Detroit Tigers, Posada was 7-for-14 with a home run and two runs batted in.

Posada had never been on the disabled list until 2008, when he suffered a shoulder injury that limited him to 51 games. Posada's last game was July 19, and the Yankees missed the playoffs for the first time in 14 seasons.

Heading into the 2009 season, the Yankees were able to take it slow with their switch-hitter because they had a solid backup in José Molina, who was in the second year of a two-year, free agent deal. Posada bounced back in 2009 to help the Yankees win their 27th world championship. He played in 111 games and batted a career-high .285 with 22 home runs and 81 RBIs. Posada was 4-for-11 (.364) and had an OPS of 1.000 in the three-game sweep of the Minnesota Twins in the 2009 American League Division Series.

Father time caught up to Posada in his final two seasons. He underwent arthroscopic knee surgery after the 2010 season and was used primarily as a designated hitter in his final season of 2011.

In May, he asked out of the lineup after being listed (ironically by his manager, Joe Girardi, who he succeeded as the starting catcher) as the number nine hitter. In August, he made his one and only appearance as a second baseman and threw out the final runner of a 22–9 Yankees win over Oakland. Posada ended his career by hitting .429 in the 2011 American League Division Series loss in five games against the Tigers.

Posada announced his retirement in January 2012. The Yankees retired his #20 in 2015.

Babe Ruth hit the first Yankee home run at the original Yankee Stadium on April 18, 1923. Who hit the first Yankee home run at the remodeled Stadium when it opened in 1976?

In the second ever game at the refurbished Yankee Stadium, Thurman Munson became the first Yankee to hit a home run in the remodeled ballpark.

On April 17, 1976, Munson clubbed a solo home run in the bottom of the first off of Twins pitcher Jim Hughes. (The Stadium reopened on April 15, 1976, but no Yankees homered in the first game. Minnesota Twins right fielder Dan Ford became the first player to hit a home run at the refurbished Stadium.)

Munson was one of the most beloved Yankees of his era, one that tragically ended when he was killed in a plane crash on August 2, 1979. Munson played his entire 11-year career with the Yankees and was a seven-time All-Star and three-time Gold Glove winner. Munson, who was named the second ever Yankee captain after Lou Gehrig in 1976, was considered the heart and soul of the team, as he led them out of a down period in Yankee history to become champions once again in the late 1970s.

The Yankees chose Munson, out of Kent State, with the fourth overall pick of the 1968 Major League Baseball June Amateur Draft. Munson played one full minor-league season in 1968 for the Binghamton Triplets, the Yankees' Double-A affiliate in the Eastern League. In 1969, Munson was batting .363 for the Yankees' Triple-A affiliate at Syracuse and was promoted to the big club in August.

In his major-league debut on August 8, 1969, Munson was 2-for-3 with an RBI and two runs scored. Two days later, Munson slammed his first big-league home run off of Oakland A's pitcher Lew Krausse. The Yankee catcher had only 86 official at-bats in 1969, so he was technically still a rookie in 1970. Munson hit .302 with seven home runs and 57 RBIs in his first full season in 1970 and was named the American League Rookie of the Year, becoming the sixth Yankee, at the time, to be so honored.

In the 1970s, Munson had a well-publicized feud with Boston Red Sox catcher Carlton Fisk. The competing backstops were considered the two best catchers in the American League, but their rivalry peaked on August 1, 1973, at Fenway Park.

With the score tied at 2 in the top of the ninth, Munson tried to score from third on a squeeze bunt attempt by Yankee shortstop Gene Michael. The bunt was missed, and Munson barreled into Fisk at home plate, sparking a 10-minute, benches-clearing brawl between the two teams. Both catchers were ejected, and that incident set the tone for the rivalry between the two that lasted until Munson's death.

Munson was named Yankee captain to start the 1976 season, and he responded by hitting .302 with 17 home runs and 105 runs batted in while leading the Yankees to their first American League East Division title and their first American League pennant in 12 years.

Munson played superbly in the postseason. He batted .435 in the American League Championship Series win over Kansas City that ended on Chris Chambliss's pennant-winning home run in Game 5. In the World Series loss to Cincinnati, Munson was spectacular, hitting .529 in the four-game sweep.

After the final game, Reds manager Sparky Anderson disparaged Munson by saying, "You don't ever compare anyone to [Reds catcher and Hall of Famer] Johnny Bench. Don't never embarrass nobody by comparing them to Johnny Bench." Those remarks did not sit well with Munson, who ripped Anderson afterward.

When Reggie Jackson was signed as a free agent and joined the team in 1977, there was friction between the two stars. An article published in *Sport* magazine quoted Jackson saying that he was the "straw that stirs the drink, but he [Munson] could only stir it bad." Munson was the one who had encouraged Yankee owner George Steinbrenner to sign Jackson, but the quotes set off a firestorm in spring training where the veteran Yankees took Munson's side and soured on Jackson. Eventually, the two men came to respect each other and were a driving force behind back-to-back World Series championships in 1977 and 1978.

In 1978, the Yankees rallied from 14 games back in July to beat the Red Sox in a one-game playoff for the division title and a berth in the American League Championship Series against Kansas City for a third straight season.

Munson was dealing with a sore shoulder for much of that season, but he authored a memorable moment in Game 3. With the Series tied at a game apiece, the Yankees trailed the Royals 5–4 in the bottom of the eighth. Roy White was on first base with one out when the gritty catcher slammed a two-run home run off of Royals pitcher Doug Bird. The ball went over the left-center field wall in "Death Valley" at Yankee Stadium and traveled 475 feet. It was the longest home run of Munson's career, made all the more remarkable because of his shoulder injury, as the Yankees won 6–5.

The Yankees eventually captured their second consecutive world championship and 22nd overall. At the time, Munson became only the second catcher in major-league history to win a Rookie of the Year Award, MVP, Gold Glove, and World Series title in his career. (Bench was the first and San Francisco Giants catcher Buster Posey became the third to join that list.)

The day after his death, the Yankees honored Munson with an emotional pregame ceremony at Yankee Stadium. The Yankees were playing the Baltimore Orioles and initially took the field without a catcher. Cardinal Terence Cooke offered a prayer and after Robert Merrill sang, "America the Beautiful," more than 51,000 fans honored Munson with an eight-minute standing ovation.

Munson's #15 was immediately retired, and his locker remained as a tribute to the Yankees' late captain until the Stadium closed after the 2008 season. Munson's locker was moved to the new Yankee Stadium where it resides in the New York Yankees Museum.

During the 1974 and 1975 seasons, Yankee Stadium was undergoing a renovation so the Yankees reached an agreement to play their home games at Shea Stadium in Queens, New York, the home of the New

York Mets. On April 6, 1974, the Yankees beat the Cleveland Indians 6–1 in their first ever regular-season game as the home team at Shea Stadium. Name the Yankee who hit the first home run at Shea Stadium in that game. Bonus: Who had the first Yankee hit in that game?

In the bottom of the fourth inning of their first ever game at Shea Stadium as the home team in 1974, Yankees third baseman Graig Nettles hit the first home run.

Nettles's home run went to left field and scored Thurman Munson, who had singled for the first Yankee hit as the home team at Shea. The irony of the left-handed-hitting Nettles hitting the first home run at Shea was that it may not have gone out at the original Yankee Stadium, where it was harder for a left-handed batter to hit a home run to the opposite field. Nettles went on to hit 11 home runs in April to set an American League record for that month that has since been broken.

The Yankees acquired Nettles and catcher Jerry Moses in November 1972 from the Cleveland Indians in exchange for catcher John Ellis, infielder Jerry Kenney, and outfielders Rusty Torres and a highly touted prospect, 21-year-old Charlie Spikes.

Nettles had hit 71 home runs in three previous seasons with the Indians, so the Yankees, who had been seeking a power bat for their lineup, knew his left-handed swing would play well at Yankee Stadium with the short porch in right field. During his 11 years with the Yankees, Nettles hit 250 home runs and was a key cog of the team that won back-to-back World Series championships in 1977 and 1978.

Nettles's defense came under question early in his big-league career, but in his first few years with the Indians he had the full support of manager Alvin Dark. Buoyed by Dark's faith in him, Nettles developed into one of the best defensive third basemen of his era.

In his first season with the Yankees in 1973, Nettles hit 22 home runs to begin a streak of seven consecutive seasons with 20 or more homers. Two of those seasons were played at Shea Stadium, where Nettles hit a total of 43 home runs.

In August 1975, Yankee owner George Steinbrenner fired manager Bill Virdon and hired the fiery and enigmatic Billy Martin to replace him. In 1968, Nettles played for Martin when he managed the Twins'

Triple-A affiliate in Denver, so he knew what to expect out of the controversial skipper. Nettles respected Martin's knowledge of the game and had his best seasons under his leadership.

The Yankees moved back to the Bronx in the 1976 season with a refurbished Yankee Stadium. The fences in left and center field were brought in some, but, despite the makeover, the left-handed hitters would see a welcome sight in right field.

Nettles took advantage of the Stadium's dimensions, but he was almost as good away from home as he led the American League with 32 home runs in 1976. In Game 4 of the 1976 American League Championship Series at Yankee Stadium vs. Kansas City, Nettles hit two home runs.

On May 20, 1976, Nettles was in the middle of one of the most famous brawls between the Yankees and their hated rivals, the Boston Red Sox. In the bottom of the sixth inning, Lou Piniella was trying to score when he crashed into Red Sox catcher Carlton Fisk at home plate. Fisk held the ball for the out, but the two competitors began throwing punches as both benches emptied.

Things seemed to be calming down, but Red Sox pitcher Bill Lee appeared to hurt his shoulder. Lee got up and said something to Nettles, who responded with a punch sending the Red Sox pitcher to the ground. It was a nasty incident that typified the hatred and intensity between the longtime rivals.

In 1977, everything came together for Nettles and the Yankees, although not without some obstacles along the way. Nettles was a major factor in the Yankees' success in 1977. The slugger played in 158 games and belted a career-high 37 home runs with 107 runs batted in. He also finished fifth in the voting for the American League's Most Valuable Player Award and was the first Yankee third baseman to win a Gold Glove Award.

Nettles's previous experience with Martin as his manager came in handy in a season that gave the newspapers something to write about nearly every day. Hall of Famer Reggie Jackson was signed as a free agent and there was a rift with captain Thurman Munson before the 1977 season even began. The team was embroiled in controversy all season long, but the Yankees managed to win their 21st World Series championship.

Nettles won a second consecutive Gold Glove in 1978, but his defensive brilliance was on full display in the 1978 World Series against the Los Angeles Dodgers. Many baseball observers credit Nettles's glove with turning the Series around after the Yankees had lost the first two games in Los Angeles.

Game 3 was at Yankee Stadium and the Yankees were starting their ace, left-hander Ron Guidry. The southpaw, who would go on to win the American League Cy Young Award that season, would get a lot of groundballs hit to the third base side, so Nettles expected to be busy.

The Yankees led 2–1 in the top of the third inning, but the Dodgers had the tying run on first with two out when Reggie Smith, a switch-hitter who was batting right-handed, crushed a ball down the third base line. Nettles dove to his right and got up and threw Smith out at first.

It was still 2–1 in the fifth inning when Smith came up with two on and two out and lined a single off the glove of Nettles, who prevented a run from scoring. The next batter was Steve Garvey who also hit a shot toward the third base line. Nettles somehow snagged it and threw to second for a force-out.

In the sixth, Nettles snuffed out another bases loaded rally with a similar play. This time, Davey Lopes lined the ball toward the third base line. Nettles backhanded the hard-hit one-hopper and got up and threw to second for the inning-ending force-out.

Nettles made a number of other eye-opening plays. It was an incredible display of defense that had the Dodgers scratching their heads. Nettles had two putouts and five assists. Beginning with Game 3, the Yankees proceeded to win four in a row to clinch their second consecutive World Series title.

Nettles's numbers dropped off in 1979. Munson's death essentially ended the season in early August for Nettles, who was also close to the Yankee captain. After hepatitis limited Nettles to 89 games in 1980, he came back in the strike-shortened 1981 season to help the Yankees reach the World Series, his fourth with the team.

Nettles had his greatest postseason success in the 1981 American League Championship Series when the Yankees swept the Oakland A's in three games. Nettles drove in nine runs, three in each game, and was named the Most Valuable Player. In Game 2 at Yankee Stadium, Nettles had a postseason career high four-hit game.

On March 30, 1984, the Yankees traded the 39-year-old Nettles to the San Diego Padres in exchange for left-handed pitcher Dennis Rasmussen. Nettles's Yankee career was over, but he left a legacy as arguably the greatest third baseman in franchise history.

Who hit the first grand slam home run when the Yankees were the home team at Shea Stadium?

On June 11, 1974, DH Bill Sudakis became the first Yankee to hit a grand slam home run as part of the home team at Shea Stadium. It was the only grand slam that the Yankees would hit at the ballpark in Queens, New York.

The Yankees were trailing the California Angels 4–0 in the bottom of the fifth inning. Thurman Munson led off with a single. After Graig Nettles walked, Chris Chambliss reached on an error to load the bases. Sudakis cleared the bases with a home run to right field to tie the game at 4.

Sudakis played one season for the Yankees and was traded to the Angels after the 1974 season for reliever Skip Lockwood.

Chambliss is best known in Yankee lore for his dramatic, walkoff, pennant-winning home run against the Kansas City Royals in the ninth inning of Game 5 of the 1976 American League Championship Series at Yankee Stadium.

Chambliss was in his first season with the Yankees in 1974. The left-handed-hitting first baseman was acquired in a seven-player deal with the Cleveland Indians in late April. Five of the players involved were pitchers. The Yankees also acquired pitchers Dick Tidrow and Cecil Upshaw in exchange for four pitchers, including veteran left-hander Fritz Peterson.

Chambliss was the 1971 American League Rookie of the Year when he batted .275 with nine home runs and 48 RBIs. The Yankees liked his left-handed bat and his ability defensively at first base.

Some of the veteran Yankees were not pleased with the trade because they felt they gave up too much pitching. It didn't help that Chambliss struggled offensively in his first season as he only batted .243 with six home runs, but he showed the Yankees that he lived up to the billing as a defender. The Dayton, Ohio, native was much more comfortable in 1975 as he batted .304 with nine home runs and 72 runs batted in and 66 runs scored.

The Yankees moved back to a renovated Yankee Stadium in 1976 and Chambliss had a chance to swing for the short right field porch. The big first baseman hit .293 with 17 home runs and a career-high 90 runs batted in and was named an All-Star for the first time.

Chambliss was nearly unstoppable in the ALCS vs. Kansas City, batting .524 with two home runs and eight runs batted in during the five games.

In Game 5 the Yankees and Royals were tied at 6 when Chambliss led off the bottom of the ninth against Royals reliever Mark Littell. The game was temporarily delayed when some fans threw debris on the field, but Chambliss stepped in the box and drove Littell's first pitch over the right-center field wall to send the Yankees to their first World Series since 1964.

Chambliss had to run the bases through a wave of fans who had descended on the field, and he never touched home plate. Later, after things settled down, Chambliss went back out to the field and officially touched home.

Chambliss had three straight seasons of 90 or more runs batted in from 1976 to 1978. Chambliss's fielding prowess paid off with his only Gold Glove Award in 1978. He tied Baltimore Orioles' Hall of Fame first baseman Eddie Murray for the major-league lead with a fielding percentage of .997 while committing only four errors in 155 games.

Chambliss was the starting first baseman for the Yankees when they won back-to-back World Series championships in 1977 and 1978. Reggie Jackson was the star of the 1977 World Series with his three-home-run game in the clinching Game 6, but Chambliss had a pretty good Series as well. The first baseman was 7-for-24 (.292) with a home run and four runs batted in.

Chambliss's only career World Series home run came in the bottom of the second inning off of Dodgers pitcher Burt Hooton. Jackson walked in his first at-bat and scored when Chambliss hit the game-tying home run over the right-center field wall.

In November 1979, the Yankees traded Chambliss and two players to the Toronto Blue Jays for three players, including catcher Rick Cerone, who was the heir apparent to the late Thurman Munson. A little over a month later, Toronto traded Chambliss to Atlanta.

Match these Yankees with firsts at the current Yankee Stadium:

First strikeout	**Dámaso Marte**
First winning pitcher	**C. C. Sabathia**
First pitcher to give up a HR	**Joba Chamberlain**
First wild pitch	**Brian Bruney**
First stolen base	**Nick Swisher**
First Yankee starting 3B	**Mark Teixeira**
First Yankee double	**Cody Ransom**
First Yankee hit by a pitch	**Johnny Damon**

Yankee Stadium III opened on April 16, 2009. The Yankees hosted the Cleveland Indians and lost the first game, 10–2.

Left-hander C. C. Sabathia was the Yankees' first starting pitcher at Stadium III, and he recorded the first strikeout in the ballpark's history when he fanned Cleveland's first baseman Victor Martínez swinging.

In December 2008, Carsten Charles Sabathia signed a seven-year, $161 million contract to join the Yankees. In his first season of 2009, Sabathia immediately became the ace of the staff and led the Yankees to their 27th World Series championship.

The 6'6" southpaw was 19-8 with a 3.37 ERA in 2009. In the post-season, Sabathia won Game 1 of the American League Divisional Series to key a three-game sweep of Minnesota.

Sabathia was 2-0 with a 1.13 ERA in the American League Championship Series win against the Los Angeles Angels and was named the Series' Most Valuable Player. Sabathia did not earn a win in the 2009

C. C. Sabathia
KEITH ALLISON VIA WIKIMEDIA COMMONS

World Series against the Philadelphia Phillies, but was still a factor in two games of the six-game victory.

Sabathia played 11 of his 19 years with the Yankees and finished in the top 10 in franchise history in games started (306), wins (134), and is fourth all time in strikeouts with 1,700.

In the 2010 season, Sabathia tied for the league lead with a career-high 21 wins. He started 34 games and posted a 3.18 ERA and finished third in the AL Cy Young voting. Sabathia was also named an All-Star for the first time as a Yankee. The left-hander was 2-0 in the postseason, although the Yankees lost to the Texas Rangers in the American League Championship Series.

From 2011 to 2013, Sabathia won 48 games and continued to be durable as he made 93 starts over that span. In 2013, Sabathia won his 200th game in July and finished the season with a 14-13 record and a 4.78 ERA.

The Yankee ace would be 33 years old in the 2014 season, so he decided to make a life change. During the offseason, Sabathia lost 40 pounds and reported to spring training at a svelte 275 pounds.

Unfortunately, Sabathia experienced problems with his right knee. After making only eight starts, Sabathia's season was over when he underwent knee surgery in late July.

Sabathia returned in 2015 to make 29 starts, but he was 6-10 with a 4.73 ERA and was starting to show his age. The knee would continue to plague Sabathia throughout the 2016 season and for the remainder of his career, so he would eventually have to make an adjustment or else he would not be able to continue to pitch effectively. At his advanced age and with the status of his knee, Sabathia re-invented himself for the 2017 season.

After undergoing a routine cleanup procedure after the end of the 2016 season, the big hurler made the transition from being a power pitcher to one who could get hitters out, thanks in part to the development of a cutter. Sabathia took a cue from former Yankee pitcher Andy Pettitte, who went through a similar transition to help extend his career.

Sabathia made 27 starts in 2017 and was 14-5 with a 3.69 ERA. In the postseason, the Yankees trailed two games to none in the American League Division Series against the Cleveland Indians but rallied to force a Game 5.

Sabathia started the winner-take-all fifth game and left it all out on Progressive Field in Cleveland in a gritty 4⅓ innings pitched. After four dominant innings, Sabathia ran out of gas in the fifth as he gave up two runs but left the game with the Yankees leading 3-2. The bullpen of David Robertson and Aroldis Chapman kept the lead as the Yankees completed the comeback with a 5–2 win, but it was Sabathia who set the tone with his short, but effective outing.

The Yankees were trailing two games to one against the Houston Astros in the 2017 American League Championship Series, but Sabathia won Game 3 with six scoreless innings. Sabathia started Game 7 against Houston's Justin Verlander and gave up a run in 3⅓ innings as he took the loss in a 4–0, season-ending defeat.

Sabathia made 29 starts in 2018 and tossed 153 innings. In the American League Division Series loss to Boston, Sabathia was the losing pitcher in the deciding Game 4.

Following the season, Sabathia re-signed with the Yankees on a one-year deal and underwent a medical procedure in December. The left-hander had a stent inserted into his heart after a blocked artery was discovered. In January 2019, Sabathia was cleared to resume baseball activities. In February, Sabathia announced that 2019 would be his final season, but he would include a few milestones along the way.

Because of the heart procedure, Sabathia missed the first two weeks of the 2019 season. He made his season debut on April 13 and pitched five scoreless innings against the Chicago White Sox at Yankee Stadium.

On April 30, 2019, Sabathia struck out Arizona Diamondbacks catcher John Ryan Murphy for his 3,000th career strikeout. On June 19, Sabathia won his 250th career game in beating Tampa Bay. Sabathia gave up a run in six innings to become the 14th pitcher in major-league history to have 250 wins and 3,000 strikeouts.

Sabathia's troublesome knee landed him on the injured list three times in his final season. His final start and appearance at Yankee Stadium was September 18 against the Los Angeles Angels. Sabathia pitched into the third inning and received a raucous standing ovation when he was removed.

Sabathia's final appearance came in Game 4 of the 2019 American League Championship Series against the Astros. The left-hander pitched two-thirds of an inning and was removed after throwing 17 pitches in the eighth inning due to shoulder discomfort. Sabathia literally threw his arm out as he was diagnosed with a subluxated left shoulder, which is a partial dislocation of the joint.

On October 21, 2019, Sabathia announced his retirement from baseball.

Yankee relief pitcher Brian Bruney was credited with being the first Yankee winning pitcher at Yankee Stadium III.

Bruney pitched an inning of scoreless relief and was credited with the win after Derek Jeter's solo home run in the bottom of the eighth gave the Yankees a 6–5 win over the Indians for their first ever victory at Stadium III in the second game played there on April 17.

Bruney was a right-handed hard-throwing middle reliever who signed with the Yankees as a minor-league free agent. Bruney made 152 relief appearances and one start over his four-year tenure with the Yankees. Bruney's best season was 2009 when he was 5-0 with 36 strikeouts in 39 innings pitched.

Bruney is best known for an incident that took place before a game with the New York Mets in June 2009. Bruney criticized Mets reliever Francisco Rodríguez for his mound demeanor, calling it a "tired act." Rodríguez answered those comments by suggesting Bruney "better keep his mouth shut." The next day, Bruney and Rodríguez confronted each other on the field during batting practice and nearly came to blows before teammates separated the hostile pair.

Following the 2009 season, Bruney signed a free agent contract with the Washington Nationals.

In the seventh inning of the first game at Stadium III, left-handed reliever Dámaso Marte was the first Yankee pitcher to give up a home run at the new ballpark. Indians center fielder Grady Sizemore cleared the bases with a grand slam home run off of Marte to give the Indians a 9–1 lead. Marte also gave up a home run to Victor Martínez later in that inning.

Marte was acquired from the Pittsburgh Pirates in July 2008 to fill a need for another left-hander in the bullpen.

Marte had a short, but rough regular season in 2009. A shoulder injury kept him sidelined for four months from late April until his return in late August. He ended the regular season with a 9.45 ERA after giving up 14 earned runs in 13⅓ innings pitched.

Marte's best stretch as a Yankee came in the 2009 playoffs and World Series. In Game 4 of the 2009 American League Divisional Series against the Minnesota Twins, Marte faced two batters and gave up two hits. That would be his only blemish in October.

Marte faced 12 more hitters and retired them all as he made a subtle, but important contribution to the World Series winning team. Marte was used by manager Joe Girardi as an effective weapon against dangerous left-handed-hitting Phillies like Chase Utley, Ryan Howard, and Raúl Ibañez. Marte appeared in four games in the World Series, including Games 4 and 6 that the Yankees won.

In the seventh inning of Game 4, Marte relieved C. C. Sabathia, who had begun to tire and had just given up a solo home run to Utley that cut the Yankees lead to 4–3. Howard was the next hitter and Marte got him on a flyout to left field to preserve the lead.

In the clinching Game 6, Marte struck out Utley to end the seventh and then struck out Howard to start the eighth before giving way to Mariano Rivera, who got the final five outs.

Right-handed pitcher Joba Chamberlain was the first Yankee pitcher to uncork a wild pitch at Stadium III.

It occurred in the fifth inning of the second ever game at the new ballpark. Cleveland had runners on first and second after tying the game at 3. Chamberlain's wild pitch got past Yankee catcher Jorge Posada to put runners on second and third. Victor Martínez's sacrifice fly gave Cleveland a 4–3 lead at the time.

The 6'3" right-hander was the Yankees' first-round pick, 41st overall, in the 2006 MLB June Amateur Draft. In 2007, Chamberlain was a highly rated starting pitching prospect and moved quickly through the Yankees' minor-league system before being promoted to the big club in August.

On August 7, 2007, Chamberlain made his much-anticipated major-league debut in relief against the Toronto Blue Jays at Rogers Centre. The 21-year-old tossed two scoreless innings in a 9–2 win.

Chamberlain got off to a fast start in his major-league career. He had 17 strikeouts in 10 innings pitched in his first eight appearances, and the Yankees were utilizing him with a plan to not push him too hard early in his career. "The Joba Rules," as they came to be known, was a program for Chamberlain under which he would get a day of rest for every inning he pitched. Chamberlain never pitched on consecutive days, and if he pitched two innings, he would get two days off. Chamberlain pitched effectively out of the bullpen, and he even worked back-to-back days in late September as the Yankees got ready for the playoffs.

In Game 2 of the 2007 American League Divisional Series against Cleveland, the Yankees had a 1–0 lead in the bottom of the eighth. Chamberlain was on the mound with a man on first and nobody out. Suddenly, he was surrounded by a swarm of little insects known as midges.

Bug spray was used to try to repel the midges, but it wasn't helping as Chamberlain tried to pitch through it—but it was obvious that it became a distraction. A wild pitch allowed the tying run to go to second. After a sacrifice bunt moved the runner to third, the Indians tied the game when

Chamberlain threw his second wild pitch of the inning. The Yankees went on to lose Game 2 in extra innings and the Series in four.

The offseason was one of uncertainty because there was some debate whether to use Chamberlain as a starter or as a setup man for Hall of Fame closer Mariano Rivera. Chamberlain began the 2008 season in the bullpen, but the Yankees needed help for the starting rotation. In May, the Yankees decided to move Chamberlain into the rotation.

Chamberlain made his first major-league start in early June against the Baltimore Orioles. He threw 62 pitches in 2⅓ innings and gave up two runs while walking four batters. The Yankees gradually increased the workload and in late July, Chamberlain tossed seven scoreless innings with one walk and nine strikeouts against the Boston Red Sox at Fenway Park.

In August, Chamberlain hurt his shoulder, which put him out of action for a month. Chamberlain was back in the bullpen for the remainder of the season when he returned in early September, but it was the beginning of a question that plagued him and what was best for the team for the rest of his Yankee career—whether he belonged in the bullpen or the starting rotation.

In 2009, Chamberlain made 31 starts but he struggled terribly in the second half of the season and was in the bullpen for the postseason. Chamberlain never made another start for the Yankees.

In June 2011, Chamberlain underwent Tommy John surgery. In March 2012, during his rehab, the enigmatic pitcher suffered a freak leg injury while jumping on a trampoline.

Chamberlain's injury woes continued in his final Yankee season of 2013 when he suffered an oblique injury in May. Following the season, Chamberlain signed a free agent contract with the Detroit Tigers.

Johnny Damon had the first stolen base at Stadium III.

It happened in the first inning of the second game on April 17, 2009. Damon singled and stole second for the Yankees' first stolen base in the new ballpark. He did not score, but getting on base and using his speed was a prime example of what Damon brought to the Yankees during a four-year period from 2006 to 2009.

After four years with the Boston Red Sox, Damon became a free agent and signed a four-year, $52 million deal to switch sides in the rivalry

Johnny Damon
KEITH ALLISON VIA WIKIMEDIA COMMONS

and join the Yankees. There was one little detail that Damon had to take care of when he came to the Yankees. In accordance with the team's facial hair policy, Damon had his long hair cut and shaved his beard, which had become something of a trademark during his time in Boston.

Even though he didn't hit for power, and wasn't really a pull hitter, Damon was a tough out who had a left-handed swing that was tailor made for both Fenway Park and Yankee Stadium III. During his four years with the Yankees, Damon hit .285 and averaged over 100 runs scored and a little over 23 stolen bases per season.

On June 7, 2008, Damon entered the Yankee record books as he became the second Yankee in franchise history to get six hits in a nine-inning game (Gerald Williams had six hits in a 15-inning game at Tampa Bay in 1996). Damon was 6-for-6 with five singles and one double. He scored one run and drove in four, including a walkoff RBI single to beat the Kansas City Royals, 6–5.

Damon, who was a key member of the 2004 Red Sox team that came back from a 3–0 series deficit against the Yankees in the American

League Championship Series, was an integral part of the Yankees' run to the 2009 world championship.

In the American League Championship Series against the Los Angeles Angels, Damon was 9-for-30 with two home runs, five runs batted in, and four runs scored. Damon continued to be a major factor in the World Series against the Philadelphia Phillies. His ability to wreak havoc on the bases was on full display in the pivotal Game 4 at Philadelphia's Citizens Bank Park.

The Yankees had a 2–1 lead in the Series and Game 4 was tied at 4 in the top of the ninth. With two out and no one on, Damon singled on a 3-2 pitch.

With Mark Teixeira at the plate, Damon took off for second on the first pitch and slid in safely. Phillies third baseman Pedro Feliz came in front of the bag to take a two-hop throw from catcher Carlos Ruiz. Damon noticed pitcher Brad Lidge was not covering third, so he popped up out of his slide and took off. Feliz made a futile attempt to run him down as Damon was credited with two stolen bases on the play.

The play seemed to upset Lidge, because he hit Teixeira with the next pitch to put runners on first and third. Alex Rodriguez drove in the go-ahead run with an RBI single to score Damon, and Jorge Posada added a two-run single as the Yankees won Game 4, 7–4 to take a three games to one lead in the Series.

Following the 2009 season, Damon became a free agent and did not re-sign with the Yankees.

The first Yankee lineup in the history of Stadium III featured Hall of Fame shortstop Derek Jeter, but to his right was the starting third baseman for that game, journeyman infielder Cody Ransom.

Starting third baseman Alex Rodriguez was recovering from hip surgery in March and would not be ready until May. Ransom was named as the replacement until A-Rod could return. Ransom played in 15 of the team's first 16 games, but he was struggling and was sent to the minors.

Over his two-year tenure with the Yankees, Ransom played 147 games with the Yankees' Triple-A affiliate at Scranton Wilkes-Barre and 64 games with the big club. Ransom is best known for fielding the final out in the history of Stadium II on an unassisted putout at first base.

Nick Swisher hit the first double at Stadium III in the third inning of the inaugural game on April 16, 2009.

The charismatic Swisher became a fan favorite during his four-year tenure with the Yankees. The switch-hitting outfielder was acquired as part of a multi-player trade with the Chicago White Sox after the 2008 season.

Swisher was not the Yankees' starting right fielder when the 2009 season opened. In July 2008, the Yankees acquired outfielder Xavier Nady from Pittsburgh and he was penciled in to be the starting right fielder when the season began. The season was just over a week old when Nady suffered an elbow injury that would eventually end his season and give Swisher an opportunity to start in right field.

Swisher endeared himself to the fans with his energy and upbeat personality. He would answer the traditional roll call from the "Bleacher Creatures" in right-center field by standing at attention and then give them an emphatic salute for acknowledging him.

Nick Swisher
KEITH ALLISON VIA WIKIMEDIA COMMONS

Swisher hit career highs in 2009 with 29 home runs and 82 runs batted in. He struggled in the postseason, but he did hit a big home run in Game 3 of the World Series against Philadelphia. Batting right-handed against left-handed pitcher J. A. Happ in the sixth inning, Swisher hit a solo home run to give the Yanks a 6–3 lead in a game they would go on to win, 8–5.

In 2010, Swisher batted a career-high .288 and had a career-high .511 slugging percentage, while being named an All-Star for the only time in his career. In 2011 and 2012, the switch-hitter put up some consistent numbers with 23 and 24 home runs, along with 85 and 93 runs batted in.

One of Swisher's memorable moments as a Yankee was when he pitched a scoreless inning against the Tampa Bay Rays. On April 13, 2009, the Yankees were trailing the Rays 15–5 at the Trop and did not want to go to the bullpen to use another pitcher for the bottom of the eighth inning of a blowout. Swisher started the game at first base and had hit a home run, but there he was on the mound to face the Rays' hitters in the home half of the eighth.

The inning didn't start well for the left-hand thrower as he walked Melvin Upton Jr. and gave up a single to Willy Aybar to put runners on first and second. Swisher then got the next three hitters as he struck out Gabe Kapler swinging, got Carlos Peña on a popout to second, and retired Pat Burrell on a flyout to Brett Gardner in center field.

After the 2012 season, Swisher became a free agent and signed a contract with the Cleveland Indians.

Another switch-hitter, first baseman Mark Teixeira, was the first Yankee to be hit by a pitch at Stadium III. In the bottom of the first inning of the first game, Teixeira, who was batting third, was hit by Indians pitcher Cliff Lee.

After the 2008 season, the Yankees were in need of a first baseman as Jason Giambi's contract had expired and he was not re-signed. The Yankees had initially wooed Teixeira early in the offseason but withdrew their initial offer. The Yankees were focused on pitching and had already signed free agent pitchers C. C. Sabathia and A. J. Burnett before they turned their attention to Teixeira.

Other teams were showing interest in signing the free agent first baseman, including the rival Boston Red Sox who reportedly offered an eight-year, $168 million deal. The Yankees came in with an eight-year, $180 million offer which Teixeira accepted.

The Maryland native got off to a slow start in his first season with the Yankees, and the fans were letting him know about it. In mid-May, the switch-hitting first baseman was hitting under .200, and the Yankees were 15-17 and 6½ games behind the first-place Toronto Blue Jays. It was a similar situation to what Tino Martinez experienced when he came to the Yankees in 1996. Martinez, who was replacing a legend in Don Mattingly, also got off to a terrible start in his first season.

Teixeira finished the month of May on a tear that jumpstarted his season. From May 13 to June 1, Teixeira slashed .410/.472/.859 with an OPS of 1.331 with nine home runs and 27 runs batted in. His season batting average rose from .191 to .282, and the Yankees went 15-4 in that stretch and took over first place in the AL East.

In August, the Yankees took charge of the AL East as they won 21 of 28 games to open up a 6½-game lead over the second-place Boston Red Sox. Teixeira hit .294 with 26 RBIs in the month and was putting together an outstanding first season in New York.

"Tex" led the American League with 39 home runs and 122 runs batted in and was an All-Star for the second time and the first as a Yankee. The slugging first baseman won a Gold Glove and Silver Slugger Award and finished second in the voting for the American League's Most Valuable Player Award.

On October 9, 2009, first baseman Mark "Tex" Teixeira became the first Yankee to hit a walkoff home run in an American League Division Series game. It was also the first walkoff hit by a Yankee in an ALDS game.

The Yankees were hosting the Minnesota Twins in Game 2 of the best of five series. The switch-hitting first baseman led off the inning, batting right-handed against Twins' left-handed reliever José Mijares. On a 2-1 pitch, Teixeira smoked a line drive down the left field line. The ball had enough height to clear the wall as the Yankees beat the Twins, 4–3.

Teixeira was known as a durable player for most of his major-league career. In the first three years of his Yankee career, Teixeira missed a total

Mark Teixeira

of 16 games, but in 2012, he was limited to 123 games due to a calf injury. It was the beginning of a wave of injuries for Teixeira that would eventually derail his career.

In March 2013, Teixeira was playing for the US team in the World Baseball Classic when he suffered a strained wrist tendon. The first baseman did not get back in the lineup until late May, but he reaggravated the injury in mid-June and missed the remainder of the season after having played in 15 games.

The wrist continued to bother Teixeira in 2014, but he played in 123 games and hit 22 home runs. In 2015, his last big season, he slammed 31 home runs in 111 games and was named an All-Star for the third time in his career, second as a Yankee.

The injuries continued to plague Teixeira in what would be his final season in 2016. Teixeira dealt with neck spasms in May. In early June, he dealt with right knee soreness and an MRI revealed a meniscus tear. Teixeira did not undergo surgery and returned late in the month.

On July 3, Teixeira hit two home runs against the San Diego Padres at Petco Park to become the fifth switch-hitter to hit 400 home runs. "Tex" hit his 400th home run in the eighth inning off of Padres pitcher Carlos Villanueva and added his 401st home run in the ninth.

In early August, Teixeira, who cited the injuries and wanting to spend more time with family, announced that he would retire at the end of the season.

On September 28, in a game against the Boston Red Sox at Yankee Stadium, Teixeira hit a walkoff, grand slam home run to give the Yankees a thrilling 5–3 win. It was the final home run of Teixeira's career and the first game-ending home run of his career. It was also the first walkoff grand slam at the new Yankee Stadium.

The Yankees honored Teixeira before his final game on October 2. He went 0-for-3 and left the field for the final time in the seventh inning.

Yankee Stadium opened in 1923, but it wasn't until 1938 that there was a no-hitter pitched in that ballpark. A Yankee pitcher threw the first no-hitter in Yankee Stadium history. Name him.

On August 27, 1938, in the second game of a doubleheader, Yankee pitcher Monte Pearson tossed the first no-hitter in Yankee Stadium history against his former team, the Cleveland Indians, in a 13–0 win. It was the third no-hitter (George Mogridge in 1917 and Sam Jones in 1923) in Yankee franchise history, but the first ever thrown at the Stadium.

Pearson walked two and struck out seven, and he got all the offensive support that he needed from the powerful Yankee offense that produced 13 runs. The red hot Pearson won his 10th consecutive game and it was his fourth straight complete game.

Nearly 41,000 fans were on hand to see Pearson, who was pitching on two days rest and in his third game in eight days, set down the first nine Indians' hitters with only one ball leaving the infield. After issuing back-to-back walks to start the fourth, Pearson retired the next three hitters and escaped unscathed. It was the only inning that Cleveland would have a runner on base.

Pearson retired the final 18 hitters to put his name in the record books. When he got Indians outfielder Bruce Campbell to fly out to left for the final out, hundreds of fans rushed onto the field and Pearson had to battle his way back to the clubhouse.

The Yankees acquired Pearson and pitcher Steve Sundra from the Indians in exchange for pitcher Johnny Allen in December 1935. The deal was not met with rave reviews. Allen was a fiery competitor and had a temper that reportedly would get the best of him, but he endeared himself to the fans with his intensity. Reportedly, the Yankees made the deal to get Sundra and considered Pearson a throw-in, but there were some who thought Allen's behavior scared the owner, Jacob Ruppert, into dealing him away.

In his first season with the Yankees, Pearson got off to a fast start as he won eight of his first nine decisions. The Yankees rolled to the American League pennant, and Pearson finished with a career-high 19 wins with a 3.71 ERA and was named an All-Star for the first time.

In the 1936 World Series against the crosstown New York Giants, Pearson got the start in Game 4 at Yankee Stadium. Before over 66,000 fans, Pearson went the distance and beat Hall of Famer Carl Hubbell as the Yankees took a 3–1 lead in the Series with a 5–2 win.

Hubbell was red hot coming into the game, having won his last 16 regular-season decisions, and he had also beat the Yankees 6–1 in Game 1 at the Polo Grounds. In Game 4, Pearson outpitched the Hall of Famer and was supported by Lou Gehrig, who had two hits and two runs batted in.

The Yankees went on to win the World Series in four consecutive seasons from 1936 to 1939. Pearson made one start in each of those four series and won all four games that he started, while coming up one-third of an inning short of four complete games.

In the 1939 World Series against the Cincinnati Reds, Pearson made his final Series appearance a memorable one. Pearson started Game 2 at Yankee Stadium and was no-hitting the National League champions for 7⅓ innings, until catcher Ernie Lombardi singled to break up the bid. Pearson walked one and struck out eight in blanking the Reds 4–0 to give the Yankees their second win, en route to a four-game sweep. Pearson's career World Series ERA was 1.01.

In 1940, Pearson made the All-Star team with a 6-4 record and 3.32 ERA through the month of June. In late July, Pearson pitched 13 innings to beat the Indians and Hall of Famer Bob Feller, 4–3. Unfortunately, Pearson hurt his right shoulder and tried to make one more appearance seven days later before shutting it down for the season.

After the season, the Yankees traded Pearson to the Reds.

Sometimes, a pitcher's major-league debut doesn't go as planned. Who was the first Yankee pitcher to give up a home run to the first major-league batter that he faced at Yankee Stadium?

On May 12, 1944, pitcher Bill Bevens made his major-league debut against the Detroit Tigers at Yankee Stadium and became the first Yankee rookie pitcher to give up a home run to the first batter he faced.

The Tigers had a 6–2 lead with two on and one out when Bevens relieved Yankees starting pitcher Bill Zuber. Tigers outfielder Jimmy Outlaw was the first batter that the 27-year-old faced, and he took the Yankee rookie deep for a three-run home run.

Bevens played his entire four-year career with the Yankees from 1944 to 1947. His best season was 1946 when the right-hander was 16-13 with a 2.23 ERA.

Bevens' moment in the sun came in Game 4 of the 1947 World Series against the Brooklyn Dodgers.

Bevens took a no-hitter into the bottom of the ninth and was three outs away from throwing the first no-hit game in World Series play. The Yankees were leading 2–1, but Bevens had lapses of control (he walked 10 batters, one intentional) during the game and that led to Brooklyn scoring a run in the fifth and contributed to the famous finish.

Dodgers catcher Bruce Edwards led off the ninth by flying out to deep left field. After Carl Furillo walked, Bevens got Spider Jorgensen on a foulout to first base, putting him one out away from the no-hitter.

Pete Reiser pinch-hit for pitcher Hugh Casey. After pinch-runner Al Gionfriddo stole second, Yankee manager Bucky Harris decided to put the winning run on base, so he intentionally walked Reiser to put runners on first and second. It was a bold move by Harris, who went against "the book" by putting the winning run on base.

Eddie Miksis ran for Reiser and the Dodgers sent up pinch-hitter Cookie Lavagetto to bat for Eddie Stanky. Lavagetto spoiled Bevens's bid for greatness when he lined a double over Yankee right fielder Tommy Henrich's head, off of the right field wall to score the tying and winning runs to give Brooklyn a stunning 3–2 win that tied the Series at two games apiece.

Bevens got some payback, three days later in Game 7 at Yankee Stadium. When Bevens entered the game in the second inning in relief of starter Spec Shea, the Yankees were trailing 1–0 and the Dodgers had two on and one out. Jorgensen's ground-rule double scored a second run, but Bevens got the next two outs to keep the score at a two-run deficit.

Bevens pitched two more scoreless innings and the Yankees took the lead while he was the pitcher of record. Joe Page pitched shutout ball over the final five innings and was awarded the win as the Yankees won the Series with a 5–2 win.

That game was Bevens's final appearance in the major leagues. Bevens was unable to pitch in 1948 and afterwards, he made a number of unsuccessful comeback attempts. A number of years after his final game, Bevens reportedly said that his "arm went dead during the World Series."

What three players became the first trio to hit a grand slam in the same game at Yankee Stadium, as well as the first to do so in major-league history?

On August 25, 2011, the Yankees were hosting the Oakland Athletics at Yankee Stadium when Robinson Canó, Russell Martin, and Curtis Granderson became the first trio in major-league history to hit grand slam home runs in the same game.

Cano got the party going with a grand slam in the bottom of the fifth inning off of A's pitcher Rich Harden. In the sixth inning, Martin cleared the bases with a home run against A's pitcher Faustino De Los Santos. Granderson completed the trifecta with a slam off of A's pitcher Bruce Billings in the eighth inning. Martin had six runs batted in total, while Canó and Granderson each had five as the Yankees walloped the A's, 22–9.

Catcher Russell Martin played only two seasons with the Yankees, but he made his presence felt down the stretch of the 2012 season. The Yankees held off the Baltimore Orioles, thanks in part to Martin's red hot September when he hit seven home runs with 17 RBIs.

On September 21, Martin hit a walkoff home run in the bottom of the 10th as the Yankees beat the Oakland A's 2–1 to remain a game ahead of the Orioles with 12 games remaining.

Following the 2012 season, Martin signed with the Pittsburgh Pirates as a free agent. In two years with the Yankees, Martin hit 39 home runs.

Curtis Granderson was acquired by the Yankees as part of a three-team trade with the Detroit Tigers and Arizona Diamondbacks in December 2009. Johnny Damon's contract had expired, and the Yankees were in the market for a center fielder.

In his first Yankee at-bat in the 2010 season opener at Fenway Park, Granderson hit a home run off of Boston Red Sox pitcher Josh Beckett. Injuries hampered him throughout the 2010 season, but Granderson still hit 24 home runs.

Curtis Granderson
KEITH ALLISON VIA WIKIMEDIA COMMONS

In 2011, Granderson had an All-Star season as he led the major leagues in runs scored with 136. The left-handed hitter slammed 41 home runs with an American League leading 119 runs batted in. Granderson posted a .916 OPS and finished fourth in the voting for the American League's MVP award.

"The Grandy Man" played in 160 games in 2012. He hit 43 home runs to tie Texas's Josh Hamilton for second in the major leagues, with 106 runs batted in.

Granderson's final Yankee season was plagued by injury. Granderson was hit by a pitch in spring training and fractured his forearm. He returned in May but suffered a a broken finger late in the month and needed surgery. Granderson returned in August but was limited to 61 games.

After the season, Granderson became a free agent and did not re-sign with the Yankees.

On May 5, 2005, the Yankees were 11-17. GM Brian Cashman wanted to shake things up, so he promoted second baseman Robinson Canó from the minors to replace Tony Womack as the starter for the big club. Canó had proven he could hit minor-league pitching and was batting .333 when he was brought up from Columbus, the Yankees' Triple-A affiliate.

Canó started slow and had some ups and downs in his first season, but he completed his rookie season with 132 games played. The 22-year-old left-handed hitter from the Dominican Republic slashed .297/.320/.458 with a .778 OPS with 14 home runs and 62 runs batted in and finished second in the voting for the American League Rookie of the Year Award. Canó slashed .342/.365/.525 with an OPS of .890 in 2006, making the All-Star team for the first time and winning a Silver Slugger Award.

Over the next seven seasons, Canó continued to be an impactful presence in the Yankee lineup. During the 2009 championship season, Canó hit .320 with a career high 204 hits, 25 home runs, and 85 RBIs. He finished in the top 10 in the American League in eight categories, including hits and batting average.

Canó won a Gold Glove in 2010, becoming the first Yankees second baseman to capture the award since Bobby Richardson in 1965. He was an All-Star and Silver Slugger Award winner in 2012 and 2013.

Canó left the Yankees after the 2013 season and signed as a free agent with the Seattle Mariners. During his nine years with the Yankees, Cano slashed .309/.355/.504 with an OPS of .860 with 204 home runs.

Who were the players involved in the first ever triple play turned by the Yankees at Yankee Stadium?

Yankee Stadium opened in 1923, but it wasn't until 1931 that the Yankees would turn a triple play at home.

Lou Gehrig was the first baseman when the Yankees turned the first triple play by the home team at Yankee Stadium on June 6, 1931, against the Cleveland Indians.

The Yankees were trailing 7–4 in the top of the ninth inning and Cleveland had runners on first and second with nobody out. Indians third baseman and right-handed hitter Willie Kamm lined out to Gehrig, who recorded the second out at first and threw to second to shortstop Lyn Lary to complete the 3-3-6 triple play.

Lary played parts of six seasons with the Yankees from 1929 to 1934. In 1931, Lary had a career-best 10 home runs with 107 runs batted in. He never came close to matching that RBI output in his entire career.

Lary had his playing time curtailed in 1932 as Frank Crosetti was being groomed to be the next shortstop. Lary was part of the team that swept the Chicago Cubs in the World Series, but he did not appear in any of the games.

The legendary Gehrig is considered by many to be the greatest first baseman in the history of baseball. His illustrious career was infamously cut short by amyotrophic lateral sclerosis (ALS), or what became known as "Lou Gehrig's disease."

During his 17-year career, Gehrig was a two-time American League MVP winner, seven-time All-Star, Triple Crown winner, and played on six Yankees' World Series winning teams.

Gehrig was the first Yankee to win baseball's Triple Crown (leading the league in batting average, home runs and runs batted in) in 1934 when he hit 49 home runs with 166 RBIs and slashed .363/.465/.706 with an OPS of 1.172. Despite those great numbers, Gehrig finished fifth in the AL MVP voting. The Yankees finished second to the Detroit

Lou Gehrig in 1923
LIBRARY OF CONGRESS

Tigers in 1934, and three Tigers players received more votes than Gehrig, while teammate Lefty Gomez finished third in the voting.

Gehrig played every game during the 1938 season, but that would turn out to be for the final time. His skills were starting to erode, and it was becoming apparent that his career was coming to a close. Gehrig had respectable numbers, but they weren't up to the standards he had set since he became the Yankees' starting first baseman.

During spring training in 1939, Gehrig struggled to hit and that carried over into the season. The Yankees hosted the Boston Red Sox on Opening Day in 1939. In the bottom of the first inning, Gehrig, who was hitting fifth in the lineup, came to the plate with two on and two out. The reported crowd of over 30,000 gave him a huge ovation, but he hit a weak liner to right field for the final out of the inning.

Later in the game, the proud first baseman hit into two inning-ending double plays. Gehrig played seven more games and was 4-for-24 during that span.

On May 2, 1939, Gehrig asked out of the lineup for the first time since he began his legendary streak of 2,130 consecutive games played on June 1, 1925. Later in the month, Gehrig announced his retirement.

On July 4, 1939, between games of a doubleheader against the Washington Senators, Gehrig gave his famous speech when he said he was the "luckiest man on the face of the earth," and "I might have been given a bad break, but I've got an awful lot to live for."

Gehrig compiled a career batting average of .340 with 494 home runs and 1,995 RBIs. He had more than 150 runs batted in seven times and hit 23 grand slams, an all-time record that stood until it was broken by Yankees third baseman Alex Rodriguez in 2013.

Who was the first Yankee pitcher to hit a grand slam home run at Yankee Stadium?

Hall of Famer Red Ruffing was the first Yankee pitcher to hit a grand slam home run at the Stadium.

On April 14, 1933, Ruffing hit a walkoff grand slam home run off of Red Sox pitcher Bob Weiland in the bottom of the ninth to beat the Boston Red Sox 6–2.

Ruffing was acquired in a trade with the Red Sox on May 6, 1930 and went on to become one of the greatest pitchers in Yankees' franchise history.

Ruffing was 231-124 with a 3.47 ERA in 15 seasons with the Yankees. He was a six-time All-Star and a six-time world champion. In World Series play, Ruffing was 7-2 with a 2.52 ERA and was the Yankees' Game 1 starter in six of his seven World Series appearances.

Ruffing finished in the top 10 in a number of all-time franchise lists including second in wins, and innings pitched (3,168.2). He's tied for second with Mel Stottlemyre in shutouts (40), fifth in strikeouts (1,526), and first in complete games (261).

Ruffing was the Yanks' Opening Day starter in 1931, and he went on to a 16-14 record. The Ohio native put it all together in 1932 when he

Red Ruffing with the Red Sox in 1924
LIBRARY OF CONGRESS

went 18-7 with a 3.09 ERA. Ruffing led the American League with 190 strikeouts as the Yankees won their first pennant since 1928.

In August, Ruffing became the first pitcher in major-league history to toss a complete-game shutout, strike out 10 or more, and hit a home run in a 1–0 win. Ruffing allowed three hits and struck out 12 and homered in the top of the 10th off of Washington Senators pitcher Tommy Thomas for the game-deciding run.

Ruffing went the distance to win Game 1 of the four-game sweep of the Chicago Cubs in the 1932 World Series. Ruffing was not his best, but with the help of the Yankees' potent offense, he was able to pitch nine innings to get the win.

The Yankees began a run of four straight World Series championships in 1936. It's no coincidence that Ruffing began a run of four straight seasons with 20 or more wins.

In 1938, Ruffing led the American League with 21 wins and was an All-Star for the second time. In the World Series four-game sweep against the Chicago Cubs, Ruffing pitched two complete games in Game 1 and the clinching Game 4.

Ruffing dealt with an elbow injury during the 1939 season, but he still won 21 games for the second consecutive season. Ruffing sat out the last few weeks of the season but returned to go nine innings in Game 1 of the 1939 World Series at Yankee Stadium against the Cincinnati Reds.

The Yankees won 2–1 on Bill Dickey's walkoff RBI single in the bottom of the ninth. It was the first ever postseason walkoff win in franchise history, and the hit gave Ruffing his sixth career World Series win.

Ruffing made two more World Series starts for the Yankees. In 1941, the right-hander tossed a complete game to beat the Brooklyn Dodgers 3–2 in Game 1 as the Yankees won in five. In the 1942 Series against the St. Louis Cardinals, Ruffing suffered his first Series loss in the deciding Game 5.

Ruffing missed the 1943 and 1944 seasons due to military service. He returned in the middle of the 1945 season and went 7-3 with a 2.89 ERA in 11 starts.

Ruffing was a spot starter in 1946 and had a 5-1 record in late June, but he broke his kneecap as the result of a batted ball by Philadelphia Athletics third baseman Hank Majeski. Ruffing did not pitch the rest of the season and was released by the Yankees after the season.

Match the year with the first at Yankee Stadium:

First night game	**1939**
First year with uniform numbers	**1923**
First All-Star Game	**1946**
First World Series game	**1934**
First cycle by a Yankee	**1929**

The first night game in the history of Yankee Stadium was played on May 28, 1946, against the Washington Senators.

The event was delayed by a day when the game was rained out the night before. On an unseasonably cool Tuesday evening, nearly 50,000 fans were in attendance to see the first game at the Stadium under the lights. General Electric installed the lights, and their president, Charles Wilson, threw out the ceremonial first pitch.

Shortly before 9:00 p.m., the first pitch was thrown by Yankee starter Clarence "Cuddles" Marshall, who ended up on the short end of a 2–1 loss.

Snuffy Stirnweiss got the first Yankee hit in a night game at the Stadium. Joe DiMaggio drove in Stirnweiss with a single with the first Yankee RBI in a home night game.

The first Yankee home run in a home night game would not come until May 31 when the Yankees hosted the Philadelphia Athletics in the second ever night game at Yankee Stadium. In the bottom of the first inning, left fielder Charlie "King Kong" Keller hit a three-run home run off of Athletics pitcher Dick Fowler for the first long ball in a home night game.

The Yankees first began wearing numbers on their uniforms in 1929.

The jerseys were numbered according to where the players hit in the batting order. Babe Ruth batted third, so he got #3, while Lou Gehrig got #4 for hitting in the four spot.

On July 11, 1939, Yankee Stadium hosted its first All-Star Game. The American League All-Stars beat the National League All-Stars 3–1 before a crowd of over 62,000.

Six Yankees were in the American League's starting lineup including catcher Bill Dickey, third baseman Red Rolfe, center fielder Joe DiMaggio, left fielder George Selkirk, second baseman Joe Gordon, and pitcher Red Ruffing.

DiMaggio hit a solo home run in the bottom of the fifth inning off of Chicago Cubs pitcher Bill Lee, while Selkirk had a run batted in. Except for Ruffing, the Yankees' representatives played the entire game.

The original Yankee Stadium hosted three other All-Star Games including 1960, 1977, and 2008, the final year of that building's existence.

In the 2008 game, the American League beat the National League 4–3 in a record-tying 15 innings.

The Yankees won their first American League pennant in 1923 and Yankee Stadium hosted its first World Series game against the New York Giants. On October 10, 1923, the Stadium hosted Game 1 of the World Series as the Giants beat the Yankees, 5–4.

Hall of Famer Waite Hoyt threw the first World Series pitch at Yankee Stadium. Bob Meusel got the first Yankee hit at the Stadium in a World Series game in the bottom of the second, an RBI double that scored Babe Ruth with the first World Series run at the ballpark.

Third baseman Joe Dugan was the first Yankee to hit a World Series home run at Yankee Stadium. Dugan hit a three-run home run off of Giants pitcher Jack Bentley in the bottom of the second inning to give the Yankees a 6–1 lead.

Dugan played parts of seven seasons with the Yankees and won seven American League pennants and three World Series championships. Dugan was an exceptional fielding third baseman, who didn't hit with much power.

Dugan's best overall season with the Yankees was 1923 when he batted .283 with career highs in runs scored (111) and RBIs (65), while leading the American League with 644 at-bats. He followed up in 1924 with a .302 average and 105 runs scored.

Chronic knee problems and other assorted injuries hampered Dugan in his later years with the Yankees. In his final season with the Yankees in 1928, Dugan appeared in 94 games. Besides his knee problem, Dugan was hit by a pitch on the elbow in May, leading to a problem that lingered all season long. After the season, Dugan was placed on waivers and was claimed by the Boston Braves.

On June 25, 1934, Hall of Famer Lou Gehrig became the first Yankee to hit for the cycle at Yankee Stadium. Gehrig had a single, double, triple, and home run against the Washington Senators before a reported crowd of 4,000 at the Stadium.

Left fielder Bert Daniels was the first player in franchise history to hit for the cycle. Daniels accomplished the feat on July 25, 1912, when the franchise was known as the New York Highlanders.

On April 18, 1929, the Yankees wore numbered uniforms for the first time. A player's number reflected his position in the batting order. Who was the first Yankee to come to bat wearing a numbered uniform?

On April 18, 1929, the Yankees played the season opener against the Boston Red Sox at Yankee Stadium. It was an historic day as the Yankees wore numbered uniforms for the first time.

The players' numbers reflected their position in the batting order. Hall of Fame center fielder Earle Combs led off for the Yankees, so he was wearing #1 as the first Yankee to come to bat.

Shortstop Mark Koenig was second in the order, so he wore #2, Babe Ruth was #3, Lou Gehrig #4. Bob Meusel, Tony Lazzeri, Leo Durocher, Johnny Grabowski, and starting pitcher George Pipgras, respectively, wore #5 through #9.

Combs played his entire 12-year, major-league career with the Yankees. He was the leadoff hitter for the Yankees famed "Murderers' Row"

From left to right, Lou Gehrig, Babe Ruth, Earle Combs, and Tony Lazzeri at Fenway Park

lineup in 1927 that featured three other Hall of Famers besides himself, including Ruth, Gehrig, and Lazzeri.

Combs was a speedy outfielder who hit .300 and got on base at over a .400 clip for most of his career. He also scored over 100 runs in eight consecutive seasons from 1925 to 1932. Combs led the league in triples three times and is second in franchise history with 154 triples (Lou Gehrig is first with 163).

Combs's career got off to a flying start in 1924 as he was batting .400 in his first 23 games. However, he suffered a fractured ankle in June and got into only one more game in September.

In 1925, Babe Ruth missed a third of the season, but Combs was healthy and he had a breakout season. The left-handed hitter batted .342 with 203 hits and 117 runs scored. The Yankees finished under .500, but Combs's season was one of the few highlights.

The Yankees rebounded to win the pennant in 1926. Combs's numbers fell off somewhat, but he still scored 113 runs and had a good World Series against the St. Louis Cardinals, despite the Yankees losing. In six games, Combs hit .357 and was on base 15 times in 33 plate appearances.

In 1927, Combs had one of the greatest seasons ever by a leadoff hitter. Combs played in 152 games and, except for four games, hit leadoff in every one. The Yankee center fielder led the American League with 726 plate appearances, 648 at-bats, a franchise-record 231 hits (later broken by Don Mattingly with 238 in 1986), and a career-high 23 triples.

In the four-game sweep of the Pittsburgh Pirates in the World Series, Combs continued to be a consistent performer as he hit .313 with six runs scored.

Year in and year out, Combs was always one of the most consistent Yankees. He never batted lower than .300 until his final year in 1935 when injuries took their toll. Combs led the league with 21 triples in 1928 and 22 in 1930.

The Yankees repeated as world champions in 1928, but Combs only appeared in one game in the World Series win over the St. Louis Cardinals as he dealt with a wrist injury.

The Yankees went three years without winning a pennant but returned to the World Series in 1932 against the Chicago Cubs. The

33-year-old Combs batted .375 in the four-game sweep with his only career World Series home run, eight runs scored, and six runs batted in.

Combs suffered a serious injury that curtailed his 1934 season. The Yankees were playing the St. Louis Browns at Sportsman Park and had a 2–1 lead in the bottom of the seventh. Browns third baseman Harlond Clift hit a ball toward the left field line. Combs slammed into the left field wall trying to make a play and suffered a fractured skull, broken shoulder, and a knee injury that put him out for the rest of the season.

Combs returned in 1935, but the 36-year-old broke his collarbone, thus ending his career.

Name the first Yankee to hit a pinch-hit grand slam on Opening Day. Bonus: Who was the first Yankee to hit a grand slam on Opening Day?

Bobby Murcer—who played 13 years with the Yankees in two separate stints—was the first Yankee to hit a pinch-hit grand slam home run on Opening Day.

On April 9, 1981, the Yankees hosted the Texas Rangers at Yankee Stadium. With the bases loaded in the bottom of the seventh, Murcer was sent up as a pinch-hitter and he cleared the bases with a home run off of Rangers pitcher Steve Comer.

Murcer, who was one of the most popular Yankees of all time, was a highly touted prospect. When he debuted in 1965, the 19-year-old was being labeled as the heir apparent to Mickey Mantle, who was in the twilight of his career. Like Mantle, Murcer was from Oklahoma, and like Mantle, he began his pro career as a shortstop but eventually moved to center field.

After spending two years in military service, the Oklahoma native joined the Yankees for the 1969 season. He began the year as the starting third baseman, but was moved to the outfield in May. By September, Murcer was ensconced in center field. Even with the distraction of changing defensive positions, Murcer hit 26 home runs with 82 runs batted in during the 1969 season.

Murcer was the starting center fielder in 1970, as the Yankees won 93 games and finished in second place in the American League East.

Bobby Murcer

The left-handed hitter posted similar power numbers as he finished with 23 home runs.

The highlight of the 1970 season for Murcer occurred on June 24. Murcer tied a major-league record by smacking four consecutive home runs in four consecutive official at-bats, in a doubleheader against the Cleveland Indians at Yankee Stadium.

In the first game, Murcer homered off of Indians pitcher Sam McDowell in his final at-bat. In the second game, the Yankee center fielder hit a home run off of Indians pitcher Mike Paul in the bottom of the first inning. Murcer walked in the fourth inning but homered off Paul again in the fifth.

In the bottom of the eighth inning, Murcer hit a home run off of Indians pitcher Fred Lasher to tie a major-league record with four home runs in four consecutive at-bats. The following day, Murcer walked in his first at-bat, but popped out in his succeeding at-bat to end his record-tying streak.

Murcer had his best all-around season in 1971. He hit a career-high .331 to finish second to Hall of Famer Tony Oliva (.337) for the American League batting title. Murcer led the league in OBP (.427) and OPS (.969) and was second in the league with a .543 slugging percentage.

The left-handed-hitting Murcer was able to take advantage of the short right field porch at Yankee Stadium when he slammed a career-high 33 home runs and drove in a career-high 96 runs in 1972. Murcer hit 22 home runs in 1973, the final year of the original Yankee Stadium. The famous ballpark was scheduled to be renovated in 1974 and 1975, so the Yankees would play their home games during that two-year period at Shea Stadium in Queens. Shea Stadium's right-field dimensions were not as friendly to Murcer as Yankee Stadium, and it showed as his numbers dropped off drastically.

In 1974, Murcer's batting average went from .304 to .274. The Oklahoma native hit only 10 home runs, the first time he had less than 20 since he became a regular player. His on-base percentage went from .357 to .332, his slugging percentage went from .464 to .378, and his OPS was .710 after it was .821 in the previous season.

After the 1974 season, the Yankees swung a blockbuster trade with the San Francisco Giants. Murcer was dealt to San Francisco in exchange for star outfielder Bobby Bonds. Murcer played two seasons with the Giants, who traded him to the Chicago Cubs before the start of the 1977 season. After two-plus seasons with the Cubs, Murcer was traded back to the Yankees in late June 1979.

Murcer was happy to be back, but tragedy struck on August 2 when his good friend and Yankee catcher and captain Thurman Munson perished in a plane crash in Canton, Ohio.

Four days later, Murcer delivered a eulogy at Munson's funeral and was in the lineup that night when the Yankees hosted the Baltimore Orioles at Yankee Stadium. As if drawing inspiration from his late friend, Murcer drove in all five runs, including a walkoff two-run single in the bottom of the ninth as the Yankees rallied for an emotional 5–4 win.

The Yankees were trailing 4–0 in the bottom of the seventh when Murcer hit a three-run homer off of Orioles pitcher Dennis Martínez to cut the deficit to one. In the ninth, the Yankees had runners at second and third with no one out, when Murcer singled to left field off of Orioles pitcher and former Yankee Tippy Martinez to score both runs to win the game.

Murcer's last season as a semi-regular player was 1980, when he helped the Yankees win the American League East Division. In his first taste of postseason play, Murcer went 0-for-4 in Game 2 of the American League Championship Series loss to Kansas City in three games.

Murcer was a part-time player by the time the Yankees returned to the World Series in 1981 against the Los Angeles Dodgers. Murcer was used as a pinch-hitter in four of the games but failed to get a World Series hit.

Murcer played in only nine games during the 1983 season when he was convinced to retire to allow the Yankees to promote Don Mattingly. Murcer announced his retirement in June. On August 7, the Yankees held Bobby Murcer Day to honor the popular player.

Murcer went right from the field to the broadcast booth in 1983 where his popularity with the fans grew even larger. In 2006, Murcer was diagnosed with a malignant brain tumor. He passed away on July 12, 2008 at the age of 62.

On April 17, 1945, journeyman outfielder Russ Derry became the first Yankee to hit a grand slam home run on Opening Day. Derry cleared the bases with a home run off of Red Sox pitcher Rex Cecil at Yankee Stadium.

With the game tied at 4 in the bottom of the seventh, Derry hit a ball deep into the right field stands at the Stadium to clear the bases and give the Yankees an 8–4 lead. It was the highlight of Derry's career with the Yankees, which lasted only two seasons.

The Princeton, Missouri, native hit only 17 home runs during his big-league career, but 13 of those came with the Yankees in 1945. In April 1946, the Yankees sold Derry's contract to the Philadelphia Athletics.

The other Yankees to hit a grand slam home run on Opening Day were Alfonso Soriano in 2003 and Alex Rodriguez in 2006.

Yankee Stadium opened on April 18, 1923. Who threw the very first pitch in Yankee Stadium history?

Right-hander Bob Shawkey, a four-time 20-game winner and two-time world champion with the Yankees, threw the first ever pitch at Yankee Stadium.

The Yankees hosted the Boston Red Sox in the first ever game, and Shawkey was the first starting pitcher. The first batter that Shawkey faced was Red Sox shortstop Chuck Fewster, and the first ever pitch was reportedly off the plate for ball one.

Shawkey went the distance and gave up a run on three hits as the Yankees beat the Red Sox 4–1 in the inaugural game at Yankee Stadium. Shawkey also scored the first ever run at Yankee Stadium as he came home from third on a fielder's choice.

After pitching parts of three seasons with the Philadelphia Athletics, Shawkey's contract was bought by the Yankees in June 1915 for $3,000. After coming to the Yankees, Shawkey appeared in 16 games and was 4-7 with a 3.26 ERA.

The Syracuse, New York, native had a breakout season in 1916 when he won 24 games with a 2.21 ERA. Shawkey had 21 complete games, but he also recorded eight saves and led the American League with 24 games finished.

In 1920, Shawkey won 20 games and led the American League with a 2.45 ERA, but he had an ugly incident that resulted in a suspension.

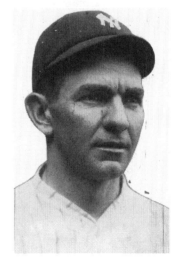

Bob Shawkey
LIBRARY OF CONGRESS

On May 27, Shawkey was facing the Boston Red Sox at Fenway Park. In the bottom of the fourth inning, the Yankees led 3–0, but the Red Sox had the bases loaded and two out and Shawkey walked in a run, on a pitch that he felt was strike three. Home plate umpire George Hildebrand ruled ball four, forcing in the run.

Shawkey struck out the next batter to end the inning, but he wasn't done debating the ball four call. Hildebrand ejected the Yankee pitcher, who proceeded to violently confront Hildebrand. In an act of self-defense, the umpire whacked Shawkey on the side of his head with his mask, leaving him bloodied behind his ear. American League president Ban Johnson suspended Shawkey. He was reinstated one week later after Shawkey wrote a letter of apology and paid a fine.

Shawkey pitched for back-to-back American League pennant winners in 1921 and 1922, but the Yankees lost the World Series in both seasons.

In the 1923 World Series win over the New York Giants, Shawkey won Game 4 at the Polo Grounds to even the Series at two games apiece. The Yankee right-hander gave up three runs in 7⅔ innings pitched as the Yankees beat the Giants, 8–4.

Shawkey was getting older, and in 1926, he was 35 years old when the Yankees faced the St. Louis Cardinals in the World Series. Shawkey appeared in three games, all losses, as the Yankees were beaten in seven games.

Shawkey was a member of the great 1927 World Series team, but he didn't pitch in the postseason. In his final two seasons, Sharkey served as a pitching coach and mentored the team's young arms.

The Yankees released Shawkey after the 1927 season.

Who had the first Yankee hit at the original Yankee Stadium?

Second baseman Aaron Ward got the first Yankee hit at the original Yankee Stadium.

Ward led off the bottom of the third inning with a single off of Red Sox pitcher Howard Ehmke, who had set down the first six Yankee hitters including Babe Ruth.

Ward joined the Yankees in 1917 as a utility infielder who could play all four positions. He played sparingly in his first three seasons but got an opportunity in 1920.

Starting third baseman Frank "Home Run" Baker stepped away from the game to care for his children following the untimely death of his wife. Ward became the starting third baseman in 1920 and finished with the second-highest fielding percentage (.965) for American League third basemen while he hit a career-high 11 home runs.

In 1921, Baker returned to the Yankees, and Ward became the starting second baseman. The Yankees won their first ever American League pennant but lost the World Series to the New York Giants in eight games. (The Series was a best of nine in 1921.)

Ward had a tough time in the final two games against the Giants. In Game 7, the score was tied at 1 in the bottom of the seventh when Ward committed a two-out error that allowed the Giants' Johnny Rawlings to reach first base. Rawlings scored the go-ahead run on a two-out double by Frank Snyder. That unearned run stood as the game-winner as the Giants took a four games to three lead in the Series with a 2–1 win.

In the final game, the Yankees trailed 1–0 in the bottom of the ninth when Ward drew a one-out walk. Baker hit a groundball toward the hole between first and second, but Rawlings, the Giants' second baseman, made a diving stop and threw to first baseman George Kelly for the second out.

Ward did not stop at second and tried to go to third, but Kelly fired a strike to Hall of Famer Frankie Frisch at third base to nail Ward for the final out of the Series.

The Yankees lost to the Giants again in 1922, but finally broke through in 1923 and beat their rivals from upper Manhattan in six games to win their first World Series championship.

Ward was a big part of that championship team. During the regular season, the Yankees second baseman batted .284 with 81 runs batted in. Ward had 47 extra-base hits including 26 doubles, 11 triples, and 10 home runs.

Ward was spectacular in his third consecutive World Series against the Giants as he had a hit in all six games and was 10-for-24 (.417) with a home run, two RBIs, and two runs scored.

Ward played three more seasons with the Yankees, but in 1926 he lost his starting job to Hall of Famer Tony Lazzeri and was traded to the Chicago White Sox in January 1927.

Who was the first Yankee to hit a home run in the final at-bat of his career?

Tony Kubek was the first and only Yankee to hit a home run in his final career at-bat. On October 3, 1965, Kubek homered in the ninth inning at Fenway Park.

Kubek was the third Yankee to be named the American League Rookie of the Year when he copped the award in 1957. During his first season, Kubek had a 17-game hitting streak beginning in late June and he finished the season with a .297 batting average.

The Yankees used the versatile Kubek at a number of positions during his rookie season. Kubek started 41 games at shortstop, 38 games at third base, and a total of 53 games in left field and center field. He won seven American League pennants, three World Series championships, and was a four-time All-Star during a modest nine-year career with the Yankees.

The Milwaukee, Wisconsin, native played in his first World Series against his hometown Milwaukee Braves in 1957. In Game 7, Kubek, playing third base, made a key error in the top of the third inning that led to a four-run rally for the Braves. Milwaukee went on to beat the Yankees in Game 7, 5–0.

In 1958, the Yankees moved incumbent shortstop Gil McDougald to second base and named Kubek as the starter. Despite an injury-plagued season, Kubek was named an All-Star for the first time.

The Yankees avenged their loss to the Braves from the season before as they rallied from a three games to one deficit to win the 1958 series in seven games. Kubek wasn't much of a factor as he hit .048 (1-for-21), but he did have a sacrifice fly in Game 7.

During the 1959 season, Yankee manager Casey Stengel platooned the left-handed-hitting Kubek with the right-handed-hitting McDougald, but the Milwaukee native was back as the starting shortstop in 1960.

Kubek had his best season in 1960 as he had career highs in home runs (14) and runs batted in (62), but it was in the World Series that the Yankee shortstop was an unfortunate victim of a cruel fate.

The Yankees had a 7–4 lead over the Pittsburgh Pirates in the bottom of the eighth inning of the seventh game at Forbes Field. With a man on and no one out, Pittsburgh's Bill Virdon hit a groundball to shortstop that looked like it was going to be a double play, but the ball took a bad hop and hit Kubek in the throat.

Kubek left the game and the Pirates proceeded to score five runs after that to take a 9–7 lead. The Yankees tied the game in the ninth, but Bill Mazeroski ended the Series with his famous walkoff home run.

Kubek was back as a full-time shortstop during the 1961 season. Roger Maris and Mickey Mantle were chasing Babe Ruth's single-season home-run record while Kubek was a steady presence in the infield. Kubek hit .276 in 1961 and had 38 doubles, which was tied for second in the American League and was a franchise record for shortstops.

Going into the 1962 season, the Yankees did not know if they would have Kubek available. The Milwaukee native was committed to military service as a member of the Wisconsin National Guard. The Yankees were fortunate in that rookie Tom Tresh filled in admirably at shortstop (1962 American League Rookie of the Year) until Kubek was ready to return.

Kubek was discharged earlier than expected and made his season debut on August 7, 1962, against the Minnesota Twins at Yankee Stadium, playing left field and batting eighth in the lineup. In his first at-bat of the season, Kubek hit a three-run home run off of Twins pitcher Camilo Pascual in the bottom of the first inning to give the Yankees a 5–0 lead in a game they went on to win, 14–1. Stengel kept Tresh at shortstop and played Kubek in left field until August 17, when they flip-flopped. Kubek went to short and Tresh was the starting left fielder for the rest of the season.

In Game 7 of the 1962 World Series against the San Francisco Giants at Candlestick Park, the game was scoreless when Kubek batted against Giants pitcher Jack Sanford with the bases loaded and nobody out. Kubek bounced into a 6-4-3 double play that scored Bill Skowron from third in what proved to be the only run of the game. The Yankees won 1–0 to capture their second consecutive World Series championship.

Injuries began to plague Kubek in 1963. He hurt his back in spring training, and his batting average plummeted from .314 in 1962 to .257. In 1964, he batted .229 and in his final season of 1965, Kubek hit .218.

Following the 1965 season, Kubek visited the Mayo Clinic and was diagnosed with nerve damage at the top of his spinal column. The Yankee shortstop was told by doctors that a sudden move or a jolt could cause paralysis. Kubek was 29 years old when he played his final season in 1965. He officially retired in January 1966.

Kubek went on to a successful career in the broadcast booth with NBC Sports as part of their Saturday *Game of the Week* and World Series telecasts. Kubek also worked Yankee games for the Madison Square Garden Network from 1990 to 1994.

In 2009, Kubek was named the winner of the Ford C. Frick Award, emblematic of the broadcaster who made major contributions to baseball. The award is presented each year at the Baseball Hall of Fame in Cooperstown.

Who was the first Yankee to hit for the cycle at the remodeled Yankee Stadium II?

Hitting for the cycle (single, double, triple, and home run in the same game) is a rare occurrence. Shortstop Tony Fernández was the first Yankee to hit for the cycle at the remodeled Yankee Stadium II.

On September 3, 1995, Fernández had four hits and hit for the cycle against the Oakland Athletics. The Yankees lost the game, 10–9.

Fernández fouled out in his first at-bat in the second inning, but in the bottom of the fourth inning, he hit a two-run home run. In the fifth, Fernández added an RBI single to give him three runs batted in.

Fernández hit a triple in the bottom of the seventh and was only a double shy of the cycle. The Yankee shortstop completed the cycle in the bottom of the ninth with a leadoff double.

The Dominican native was already a five-time All-Star, four-time Gold Glove Award winner, and World Series champion with the Toronto Blue Jays in 1993 when he signed a two-year, free agent contract with the Yankees in December 1994.

Fernández hit .245 with five home runs and 45 runs batted in during the 1995 season, as the Yankees made a run for the American League wild card. Despite his low overall batting average, Fernández was better with men on base (.260), and with runners in scoring position, he batted .287.

Heading into the 1996 season, the plan was to have Fernández begin the season at shortstop with Derek Jeter slated to eventually take over as the starter. Those plans went awry when Fernández broke his right elbow diving for a ball in spring training and missed the entire 1996 season. Jeter took over at shortstop and the rest is history.

The only other Yankees to hit for the cycle at Yankee Stadium are Lou Gehrig (1934), Joe DiMaggio (1937), Buddy Rosar (1940), and Mickey Mantle (1957). Mantle was the first Yankee switch-hitter to hit for the cycle.

On July 23, 1957, against the Chicago White Sox, Mantle hit for the cycle for the only time in his career. Mantle doubled in the first inning, homered off White Sox pitcher Bob Keegan in the third, singled in the sixth, and tripled in the seventh.

POSTSEASON FIRSTS

In the 120-year history of the franchise, the Yankees have won 27 World Series and have made 58 appearances in the postseason. There are Yankees' World Series firsts, but also a number of Yankee firsts in the other postseason series (ALDS and ALCS). Use your baseball knowledge to figure out which Yankees can say they were the first.

In Game 5 of the 1956 World Series at Yankee Stadium, Yankees pitcher Don Larsen threw a perfect game against the Brooklyn Dodgers. Brooklyn's starting pitcher Sal Maglie retired the first 11 Yankees that he faced. Who was the first Yankee to get a hit in that historic game?

Hall of Famer Mickey Mantle got the first Yankee hit in Don Larsen's perfect game against the Brooklyn Dodgers in Game 5 of the 1956 World Series at Yankee Stadium. In the bottom of the fourth inning, Mantle pulled a 2-2 pitch down the right field line against Dodgers pitcher Sal Maglie for a homer and a 1–0 lead.

Mantle also made a huge defensive play in the top of the fifth to preserve Larsen's perfect game. Dodgers first baseman Gil Hodges lined a ball into the left-center field gap that looked like it was going to be Brooklyn's first hit. Mantle raced over and was able to backhand the ball for a spectacular catch in the historic game.

Mantle is considered by many to be the greatest switch-hitter in the history of baseball. Mantle played his entire 18-year career with the Yankees. His career slash line was .298/.421/.557 with an OPS of .978. Mantle slammed 536 career home runs, which, at the time of his retirement in 1969, was third all time.

Mickey Mantle in 1951, his rookie season
WIKIMEDIA COMMONS

Mantle wowed baseball fans with his prodigious power from both sides of the plate. The switch-hitter produced mammoth home runs while batting from the left side or right side.

On April 17, 1953, Mantle hit a home run that sailed out of Griffith Stadium in Washington, DC, and was reportedly measured at 565 feet. That home run is credited with the coining of the phrase "tape measure home run."

With Yogi Berra on first, Mantle, batting right-handed, crushed a letter-high fastball from Washington Senators left-hander Chuck Stubbs, way over the 391 mark in left field. The ball cleared the bleachers and Fifth Street, which ran directly behind the left field wall. After hitting a sign that was a reported 460 feet away, the ball rolled and ended up in a backyard that was a few blocks away from the stadium.

Yankee press secretary Red Patterson left the ballpark and met a 10-year-old boy who had found the ball. After negotiating an exchange, the ball and Mantle's bat eventually ended up in Cooperstown at the Baseball Hall of Fame.

No one had ever hit a fair ball completely out of the original Yankee Stadium, but Mantle came excruciatingly close twice. Both times, Mantle hit a ball that struck the facade that adorned the right field stands.

The first time was May 30, 1956, in the first game of a doubleheader against Washington. Mantle, hitting left-handed, connected off of Senators pitcher Pedro Ramos and hit a high drive that had reached a distance of 370 feet and a height of 112 feet when it struck the facade.

The second one was more notable in that it was a game-winning home run. On May 22, 1963, Mantle, hitting left-handed, smashed a walkoff home run in the bottom of the 11th inning of an 8–7 win. Mantle took Kansas City Athletics pitcher Bill Fischer deep when he struck the facade a second time, in nearly the same spot he had hit seven years earlier.

Those who were there claim the ball would have traveled about 620 feet. Mantle's teammate, first baseman Joe Pepitone said, when the ball struck the facade, he could "hear the boom." Fischer said the ball was still rising when it made impact. "It wasn't coming down, it was going up, like a jet taking off."

Mantle's career accomplishments are even more remarkable when you consider that he was never really fully healthy. As a youngster, Mantle had tremendous speed, but he developed osteomyelitis (an infection of the bone) in his ankle while playing football and nearly had his leg amputated. In Game 2 of the 1951 World Series, he tore ligaments in his knee after stepping in a drain pipe in right field at Yankee Stadium.

In the 1957 World Series against Milwaukee, Mantle suffered a shoulder injury that plagued him throughout the rest of his career. In Game 3, Mantle was on second base when, on a pickoff attempt, Braves second baseman Red Schoendienst fell right onto Mantle's right shoulder with the full force of his body. Mantle later admitted that his left-handed swing was never the same after that, and he was reportedly considering hitting right-handed full-time but it never came to that.

Mantle's pregame ritual became well publicized. He would need to apply large wraps on both of his knees before every game, and by the end of his career, he would be in such pain that he couldn't even swing the bat without falling to one knee.

Mantle was at his best in World Series play. The slugger played in 12 World Series and was a seven-time winner. Mantle holds a number of World Series records that still stand today, including most World Series home runs (18), runs batted in (40), runs (42), walks (43), total bases (123), and strikeouts (54).

In the 1952 World Series, Mantle homered in Games 6 and 7 as the Yankees rallied from a three games to two deficit to beat the Brooklyn Dodgers for their fourth straight championship.

In Game 3 of the 1964 World Series against St. Louis, Mantle hit a record-setting, game-winning home run in the bottom of the ninth on the first pitch from Cardinals knuckleballing reliever Barney Schultz. The walkoff blow was Mantle's 16th home run in World Series play, breaking Babe Ruth's record.

The respect that Mantle had from his peers was never more evident than on September 19, 1968. The Yankees were in Detroit to play the Tigers, who had already clinched the American League pennant. Mantle came into the game tied with Hall of Famer Jimmie Foxx for third place on the all-time home-run list with 534 career home runs.

Tigers pitcher Denny McLain, who would be named the American League's Cy Young Award winner in 1968, was going for his 31st win of the season and had a 6–1 lead in the top of the eighth, when Mantle batted with one out and no on one. While he was growing up, McLain idolized Mantle and knew the gravity of the situation. Rumors of Mantle's impending retirement had begun to circulate, so McLain knew he would not have too many more chances to move ahead of Foxx, the great slugging first baseman.

During an event in 2013 that was celebrating the Tigers' 1968 World Series winning team, McLain told the story of what happened that day. McLain said he called his catcher Jim Price to come out in front of home plate. Speaking loud enough for Mantle to hear, McLain said, "Listen, we want him to hit one," and Jim looked at me and said, "What the hell are you talking about?" I said, "The only way you and I are going to get into the Hall of Fame is if we give the ball and the home run for Mantle to go over 535 with the Yankees."

According to McLain, Mantle took the first two pitches in disbelief. After Mantle fouled off the third pitch down the right field line, McLain said he yelled at Mickey, "Where the hell do you want the damn thing?" Mantle put his hand out over the plate, a gesture to signal he wanted the pitch to be over the plate, belt high, and McLain grooved a pitch that Mantle slammed, deep into the upper deck in right field at Tiger Stadium.

The next day at Yankee Stadium, Mantle hit the final home run of his career off Boston Red Sox pitcher Jim Lonborg, who was the reigning American League Cy Young Award winner.

Mantle's final game was September 28, 1968, against the Red Sox at Fenway Park, although no one knew it at the time. The speculation that Mantle would retire continued to grow and culminated with an announcement on March 1, 1969, that the Yankee great would hang up the spikes.

In 1974, Mantle was inducted into the National Baseball Hall of Fame.

In 1961, Mantle was engaged with Roger Maris in a chase for Babe Ruth's single-season record of 60 home runs. Both players captivated the country with their pursuit of the hallowed record. In September, Mantle was hospitalized with a hip infection and dropped out of the chase with 54 home runs.

Earlier in the season, baseball commissioner Ford Frick declared that Maris needed to break the record within 154 games as Ruth did. If he failed to do so and still hit more than 60 home runs, Frick said that record would be shown separately with a distinctive mark. A narrative developed that an asterisk was placed next to Maris's name in the record books, but that was a myth. There never was an asterisk in the record books.

Maris hit his 60th home run on September 26 against the Baltimore Orioles at Yankee Stadium. The tying blow came in the bottom of the third off of Orioles pitcher Jack Fisher.

Maris had one more game to try to break Ruth's record. On October 1, 1961, 23,154 fans were on hand to see history as the Yankees were playing the Boston Red Sox at Yankee Stadium on the final day of the regular season. Maris broke the record in the bottom of the fourth inning.

Roger Maris hitting his 58th home run of the season off Terry
Fox at Tiger Stadium on September 17, 1961
WIKIMEDIA COMMONS

Maris faced Red Sox pitcher Tracy Stallard and drove the record-setting home run into the lower right field stands.

After he reached the dugout, fans kept standing and cheering to urge him to come out of the dugout. Maris eventually stepped to the top step of the dugout and tipped his cap to the crowd.

Maris came to the Yankees in December 1959 in a celebrated seven-player trade with the Kansas City Athletics. The Fargo, North Dakota, native played seven seasons with the Yankees and won five American League pennants and two World Series championships. Maris was a six-time All-Star with the Yankees. He also won back-to-back Most Valuable Player Awards in 1960 and 1961 and a Gold Glove in 1960.

Maris was a standout defender in the outfield and made a key defensive play in the seventh game of the 1962 World Series against the San Francisco Giants.

The Yankees were leading the Giants 1–0 in the bottom of the ninth inning. San Francisco had Matty Alou on first and two out when Hall of Famer Willie Mays lined a ball into the right field corner. Maris cut the ball off to keep it from going to the fence, or else Alou would have scored from first. Mays took second, but the next batter, Willie McCovey, lined out to second baseman Bobby Richardson to end the game and the Series.

After the 1966 season, Maris was traded to the St. Louis Cardinals where he went on to win a World Series in 1967.

Who was the first Yankee to hit a grand slam in the World Series?

On October 2, 1936, Hall of Famer and second baseman Tony Lazzeri became the first Yankee to hit a grand slam home run in a World Series game. Lazzeri's blow capped off a seven-run rally in the third inning of Game 2 of the 1936 Series against the New York Giants at the Polo Grounds.

With Hall of Famers Lou Gehrig and Bill Dickey on base along with left fielder Jake Powell, Lazzeri homered to deep right field off of Giants pitcher Dick Coffman. The first World Series grand slam by a Yankee gave the team a comfortable 9–1 lead over their metropolitan rivals. The Yankees won Game 2, 18–4, and captured the Series in six games.

Lazzeri was born and raised in San Francisco, California, and came to New York at a time when Babe Ruth and Lou Gehrig were the faces of the Yankees franchise.

With a large number of Italian Americans having emigrated to New York City, Lazzeri had instant credibility from a portion of the fanbase that could claim him as one of their own, while introducing a number of new fans to the game. Fans would yell, "Poosh 'Em Up Tony" when Lazzeri was hitting in an effort to encourage him to hit a home run. According to Lazzeri, he received that nickname while he was in the minor leagues.

During his 12-year career with the Yankees, Lazzeri developed a reputation for being one of the best clutch hitters of his era. Despite never hitting more than 18 home runs in a season, Lazzeri had seven seasons of 100 or more runs batted in.

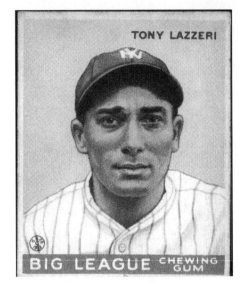

Tony Lazzeri's 1933 baseball card
WIKIMEDIA COMMONS

As a teenager in the early 1920s, Lazzeri began putting up impressive numbers in the minor leagues, and that caught the Yankees' attention. Lazzeri played in 192 games while playing at Salt Lake City of the Pacific Coast League (PCL) in 1925 (the PCL played a 197-game season that year) and batted .355, with a .721 slugging percentage. The 5'11" Lazzeri had 52 doubles, 14 triples, and 60 home runs, which, at the time was a record for professional baseball.

Salt Lake City had an arrangement with the Chicago Cubs in 1925, but they shied away from signing Lazzeri because he had epileptic episodes off the field. The Yankees did their due diligence on Lazzeri and found he didn't miss any games because of the medical disorder. They even went so far as to send a scout to Lazzeri's home in San Francisco to look into his family history.

Yankees de facto general manager Ed Barrow sent two players and $50,000 to Salt Lake City to acquire Lazzeri's contract. The Yankees signed the 22-year-old, and he reported to spring training in St. Petersburg, Florida, in 1926.

Lazzeri played shortstop at Salt Lake City, but Yankees manager Miller Huggins moved him to second base. Switch-hitting rookie Mark

Koenig was anointed the shortstop, and Huggins felt the two would combine to provide a solid keystone combination.

In his first season with the Yankees, Lazzeri found himself in a lineup with three other Hall of Famers in Ruth, Gehrig, and outfielder Earle Combs. The second baseman made his own impact as he hit .275 with 18 home runs and 117 RBIs, while finishing 10th in the voting for the American League's Most Valuable Player Award.

In the 10th inning of Game 5 of the 1926 World Series against the St. Louis Cardinals, Lazzeri's sacrifice fly plated the go-ahead run to give the Yankees a 3–2 win and a three games to two lead in the Series.

The Yankees trailed 3–2 in the seventh inning of Game 7 when Lazzeri batted with two out and the bases loaded. Cardinals player/manager Rogers Hornsby went to the bullpen to bring in Grover Cleveland Alexander. The Hall of Fame pitcher had tossed a complete game the day before in the Cards' 10–2 win in Game 6 and reportedly went out partying afterward.

Alexander proceeded to strike out Lazzeri to snuff out the rally. The Cardinals went on to beat the Yankees 3–2 in Game 7, which famously ended when Babe Ruth was thrown out trying to steal second base in the bottom of the ninth.

Lazzeri was constantly reminded of that strikeout, in part because of an inscription that is on Alexander's Hall of Fame plaque. Alexander was inducted in 1938 while Lazzeri was still an active player. It reads, "He won the 1926 world championship for the Cardinals by striking out Lazzeri with the bases full in the final crisis."

Lazzeri was reportedly not very fond of being mentioned on the plaque. According to a 1945 interview with a syndicated sports columnist, Lazzeri lamented, "Funny thing, but nobody seems to remember much about my ball playing, except that strikeout."

Lazzeri was part of the famed Murderers' Row in 1927. Murderers' Row was the nickname given to the Yankee lineup that featured four Hall of Famers (including Lazzeri) and averaged over six runs per game. The 1927 Yankees finished with a 110-44 record and won the pennant by 19 games before sweeping the Pittsburgh Pirates in the World Series. Lazzeri had 104 runs batted in (52 at home, 52 on the road) and finished third in the American League with 18 home runs. Ruth (60) and Gehrig (47) were the top two finishers.

In 1928, the Yankees fielded (except for catcher) the same lineup as the previous season, and Lazzeri finished tied for third in the voting for the American League's Most Valuable Player Award. (Note: Before 1931, players who previously won the award were not eligible to win a second time.) The 24-year-old second baseman had a slash line of .332/.397/.535 with an OPS of .932.

On May 24, 1936, Lazzeri established a franchise record that still stands today. In what is arguably the greatest single game by a position player in Yankee history, Lazzeri hit three home runs, including two grand slams, and compiled a modern-day American League and franchise record 11 runs batted in as the Yankees crushed the Philadelphia Athletics at Shibe Park, 25–2. (Lou Gehrig had a four-home-run game in 1932 at the same ballpark, but only had six runs batted in.)

In the second, Lazzeri hit his first grand slam of the game to give the Yankees a 5–2 lead. Three consecutive walks to Bill Dickey, Ben Chapman, and George Selkirk enabled Lazzeri to clear the bases for his first four runs batted in.

The same three baserunners were on board in the fifth when Lazzeri smacked his second grand slam of the game to give the Yankees a 16–2 lead. Lazzeri became the first Yankee and first player to hit two slams in one game, and that gave him eight runs batted in after just five innings.

Lazzeri completed his memorable day in the eighth with a two-run triple that scored Chapman and Selkirk once again for his 10th and 11th run batted in. According to James P. Dawson of the *New York Times*, Lazzeri "missed a fourth [homer] by a matter of inches and had to be content with a triple. . . ."

Lazzeri had been in the midst of a blistering hot streak. The day before his record-setting game, Lazzeri hit three home runs against Philadelphia to give him a major-league record 15 RBIs in consecutive games. Two days before that, Lazzeri also homered against Detroit, giving him seven in a four-game stretch. He only had 14 home runs for the entire season, so half of his total came in four games.

After he dropped to a career-low .244 average in 1937, the 33-year-old Lazzeri was released by the Yankees after the season. In 1938, Lazzeri played with the Chicago Cubs and faced his old team in the 1938 World Series. In 1939, his final season as an active player, Lazzeri split 27 games between the Brooklyn Dodgers and the New York Giants.

In his 15 years on the Hall of Fame ballot, Lazzeri never got more than 30 percent of the vote. In 1991, Lazzeri was elected to the Hall by the Veterans Committee.

In Game 1 of the 1939 World Series at Yankee Stadium on October 4, 1939, the Yankees scored a run in the bottom of the ninth to beat the Cincinnati Reds, 2–1. It was the first time in franchise history that the Yankees won a World Series game with a base hit in their last at-bat. Who was the Hall of Famer who got the winning hit in that game?

Hall of Fame catcher Bill Dickey was the first Yankee to get a game-winning walkoff hit in World Series play. Dickey singled off Reds pitcher Paul Derringer to score Charlie Keller from third with the winning run in the Yankees 2–1 win in Game 1 of the 1939 World Series.

Keller tripled with one out, and after the Reds elected to intentionally walk Joe DiMaggio, Dickey stroked a single to center to give the Yankees the win in what eventually became a four-game sweep.

Dickey played his entire 17-year career with the Yankees and posted a career slash line of .313/.382/.486 with an OPS of .868. Dickey batted over .300 in 11 seasons and caught over 100 games in 13 consecutive seasons.

Dickey played on eight American League pennant winners and seven Yankees' World Series championship teams. The Little Rock, Arkansas, native was an 11-time All-Star and became the first Hall of Fame catcher in franchise history.

During their championship run in the late 1920s into the 1930s, the Yankees employed three solid catchers. Benny Bengough, John Grabowski, and Pat Collins caught most of the games until Dickey's debut with the team in August 1928. Starting in 1929, Dickey caught at least 100 games for the next 13 seasons.

Dickey debuted on August 15, 1928, against the Chicago White Sox at Yankee Stadium, but it took until his third game to get his first hit. In the ninth inning of a 3–1 loss, Dickey tripled off of St. Louis Browns pitcher George Blaeholder for his first major-league hit.

In 1929, Dickey began to live up to his potential with an outstanding rookie season. Hitting seventh in the powerful Yankee lineup, the 22-year-old catcher's slash line was .324/.346/.485 with an OPS of .832. Dickey hit 10 home runs with 65 runs batted in, and he only struck out 16 times in 474 at-bats.

Dickey also showed off his skills behind the plate. In 1929, Dickey caught 127 games and led all catchers with 95 assists. He threw out runners attempting to steal at a rate of 44 percent. Former Yankee pitcher Charlie Devens praised Dickey's work behind the dish when he said, "He not only called a great game, but had the best arm I'd ever seen."

Dickey won seven of eight (losing only in 1942 to the St. Louis Cardinals) World Series championships with the Yankees, but his first appearance in the Fall Classic would not occur until his fourth full season in 1932. By that time, Dickey had already established himself as one of the best catchers in baseball, and his performance in his first World Series didn't disappoint. In the four-game sweep of the Chicago Cubs in the 1932 World Series, Dickey batted .438 (7-for-16) with four runs batted in.

Dickey was known for being a good teammate who had an easygoing personality off the field, but on the field, he was a fierce competitor. That competitive nature was front and center when Dickey was suspended for 30 days during the 1932 season.

On July 4, 1932, the Yankees were hosting the Washington Senators in the first game of a traditional, holiday doubleheader at Griffith Stadium. In the bottom of the seventh, the Yankees had a 3–2 lead, but the Senators had runners on first and third with one out.

Senators right fielder Carl Reynolds was on third when, on a failed suicide squeeze, Dickey tried to pick him off. The throw hit Reynolds, who tried to score when the ball rolled away. Yankees third baseman Joe Sewell retrieved the ball and threw home. Reynolds collided with Dickey, who couldn't hold the ball. Reynolds went back to make sure he touched

Bill Dickey
COURTESY OF THE BOSTON PUBLIC LIBRARY, LESLIE JONES
COLLECTION

the plate. That's when Dickey, who reportedly was knocked out in a similar incident the day before in Boston, promptly got up and punched Reynolds in the face, breaking his jaw in two places.

Both players were ejected. Clark Griffith, the owner of the Senators, reportedly said he was the one who put Dickey into a taxi to get him away from the stadium and from some irate Senators who were calling for the Yankee catcher to be arrested for assault.

It was something that Dickey regretted for the rest of his career. "I was never so sorry about a thing in my life," he said years later. "There had been bad blood between the two clubs. I thought he was coming back to strike me. I struck first. That tells the whole story. I felt terrible about what I'd done and deserved the punishment, which was considerable."

The punishment was levied by American League president Will Harridge, who handed down a 30-game suspension and $1,000 fine. Dickey returned in early August after missing 31 games, but the Yankees were fortunate in that Dickey's loss did not cost them in the standings as they still had a 7½-game lead over the second-place Philadelphia Athletics.

Even though the Yankees were going through a three-year championship drought from 1933 to 1935, Dickey remained one of their most consistent players. During that span, Dickey was named to the American League All-Star team in both 1933 and 1934. Dickey did not play in the inaugural game in 1933, but he was a participant in the famous 1934 All-Star Game at the Polo Grounds.

In the second inning, New York Giants pitcher Carl Hubbell famously struck out five future Hall of Famers in a row, but Dickey ended the streak. Babe Ruth, Lou Gehrig, Jimmie Foxx, Al Simmons, and Joe Cronin had all struck out before Dickey singled. The following batter was Yankee and American League All-Star starting pitcher Lefty Gomez, and he struck out to end the inning.

In 1936, Gehrig was still a productive player, Joe DiMaggio was a rookie, and Dickey was in his prime. The Yankees began a run that netted them an unprecedented four consecutive World Series championships. Dickey had his best season in 1936. He led the Yankees and finished third in the American League with a career-high .362 batting average. Dickey was sixth in the league with a .428 on-base percentage, and fifth with a career-high slugging percentage of .617 and a career-high OPS of 1.045. Dickey was 3-for-25 (.120) in the six-game World Series win over the New York Giants, but reportedly the Yankee catcher was playing with a broken bone in his hand.

Starting with the 1934 season, Dickey began rooming with Lou Gehrig. Five years later, Dickey had a front row seat for Gehrig's tragic decline as he began to succumb to amyotrophic lateral sclerosis (ALS, aka Lou Gehrig's disease).

In 1940, the Yankees finished in third place, two games behind the pennant-winning Detroit Tigers, and Dickey's numbers plummeted (from 24 to nine home runs in 1939 and 105 runs batted in to 54), bringing into question whether he could still be a productive major-league catcher.

Dickey bounced back in 1941 to hit .284, although his power numbers were still down. In the twilight of his career in 1942 and 1943, Dickey's workload was cut in half.

Gehrig passed away during the 1941 season, and Dickey took it particularly hard. Dickey was one of a number of Yankee players, including Babe Ruth, who played themselves in the Oscar-winning Gehrig biopic, *The Pride of the Yankees.*

Dickey was drafted for military service in 1944, so he missed two seasons. He served in the US Navy as an athletic officer and also managed the US Navy team that won the 1944 Service World Series.

Dickey returned to the Yankees for what would be his final season in 1946. Manager Joe McCarthy, who was dealing with alcoholism, suddenly resigned and Dickey was named as the player/manager.

The Yankee catcher went 57-48 as a manager, but he resigned with 14 games remaining when the front office refused to commit to him for the following season. The Yankees finished 87-67, 17 games behind the American League pennant winning Boston Red Sox.

Dickey retired as an active player after the 1946 season. When Casey Stengel was brought in to manage the Yankees in 1949, Dickey became the first base coach with the intent of mentoring a young 24-year-old catcher named Yogi Berra.

Berra and Dickey both wore #8 during their careers. On July 22, 1972, the Yankees retired that number in honor of both Hall of Fame players.

In the fourth and final game of the 1927 World Series, Earle Combs scored the winning run on a wild pitch in the Yanks final at-bat. It was the first time the Yankees won a World Series game in their final at-bat.

In 1995, baseball expanded the postseason, and the Yankees became the first American League team to qualify as a wild card entrant. The Yankees played the AL Western Division champion Seattle Mariners in the American League Division Series. Who was the first Yankee pitcher to start an American League Division Series game? Bonus: Who was the first Yankee to hit a home run in an ALDS game?

On October 3, 1995, the Yankees hosted the Seattle Mariners in Game 1 of the American League Division Series at Yankee Stadium. It was the first postseason game at the Stadium since Game 6 of the 1981 World Series.

Right-hander David Cone was the Yankees' first starting pitcher in an ALDS game as he took the mound against Seattle. Cone gave up four runs (three on two home runs by Ken Griffey Jr.) in eight innings and got the win as the Yankees outscored Seattle 9–6 to capture Game 1 before over 57,000 playoff-starved fans.

Cone started the fateful Game 5 and threw 147 pitches over 7⅔ innings, but he gave up the tying run in the eighth inning when he walked Seattle's Doug Strange on a 3-2 pitch with two out and the bases loaded. The Yankees went on to lose the game and the Series in 11 innings.

On July 28, 1995, the Yankees acquired Cone, who was an impending free agent, from the Toronto Blue Jays for pitcher Marty Janzen and two minor leaguers, to add some depth and experience to a rotation that featured 23-year-old Andy Pettitte.

Cone went 9-2 with a 3.82 ERA with the Yankees and helped them end a 14-year postseason drought. In December, Cone signed a three-year deal to remain with the Yankees.

The 33-year-old got off to a fast start in 1996, but after tossing a complete-game win over the Chicago White Sox in early May, Cone was diagnosed with a potentially life-threatening aneurysm. Cone underwent surgery and missed four months.

Cone returned on September 2 and had a no-hitter through seven innings against the A's in Oakland. Cone was on a strict pitch limit, so Yankee manager Joe Torre lifted him after seven innings. A one-out single in the ninth spoiled a combined no-hit bid, but Cone's return provided a spark for the Yankees, who were looking for their first division title since 1981.

In Game 3 of the 1996 World Series against the Atlanta Braves, Cone gave up a run in six innings to key a 5–2 win that got the Yankees back in the Series after they had lost the first two games at home. Cone went on to be a member of four Yankee championship teams in 1996, 1998, 1999, and 2000.

Hall of Famer Wade Boggs was the first Yankee to hit a home run in an American League Division Series game. Boggs broke a scoreless tie with a two-run home run in the third inning of Game 1 vs. Seattle.

The Yankees signed Boggs to a free agent contract in December 1992 after he played 11 seasons with the rival Boston Red Sox and won five American League batting titles.

Yankees GM Gene Michael felt Boggs's plate discipline would rub off on the rest of the lineup. That discipline helped the Yankees win Game 4 of the 1996 World Series when he walked as a pinch-hitter with the bases loaded in the top of the 10th to force in the go-ahead run.

During his five seasons with the Yankees, Boggs was a four-time All-Star and two-time Gold Glove winner.

(Note that in the strike-shortened season of 1981, the Yankees played the Milwaukee Brewers in a five-game series that was called the American League Division Series. The intra-division series was created by the owners as a result of the strike that caused the cancellation of over two months of the regular season. The abridged regular season was split into two halves with the winner of each half meeting in the division series. The first Yankee pitcher to start a 1981 Division Series game was Ron Guidry.)

Name the first Yankee pitcher to get a base hit in a World Series game after the designated hitter era began in 1973.

Kenny Rogers became the first Yankee pitcher to get a base hit in a World Series game in the designated hitter era. Rogers had a single in Game 4 of the 1996 World Series against the Atlanta Braves at Atlanta's Fulton County Stadium.

Game 4 was in Atlanta, so the DH rule was not in effect in the National League ballpark and Rogers was listed ninth in the batting order. When he came to bat in the top of the third inning, the Yankees were already trailing 4–0. With two out and no one on, Yankee manager Joe Torre did not want to waste a pinch-hitter that he might need later in the game, so Rogers was sent up to the plate to take his first major-league at-bat.

On a 1-1 pitch from Braves starting pitcher (and future Yankee) Denny Neagle, Rogers lined a ball off a diving Chipper Jones's glove at third base for an infield single. He was left stranded when Tim Raines flied out to end the inning. Rogers did better with the bat than he did on the mound in that game, as he gave up five runs in two-plus innings.

Rogers spent his first seven seasons with the Texas Rangers, the first four of those as a reliever before becoming a starter in 1993. On July 28, 1994, Rogers pitched a perfect game against the California Angels. The 31-year-old left-hander signed a four-year, $20 million contract with the Yankees.

Rogers did not have an easy time during his two-year tenure with the Yankees. He was up and down in 1996. In mid-August, Rogers tossed a complete-game, six-hit shutout against the Detroit Tigers, but in his next two succeeding starts, he gave up 18 earned runs in eight innings pitched. Rogers finished the season with a 12-8 record and a 4.68 ERA.

In the postseason, Rogers made three starts and gave up 11 runs in seven innings for a 14.14 ERA, capped off by his Game 4 performance in the World Series.

In 1997 things went even worse for Rogers as he pitched to a 5.65 ERA and did not pitch in the American League Division Series loss to Cleveland. In December 1997, the Yankees traded Rogers to the Oakland Athletics in exchange for third baseman Scott Brosius.

Brosius played four seasons with the Yankees from 1998 to 2001 and was in the World Series every year, winning three of them. The Oregon native was an outstanding defender at third base and won a Gold Glove in 1999.

As the eighth or ninth hitter in the lineup in 1998, Brosius hit 19 home runs with 98 runs batted in. In the four-game sweep of the San Diego Padres in the 1998 World Series, Brosius was named the Most Valuable Player after he hit .471 (8-for-17) with two home runs and six runs batted in.

In Game 3 at San Diego's Jack Murphy Stadium, Brosius hit two home runs including a three-run shot off of Hall of Famer and Padres closer Trevor Hoffman in the eighth inning that gave the Yankees a 5–3 lead. The Yankees held on for a 5–4 win and closed out the Series in Game 4.

The Yankees faced the Boston Red Sox in the 1999 American League Championship Series. Brosius had three hits and two runs scored as the Yankees took Game 1, 4–3 in 10 innings on Bernie Williams's walkoff home run off of Red Sox closer Rod Beck.

Brosius continued to provide a steady presence at third base as the Yankees went for their third consecutive World Series championship in 2000. The New York Mets had won the National League, so there would be a "Subway Series" in New York for the first time in 44 years. In Game 5 at Shea Stadium, Brosius scored a run in the top of the ninth and the Yankees went on to take the Series with a 4–2 win.

Brosius had one more great moment with the Yankees in the 2001 World Series. The Series was tied at two games apiece, thanks to the Yanks' stunning comeback in Game 4. Tino Martinez tied the game in the ninth with a two-out, two-run home run off of Arizona closer Byung-Hyun Kim, and Derek Jeter ended the game in the 10th inning with a walkoff home run.

In Game 5 the Yankees once again were trailing by two runs in the ninth with two out when Brosius tied the game with a two-run home run off Kim. The Yankees walked off a second straight win in 12 innings to take a three games to two lead in the Series, but they couldn't close the deal as they lost Games 6 and 7 in Arizona.

Brosius retired after the 2001 season.

In 1976, the designated hitter rule was used for the first time in World Series play. Who was the Yankees' first designated hitter in World Series play? Bonus: Who hit the first World Series home run as a Yankees designated hitter?

Lou Piniella was the Yankees' first ever designated hitter in World Series play.

Game 1 of the 1976 World Series between the Yankees and Reds was played in Cincinnati, so it was the first time that a DH was used in a National League ballpark.

The designated hitter rule began in 1973 in the American League, but it wasn't employed until 1976 in World Series play. The DH was in play in alternate years until 1986, when it became a staple of every World Series, but used only when the American League champion was the home team. (In 2022, the National League adopted the Universal DH.)

Piniella was batting fourth as the DH in the Yankee lineup. Cincinnati's Dan Driessen would become the first ever DH for a National League team.

After the Yankees were retired in order in the top of the first, Driessen, who was hitting fifth in the Reds lineup, got a chance to bat in the first inning. Hall of Famer Joe Morgan hit a solo home run with two out to give the Reds a 1–0 lead. Hall of Famer Tony Pérez followed with a single, but, while Driessen was batting, Pérez was thrown out stealing second so he would lead off the second.

Piniella led off the Yankee second inning and lined a double into right field to become the first DH to record an official at-bat and get a hit in World Series play.

Piniella's big-league career took off after he was selected in the expansion draft by the Kansas City Royals in 1969. The 25-year-old hit .282 and won the American League Rookie of the Year Award, becoming the first to capture the award for an expansion team in its inaugural year.

In December 1973, the Yankees acquired Piniella, along with pitcher Ken Wright from Kansas City for pitcher Lindy McDaniel. Wright pitched three games for the Yankees, but the acquisition of Piniella began to change the fortunes of the Yankees, who had fallen on hard times. Piniella was a fierce competitor with a quick temper, but that fieriness was something that the Yankees sorely needed.

Piniella spent 11 of his 18 major-league seasons with the Yankees. Not known as a power hitter, Piniella was nonetheless a reliable clutch hitter as evidenced by his career mark of .303 with runners in scoring position. Of Piniella's career RBI total, 73 percent (639 of 866) came with runners in scoring position, further justifying the label.

In his first season with the Yankees in 1974, Piniella hit a team-leading .305, with a team best .407 slugging percentage. In September, the Yankees and Baltimore Orioles were neck and neck for the American

League East Division title. Piniella hit .299 and had 19 of his 70 runs batted in during the final month as the Yankees took the race down to the penultimate day of the season before losing out to the Orioles.

An inner ear infection limited Piniella to just 74 games in 1975. The Yankee outfielder hit .196, scored seven runs, and did not hit a home run the entire season. In August, the Yankees fired manager Bill Virdon and replaced him with Billy Martin, who liked Piniella's competitive nature.

Throughout his Yankee tenure, Piniella found himself in the middle of some memorable moments in Yankee history.

On May 20, 1976, in a game against the rival Boston Red Sox at Yankee Stadium, Piniella incited a brawl between the two clubs after he slid hard into home plate and collided with Red Sox catcher Carlton Fisk. Piniella injured his right hand in the fight and reinjured it later in the season when he punched the wall in frustration after he made an out. Those injuries limited him to only 100 games that season.

Piniella had his best season as a Yankee in 1977 with a career-high slash line of .330/.365/.510. In the 1977 postseason, Piniella hit in nine consecutive games (13-for-36, .361) and was a factor in the Yankees winning their first World Series since 1962.

Bucky Dent's home run was the indelible moment in the Yankees playoff win over Boston in 1978, but Piniella was a significant factor as the team rallied from 14 games behind in July to force the one-game showdown for the AL East Division title. Piniella also made a memorable defensive play in the game that saved the historic win.

From July 19, when they were 14 games behind, to the end of the regular season, the Yankees went 52-21 in their final 73 games to tie the Red Sox and force a one-game playoff at Fenway Park the day after the season ended. Piniella played in 66 of those games and batted .318 (78-for-245) with four home runs and 40 runs batted in during that span.

The Yankees led 5–4 and had Rich "Goose" Gossage, their dominant closer on the mound as the Red Sox batted in the ninth.

With one out, Rick Burleson walked to put the tying run on first. The weather at Fenway Park that day was absolutely spectacular. There was not a cloud in the bright blue sky, which was trouble for any player in right field because, late in the afternoon, that was the sun field at Fenway.

Red Sox second baseman Jerry Remy hit a line drive to right field that was going to be a single, but Piniella lost the ball in flight in the bright sunshine. If the ball got past him, Burleson would have undoubtedly taken third and maybe could have even scored the tying run, while the winning run would have been at second base.

At that point, Piniella's instinct and experience took over as he spread his arms wide to signal he had lost the ball, but he lunged to his left, grabbed it, and spun around to throw to third for a play on Burleson. The Red Sox shortstop stopped dead in his tracks after rounding second when he saw Piniella had the ball. It turned out to be a huge play because of what happened next.

Jim Rice, who would go on to be named the American League Most Valuable Player in 1978, was the next batter and he hit a deep flyball to right-center field that looked like it was headed into the Boston bullpen, but Piniella caught it in front of the warning track for the second out. There is no doubt that if Piniella had not gloved Remy's hit, Burleson would have been able to score the tying run from third base on Rice's flyball. Gossage got Hall of Famer Carl Yastrzemski to foul out to third baseman Graig Nettles for the final out, and the rest is history.

Piniella had another solid postseason in 1978 as he hit in all six World Series games and eight of 10 postseason games overall. In the bottom of the 10th inning of Game 4 of the 1978 World Series at Yankee Stadium, Piniella hit a walkoff RBI single to give the Yankees a 4–3 win to tie the Series at two games apiece. The Yankees won the next two games to beat the Dodgers for their second consecutive World Series championship.

Thurman Munson's death in 1979 hit Piniella especially hard because he was a very close friend of the Yankee captain. At the funeral, Piniella was visibly shaken as he gave an extremely emotional eulogy for his friend.

The 37-year-old outfielder/DH made his final postseason appearance in the 1981 World Series loss to the Dodgers. Piniella completed an outstanding postseason career by hitting in all six games and finishing with a slash line of .438/.438/.500 in the Series.

Piniella transitioned to a part-time player for the remaining years of his career, while serving as a part-time hitting instructor. He also dealt with a chronic shoulder injury. In June 1984, the 40-year-old announced his retirement to become a full-time hitting coach.

Piniella's final game was at Yankee Stadium on June 16, 1984, and he went on to a successful managerial career that began with the Yankees in 1986 and 1987. Following the 1987 season, Piniella was promoted to general manager to start the season, but he replaced Billy Martin as the manager in June.

Piniella left the Yankees after the 1989 season to manage the Cincinnati Reds to a World Series title in 1990. Piniella also managed the Seattle Mariners to three division titles, the Tampa Bay Devil Rays, and the Chicago Cubs to back-to-back NL Central Division titles in 2007 and 2008.

Three Yankees have led off a World Series game with a home run. Who was the first Yankee to lead off a World Series game with a home run?

Hall of Famer Phil Rizzuto was the first player in Yankee history to lead off a World Series game with a home run.

In the first inning of Game 5 of the 1942 World Series at Yankee Stadium, Rizzuto hit a leadoff home run off of St. Louis Cardinals pitcher Johnny Beazley. St. Louis went on to win the game 4–2 and the Series in five games.

Rizzuto played his entire 13-year career with the Yankees. The Hall of Famer was a five-time All-Star, seven-time World Series winner, and the American League MVP in 1950.

Rizzuto was born in Brooklyn, but grew up in Queens where he played high school ball at Richmond High. At 5'6", Rizzuto had to always prove himself to those who doubted him, but the Yankees signed the 19-year-old as an amateur free agent in 1937.

From his first days as a pro, Rizzuto showed he had the credentials to be an outstanding major-league shortstop. While playing for the Yankees' American Association (AA) affiliate at Kansas City in 1940, Rizzuto hit .347 and was named the league's MVP while the *Sporting News* also named him Minor League Player of the Year.

Rizzuto was being counted on to fill some big shoes when he was tabbed to be the Yankees' starting shortstop in 1941. Frank Crosetti had been the Yankees' starting shortstop since 1932, but the Yankees felt that the 29-year-old veteran was on the downside of his career after he hit .194 in 1940.

Rizzuto, whose nickname was "the Scooter" (he reportedly earned that moniker for the way he ran the bases), had to earn the acceptance of the veteran Yankee players, who were supportive of Crosetti, including Joe DiMaggio. After starting slowly, Rizzuto settled in nicely to hit .307 in his first full season as the Yankees went on to beat the Brooklyn Dodgers in five games in the 1941 World Series.

From 1943 to 1945, Rizzuto served in the military. He returned to the Yankees in 1946, but Rizzuto had a down year and so did the team as they finished in third place. The Yankees returned to the World

Phil Rizzuto, second from right, with Johnny Sturm, Joe Gordon, and Red Rolfe at Fenway Park in 1941
COURTESY OF THE BOSTON PUBLIC LIBRARY, LESLIE JONES COLLECTION

Series in 1947, and Rizzuto played a big role in beating the Brooklyn Dodgers in seven games. Rizzuto hit .308 for the Series, but he really shined in the seventh and final game at Yankee Stadium. The Yankee shortstop had three hits, an RBI, and he scored two runs as the Yankees beat the Dodgers, 5–2.

From 1949 to 1953, the Yankees won five consecutive World Series championships and Rizzuto was the starting shortstop and a key contributor during that historic run.

In 1949, Rizzuto keyed the Yankee offense from the leadoff or number two slot in the batting order. Rizzuto scored 110 runs and finished second to Red Sox outfielder and Hall of Famer Ted Williams in the voting for the American League MVP award.

Rizzuto captured the award in 1950 with 125 runs scored and 200 hits. Despite hitting only seven home runs, Rizzuto drew 92 walks and had a slash line of .324/.418/.439 with an OPS of .857.

Rizzuto also beat out his own teammates, Yogi Berra and Joe DiMaggio, for the award. Berra hit .322 with 28 home runs, 116 runs scored, and 124 RBIs and finished third in the voting. DiMaggio was ninth in the voting despite 32 home runs, 114 runs scored, 122 RBIs, and a league-leading .585 slugging percentage.

Rizzuto's skills were starting to decline in the mid-1950s. The Scooter batted .195 in 1954 and then played only 81 games in 1955 as the Yankees began transitioning to a younger shortstop in Gil McDougald. The 38-year-old shortstop appeared in only 31 games, 15 starts, during the 1956 season before he was shockingly released in August.

Following his playing career, Rizzuto began a broadcasting career that would span 40 years. In 1957, Rizzuto worked with two of the best in Mel Allen and Red Barber. Over the years, Rizzuto became very popular with the fans as a broadcaster. Rizzuto's voice can also be heard narrating simulated play-by-play on the popular song "Paradise by the Dashboard Light," released in 1977 by the rock singer Meat Loaf.

In August 1985, the Yankees retired Rizzuto's #10.

Two other Yankees have led off a World Series game with a home run. Hall of Famer Derek Jeter hit a home run off of New York Mets pitcher Bobby Jones to lead off Game 4 of the 2000 World Series, and outfielder

Gene Woodling homered off Brooklyn Dodgers pitcher Johnny Podres to lead off Game 5 of the 1953 World Series at Yankee Stadium.

The left-handed-hitting Woodling did not hit for power but was known as a clutch hitter throughout his career. He played six seasons with the Yankees and was a member of the team that won five straight World Series championships from 1949 to 1953. During that five-year run, Woodling batted .318 in 26 World Series games and scored 21 runs.

Woodling began his major-league career with the Cleveland Indians in 1943. After two years of military service, Woodling returned to the States for one more season with Cleveland in 1946 before playing with the Pittsburgh Pirates in 1947.

In 1948, Woodling played for San Francisco in the Pacific Coast League where he was named the *Sporting News* Minor League Player of the Year after he batted .386 with 22 home runs and 107 RBIs.

Yankee manager Casey Stengel's first season was 1949, but he saw a lot of Woodling in 1948 when he managed Oakland of the PCL. After the season, the Yankees purchased Woodling's contract for a reported $100,000.

In Woodling's first season with the Yankees, Stengel used him in a platoon with right-handed-hitting outfielder Johnny Lindell. In 1949, Woodling played in 112 games and scored 60 runs. The Yankee outfielder hit .400 in the 1949 World Series win over the Brooklyn Dodgers.

In the 1950 season, Woodling scored 81 runs in 122 games. His best season with the Yankees was 1951 when the Yankee outfielder batted .281 with 15 home runs and 71 RBIs. In 1953, Woodling had 82 walks and led the American League with a .429 OBP.

Woodling played one more season with the Yankees. In November 1954, Woodling was traded to the Baltimore Orioles as part of a 17-player deal that brought Don Larsen and Bob Turley to the Yankees.

Four Yankees have hit a walkoff home run to end a World Series game. Who was the first Yankee to hit a walkoff World Series home run?

In Game 1 of the 1949 World Series against the Brooklyn Dodgers at Yankee Stadium, Tommy Henrich became the first Yankee and the first player ever to hit a walkoff home run to end a World Series game.

Henrich homered off of Dodgers pitcher Don Newcombe to lead off the bottom of the ninth for the only run of the game in a 1–0 win.

The left-handed-hitting Henrich was known as "Ol' Reliable" for being a consistent clutch hitter and he was a versatile player, manning the outfield and first base during his 11-year career with the Yankees.

Henrich made his major-league debut in 1937 and was a five-time All-Star and four-time World Series winner. Henrich was a terrific defensive outfielder who averaged double digits in assists.

Henrich is well known for an at-bat in the 1941 World Series against the Brooklyn Dodgers at Ebbets Field.

The Dodgers were leading the Yankees 4–3 in Game 4 and were one out away from tying the Series at two games apiece. With two out and no one on base, Henrich swung and missed a 3-2 pitch, but the ball got away from Dodgers catcher Mickey Owen to keep the game alive. The Yankees took full advantage of the mistake as they scored four runs to steal a 7–4 win and won the Series the next day in Game 5.

Henrich lived up to his nickname on the final day of the 1949 season.

The Yankees and Boston Red Sox were tied for first place in the American League and with the pennant on the line, the teams met at Yankee Stadium. The Yankees had beaten Boston the day before to set up this showdown, and Henrich played a big role in the final game. Henrich drove in two and scored one as the Yankees beat the Red Sox 5–3 to win the American League pennant. With the Yankees leading 1–0 in the eighth inning, the Yankee first baseman homered off of Red Sox pitcher Mel Parnell to give the Yankees some breathing room and a 2–0 lead at the time.

In his final season of 1950, Henrich was relegated to a role off the bench, but was an All-Star for the final time. Henrich retired in December 1950.

Other Yankees who have hit a walkoff home run to win a World Series game include Mickey Mantle (1964 Game 3), Chad Curtis (1999 Game 3), and Derek Jeter (2001 Game 4).

The Yankees won their first ever American League East Division title and played in their first ever American League Championship Series

in 1976. Who was the first Yankee winning pitcher in an ALCS game? Bonus: Who was the first Yankee to get a hit in an ALCS game?

In 1976, Hall of Famer Catfish Hunter became the Yankees' first winning pitcher in an American League Championship Series game.

The Yankees ended a 12-year postseason drought in 1976 as they won their first American League Eastern Division title.

Hunter, who was the Yankees' first starting pitcher in an ALCS game, tossed a complete game to beat the Kansas City Royals in Game 1 at Royals Stadium. Hunter gave up one run on five hits as he continued to add to his reputation as a big-game pitcher.

Hunter made his major-league debut as a 19-year-old in 1965 with the Kansas City Athletics. By the time the team moved to Oakland for the 1968 season, Hunter had established himself as one of the best pitchers in the American League. Hunter was the ace of the Oakland staff, and his big-game reputation blossomed when the A's won three straight world championships from 1972 to 1974.

In the 1972 World Series against the Cincinnati Reds, Hunter came within one out of a complete game in Game 2 as he won 2–1. After pitching in Game 5, Hunter came back on one day of rest to pitch 2⅔ innings in relief and earn the win in Game 7 as the A's beat the Reds 3–2.

The A's were trailing the New York Mets three games to two in the 1973 World Series when Hunter delivered a clutch performance. The Hall of Fame right-hander tossed 7⅓ innings of one-run ball to beat Hall of Famer Tom Seaver and even the Series at three games apiece, before the A's won Game 7 and their second straight World Series title.

The A's capped off their third straight world championship in 1974 by beating the Los Angeles Dodgers in five games. Hunter got a save in Game 1 and his fourth World Series win in Game 3.

Hunter won the 1974 AL Cy Young Award by going 25-12 with a 2.49 ERA. Before the season, he signed a two-year contract with the A's for $100,000 per season, but owner Charles Finley was accused by Hunter of a breach of contract. The case went to an arbitrator, who ruled Finley had not lived up to a stipulation in the contract that called for him to defer half of Hunter's salary into insurance annuities.

Hunter became a free agent and over 20 teams were in the running for his services, but the Yankees wanted him badly. On December 31, 1974, the Yankees held an impromptu press conference to announce the signing of Hunter to a record five-year, $3.35 million contract. Now, he was the highest paid player in baseball and the highest paid pitcher in history.

Hunter started slow as he lost his first three starts, but finished his first season with a 23-14 record and a 2.58 ERA. The Hall of Famer also led the major leagues with 328 innings pitched and 30 complete games, while he finished second in the voting for the 1975 AL Cy Young Award.

Hunter was never able to match the success he had in his first year as a Yankee in 1975. From 1976 to 1979, Hunter was 40-39 with a 4.07 ERA, but he helped the Yankees win back-to-back championships in 1977 and 1978.

As the Yankees were making their historic comeback in 1978 to overtake the Boston Red Sox, Hunter was 6-0 in August, and won 12 of his final 14 decisions down the stretch. Unfortunately, on the final day of the regular season, the Yankees needed a win to clinch the AL East Division title, but Hunter did not have it and was roughed up for five runs in less than two innings. The Yankees lost to the Cleveland Indians, 9–2, and were forced to play the playoff game at Fenway Park the next day.

In the clinching Game 6 of the 1978 World Series against the Los Angeles Dodgers at Dodger Stadium, Hunter gave up two runs in seven innings as the Yankees won their second consecutive world championship.

The 33-year-old Hunter retired after the 1979 season. It was a rough year all around for the proud right-hander, who was 2-9 with an ERA of 5.31 in his final season.

Hunter was inducted into the Baseball Hall of Fame in 1987.

Center fielder Mickey Rivers was the first Yankee to get a hit in an American League Championship Series game.

Rivers led off the game with an infield single and moved to second on a throwing error by Hall of Famer and Royals third baseman George Brett. Rivers eventually came around to score the first run of the Series.

In December 1975, Rivers was acquired, along with pitcher Ed Figueroa, from the California Angels in exchange for outfielder Bobby

Bonds, who ended up playing only one season for the Yankees. The trade paid dividends for the Yankees, helping them win the AL East in 1976.

Figueroa won 19 games while Rivers's speed immediately changed the complexion of the lineup. The colorful leadoff man hit .312 and scored 95 runs. Rivers also had 43 steals in 50 attempts and finished third in the AL MVP voting.

Name the first Yankee to homer in the American League Wild Card Game.

On October 3, 2017, shortstop Didi Gregorius was the first Yankee to hit a home run in the American League Wild Card Game.

The Yankees hosted the Minnesota Twins and found themselves in an early 3–0 hole in the bottom of the first. With two on and one out, Gregorius lined a 3-2 pitch from Twins pitcher Ervin Santana into the stands in right-center field to tie the game at 3. The crowd of over 49,000 at Yankee Stadium went absolutely bonkers. The Yankees went on to beat the Twins 8–4 to advance to the American League Division Series against the Cleveland Indians.

Gregorius had some tough shoes to fill when he joined the Yankees, as he was the shortstop who succeeded Hall of Famer Derek Jeter, who retired after the 2014 season.

In December 2014, the Yankees acquired Gregorius as part of a three-team deal with the Arizona Diamondbacks and Detroit Tigers. Yankee manager Joe Girardi named Gregorius his Opening Day shortstop, but the 25-year-old struggled in the first few months of the season. By the end of May, Gregorius was hitting .221 with six errors in the field.

Things only got better from there as Gregorius began to play a lot better, both at bat and in the field. In the second half of the season, Gregorius had 37 of his 56 runs batted in. The left-handed-hitting shortstop finished with a slash line of .265/.318/.370. In a game against the Atlanta Braves in late August, Gregorius had four hits and a career-high six runs batted in as the Yankees won 15–4. Gregorius was a finalist for the AL Gold Glove Award, but it went to Kansas City Royals shortstop Alcides Escobar.

In 2016, Gregorius established himself as one of the top shortstops in the league. He batted .276 with 20 home runs and 70 RBIs. Gregorius showed a major improvement against left-handed pitching as he batted .324 and struck out only 12 times in 148 at-bats against southpaws.

Before the 2017 season Gregorius, a native of Amsterdam, represented the Netherlands in the World Baseball Classic that was played before the season, but he injured his shoulder and did not return until late April. Despite missing the first few weeks of the season, Gregorius batted a career-high .287 with 25 home runs and a career-best 87 runs batted in.

On April 3, 2018, Gregorius had a game for the ages. The Yankees were hosting the Tampa Bay Rays in the home opener and Gregorius was 4-for-4, with two home runs, three runs scored, and a career-high eight runs batted in to key an 11–4 win.

In Game 1 of the 2018 American League Division Series against the Boston Red Sox, Gregorius hurt his elbow while making a throw. He was able to play the remainder of the Series that the Yankees lost in four games, but the Yankee shortstop needed Tommy John surgery after the season.

Gregorius began the 2019 season on the disabled list and was activated in June. In Game 2 of the American League Division Series against the Minnesota Twins at Yankee Stadium, Gregorius hit a grand slam home run. Gregorius's blow keyed a seven-run third inning and made him the first Yankee shortstop to hit a postseason, grand slam home run.

The Yankees elected not to re-sign Gregorius, who became a free agent after the 2019 season and signed with the Philadelphia Phillies.

The Yankees have made 17 appearances in the American League Championship Series, beginning with their initial appearance in 1976. Who was the first Yankee pitcher to strike out at least 10 batters in a single ALCS game?

In Game 5 of the 1998 American League Championship Series against the Cleveland Indians, David Wells became the first Yankee pitcher to strike out 10 or more in a single ALCS game. Wells struck out 11 in 7⅓ innings pitched to lead the Yankees to a 5–3 win and a three games to two lead in a series that eventually ended in six games.

A talented left-handed arm who spent 21 years in the majors with nine teams and won 239 games, Wells pitched four years for the Yankees in two separate, two-year stints and posted an impressive 68-28 record with a 3.90 ERA.

Yankee owner George Steinbrenner longed to have Wells in a Yankee uniform. The feeling was mutual as the Yankees were Wells's favorite team because he was a huge Babe Ruth fan. The left-hander's name surfaced many times over the years in trade talk involving the Yankees, but there were concerns about Wells's weight and off-the-field behavior.

In March 1993, Wells was released by the Toronto Blue Jays (who had grown tired of his polarizing ways) and signed a free agent deal with the Detroit Tigers. Wells's major-league odyssey continued when he was traded to the Cincinnati Reds in July 1995. After the season, the Reds traded Wells to the Baltimore Orioles where he spent the 1996 season.

In the 1996 American League Championship Series, Wells beat the Yankees in Game 2 to give Baltimore their only win in the Series. After one season with Baltimore, Wells was a free agent and he signed a three-year, $13.5 million contract to join the Yankees.

Wells's fascination with Ruth took on a whole new level when he joined the team in 1997. First, he asked for the retired #3 and was denied. In late June, Wells purchased an authentic hat that Ruth wore in 1934 and wore it on the mound to start a game. Yankee manager Joe Torre made him remove it after one inning and fined his left-hander $2,500.

In the 1997 American League Division Series loss to the Cleveland Indians, Wells was outstanding as he went the distance in Game 3 to lead the Yankees to a 6–1 win in Cleveland. Wells gave up one run on five hits with no walks and only one strikeout.

Wells was the nominal ace of the 1998 Yankees team that won 114 regular-season games and the World Series. He was 18-4 with a 3.49 ERA. Wells was an All-Star and finished third in the voting for the American League's Cy Young Award. On May 17, Wells pitched a perfect game against the Minnesota Twins at Yankee Stadium.

In the 1998 postseason, Wells started the first game in each series (ALDS, ALCS, WS) and was 4-0 overall with a 2.93 ERA. In Game 1 of the American League Division Series vs. Texas at Yankee Stadium, Wells tossed eight scoreless innings.

Despite his affinity for Wells, Steinbrenner was even more fascinated with Roger Clemens. The Yankees had wooed Clemens when he became a free agent after the 1996 season, but pivoted when the seven-time Cy Young winner decided to sign with the Blue Jays. In February 1999, the Yankees traded Wells along with left-handed reliever Graeme Lloyd and infielder Homer Bush to Toronto for Clemens.

After winning a career-high 20 games for Toronto in 2000, he was dealt to the Chicago White Sox for the 2001 season. Wells made 16 starts for the White Sox but did not pitch after June because of a back issue that required surgery.

In January 2002, Wells signed up for a second stint with the Yankees. Wells got off to a fast start in 2002 by winning six of his first seven decisions. On May 16, Wells tossed a complete-game, three-hit shutout against the Tampa Bay Devil Rays to go to 6-1.

Wells finished the season with a team-leading 19 wins. In the 2003 American League Division Series win over the Minnesota Twins, Wells won the clinching Game 4 by pitching into the eighth inning of an 8–1 win.

Wells beat Boston in Game 5 of the American League Championship Series to put the Yankees up three games to two. In Game 7, Wells came on in relief and gave up a solo home run to David Ortiz in the fateful eighth inning, but the Yankees rallied to win.

In the World Series against the Florida Marlins, Wells lost Game 1. With the Series deadlocked at two games apiece, Wells got the start in the pivotal Game 5, but after pitching a perfect first inning, he had to leave the game because his back tightened up.

It turned out to be the last game that Wells pitched for the Yankees. He was a free agent after the season and was not re-signed.

Name the first Yankee to hit two home runs in the ninth inning or later in a postseason game.

Raúl Ibañez is the first Yankee to hit two home runs in the ninth inning or later of a postseason game.

Going to the bottom of the ninth of Game 3 of the 2012 American League Division Series against the Baltimore Orioles at Yankee Stadium, the Yankees trailed 2–1. Ibañez hit a pinch-hit home run to tie the game in the ninth and then won it with a walkoff home run in the bottom of the 12th inning to give the Yankees a 3–2 win and a two games to one lead in a series the Yankees eventually won in five games.

In the ninth, there was one out when Ibañez was sent up to pinch-hit for struggling designated hitter Alex Rodriguez. With Orioles closer Jim Johnson looking to seal the deal for Baltimore, Ibañez drove a 1-0 pitch over the auxiliary scoreboard in right-center field to tie the game at 2. The game was still tied when Ibañez led off the 12th inning and hit the first pitch from Orioles pitcher Brian Matusz into the second deck in right field for the game-winning home run.

In Game 1 of the 2012 American League Championship Series loss to the Detroit Tigers, Ibañez hit a two-run home run off of Tigers closer José Valverde to cap a four-run rally that tied the game at 4. The Yankees went on to lose the game 6–4 in 12 innings, but Ibañez became the first player in baseball history to hit three home runs in the ninth inning or later in a single postseason.

Ibañez made a habit of hitting big home runs during his one season with the Yankees in 2012.

The Yankees and Orioles were both making a good run for the American League East Division title. On September 22, the Yankees entered the day leading Baltimore and were hosting the Oakland A's in an important game at Yankee Stadium.

The teams were tied at 5 in the top of the 13th inning when the A's scored four runs to take a 9–5 lead. The Yankees staged a rally and Ibañez tied the game with a two-run home run in the bottom of the 13th inning off of Oakland pitcher Pat Neshek. The Yankees went on to win in 14 innings.

In the penultimate game of the regular season at Yankee Stadium, the Yankees were trailing 2–1 against the Boston Red Sox in the bottom of the ninth inning. Ibañez tied the game with a one-out, solo home run off of Red Sox pitcher Andrew Bailey.

With tough left-hander Andrew Miller on the mound for Boston, Ibañez hit a walkoff RBI single to give the Yankees a big, 4–3 win that kept them a game ahead of the Orioles with one game remaining. The next day, the Yankees won the final regular-season game to clinch the American League East Division title.

Who was the first Yankee player to win the World Series Most Valuable Player Award without hitting a home run?

Shortstop Bucky Dent was the first and only Yankee player to win the World Series Most Valuable Player Award without hitting a home run. He is also known for a famous home run that preceded his World Series honor.

In the 1978 World Series, Dent hit .417 (10-for-24) with three runs scored and seven RBIs in the six-game win over the Los Angeles Dodgers. Dent did not hit a home run in his entire postseason career (24 games).

The Yankees acquired Dent in a trade with the Chicago White Sox, just two days before the 1977 season began. Outfielder Oscar Gamble and pitcher LaMarr Hoyt (who won a Cy Young Award in 1983) went to the White Sox.

Dent was a solid defensive shortstop and was acquired by the Yankees to shore up an infield that already had defensive stalwarts in third baseman Graig Nettles, second baseman Willie Randolph, and first baseman Chris Chambliss. The Yankees had a deep lineup keyed by Thurman Munson and the newly acquired Reggie Jackson, so whatever Dent could contribute offensively was a bonus.

Dent's moment in the sun occurred during the 1978 season.

In 1978, the Yankees and Red Sox were tied for first place in the American League East after 162 games at 99-63. A one-game playoff was scheduled for Fenway Park on Monday, October 2 to decide the division title.

The Yankees were behind 2–0 in the top of the seventh. Red Sox pitcher Mike Torrez, who was on the mound for the Yankees when they clinched the 1977 World Series, was shutting out his former team, when Dent came to the plate with two on and two out.

With the count 1-0, Dent fouled a pitch off of his foot and was in a lot of pain. After a few minutes of treatment from the medical staff, Dent stepped back in the batter's box.

Dent stunned the sellout crowd at Fenway as he hit the 1-1 pitch over the left field wall (aka "The Green Monster") to give the Yankees a 3–2 lead. Dent's surprising blow was the turning point as the Yankees went on to beat the Red Sox, 5–4.

Thanks to Dent's home run, the Yankees went on to beat the Kansas City Royals for the third straight season in the American League Championship Series and then won the World Series in six over the Dodgers.

Dent played three and a half more seasons for the Yankees. Late in the 1981 season, Dent tore ligaments in his hand and missed the remainder of the season and the World Series loss to the Dodgers. The 30-year-old shortstop began the 1982 season with the Yankees but was traded to the Texas Rangers on August 8 for outfielder Lee Mazzilli.

The Yankees became the first team to hit three consecutive home runs in a postseason game. Hall of Famer Derek Jeter and Paul O'Neill were the final two batters of the trio to be a part of history. Who was the Hall of Fame player who led off the historic trifecta of home runs in a postseason game?

In the sixth inning of Game 1 of the 1997 American League Division Series vs. the Cleveland Indians at Yankee Stadium, three consecutive New York batters hit home runs, making the Yankees the first team to accomplish the feat in major-league history.

With a runner on first and two out, and the Yankees trailing 6–4, Yankee designated hitter Tim Raines was the Hall of Fame player who began the barrage with a two-run home run off of Indians pitcher and former Yankee Eric Plunk, to tie the game at 6. Yankee shortstop and Hall of Famer Derek Jeter was the next batter, and he took Plunk's 0-2 pitch deep into left field to give the Yankees a 7–6 lead.

Indians manager Mike Hargrove replaced Plunk with left-hander Paul Assenmacher to pitch to left-handed-hitting Yankee right fielder Paul O'Neill, but it didn't work. O'Neill drove the ball over the center field wall for a history-making, third straight home run and an 8–6 lead.

Raines, who was nicknamed "Rock," was a switch-hitting outfielder who played 23 years in the major leagues. Raines joined the Yankees in 1996 for a three-year run that featured the only two world championships in the Hall of Famer's career.

Raines was a timely addition to a Yankee team that was on the verge of being a perennial winner and featured a relatively young and inexperienced roster. Raines was noted for his sense of humor and was well respected in the clubhouse. Jeter credited Raines for being a mentor and a friend. Despite just playing three seasons with Jeter, Raines was one of the invited guests when the Yankees honored their legendary shortstop with Derek Jeter Day in 2014.

After playing his first 13 seasons with the Montreal Expos, Raines spent five seasons with the Chicago White Sox. Rock was traded to the Yankees after the 1995 season for relief pitcher Blaise Kozeniewski, who never appeared in a major-league game.

Because of recurring injuries, Raines averaged a little over a half a season of playing time during his tenure with the Yankees, but he made the most of the time that he did play.

In 1996, Raines missed the first two weeks of the regular season with a finger injury. When he returned in mid-April, he started slow but he eventually got hot and by the end of May, Raines had scored 20 runs in 23 games and was making his presence felt in the Yankee lineup.

Unfortunately, Raines suffered a hamstring injury that kept him out nearly three months. By the time Raines returned in mid-August, the Yankees were in first place in the American League East by 5½ games over the second-place Baltimore Orioles, but he was a big factor in September. Raines's slash line in September was .298/.412/.595 as the Yankees went 16-11 to capture their first American League East Division title in 15 years.

In Game 4 of the 1996 World Series against the Atlanta Braves, Raines drew a walk to start a two-out rally in the 10th inning and scored the go-ahead run on Wade Boggs's pinch-hit, bases loaded walk. Raines also caught the final out in left field but not without a little excitement.

The Yankees were leading 8–6 but, with two out and a man on first, the Braves had the tying run at the plate. Braves third baseman Terry

Pendleton lifted a deep drive to left field. Raines went back on the ball and was falling as he caught it with two hands to seal the win.

In 1997, Raines again missed significant time due to a hamstring injury and, like the previous season, had a great September to help the Yankees make the playoffs as the American League wild card team.

Raines was a free agent after the 1997 season, but he re-signed with the Yankees on a one-year deal and played in 109 games in 1998. One of the highlights of the 1998 season for Raines was when he made his first trip back to Montreal since he was traded from the Expos after the 1990 season. In that game at Olympic Stadium, Raines had his 800th career stolen base.

In 1999, Raines signed with the Oakland A's, but midway through the season he was diagnosed with lupus, an autoimmune disease that can cause inflammation in many parts of the body. Raines's lupus caused kidney problems, and he had a tough time dealing with radiation and medication to treat this incurable, but treatable disease.

In the spring of 2000, Raines signed a free agent contract with the Yankees as he attempted a comeback, but he was released in March. Raines returned to the Expos for the 2001 season but was traded to Baltimore in early October so he could play with his son, center fielder Tim Jr., who had made his major-league debut for the Orioles a few days before.

On October 3, 2001, the elder Raines was in the lineup as a DH, while his son was in the outfield, as they became the second father-son duo (Ken Griffey and Ken Jr.) to play in the same game. The next day, they both started in the same outfield.

Raines played one more season with the Orioles in 2002 and was inducted into the Hall of Fame in 2017.

OTHER NOTABLE FIRSTS

WE COVER A NUMBER OF UNUSUAL FRANCHISE RECORD–SETTING EVENTS in this chapter, including the first Yankee to hit two home runs in one inning, the first Yankee to do that twice, and the first Yankee to strike out four batters in one inning. Think you know the answers to those questions? Take the challenge.

Who was the first Yankee to hit two home runs in one inning?

Hall of Famer Joe DiMaggio was the first Yankee to hit two home runs in one inning, and he did it in his rookie season.

On June 24, 1936, DiMaggio hit two home runs in the fifth inning of an 18–11 win over the Chicago White Sox at Comiskey Park to become the first Yankee to accomplish the feat. DiMaggio hit a two-run home run and later in the inning, he slammed a three-run homer as the Yankees scored 10 times.

DiMaggio played his entire 13-year career with the Yankees and won 10 American League pennants and nine world championships. The "Yankee Clipper" won three American League MVP Awards, two batting titles in 1939 and 1940, and was a 13-time All-Star.

DiMaggio is best known for his 56-game hitting streak in 1941, a record that has stood the test of time. The streak began on May 15 and it captivated the entire country. In July, *Time* magazine wrote, "Big Joe's hits have been the biggest news in U.S. sport. Radio programs were interrupted for DiMaggio bulletins."

On July 2, DiMaggio homered to break Wee Willie Keeler's all-time record by hitting in 45 consecutive games. The streak came to an end on July 17 in Cleveland. A record crowd of 67,468 packed Cleveland's

Joe DiMaggio hitting at Fenway Park
COURTESY OF THE BOSTON PUBLIC LIBRARY, LESLIE JONES COLLECTION

Municipal Stadium to see if DiMaggio would keep the streak going, or to witness its end.

Indians third baseman Ken Keltner robbed DiMaggio twice with two sparkling defensive plays. The Yankee Clipper also walked, and in his final at-bat in the eighth inning, he grounded into an inning-ending double play with the bases loaded. During the streak, DiMaggio had 91 hits and raised his batting average from .306 to .371. The Yankee Clipper won his second MVP award in 1941 as he garnered 15 first-place votes to beat out Red Sox Hall of Famer Ted Williams, who hit .406.

From 1943 to 1945, DiMaggio served in the military. During his absence, the Yankees won the World Series in 1943, but finished in third and fourth in 1944 and 1945, respectively.

DiMaggio was starting to show signs of wearing down when he returned as a 31-year-old in 1946. He had his worst year, offensively, since he debuted in 1936 and the Yankees finished in third place, 17 games behind the AL pennant–winning Boston Red Sox.

In 1947, DiMaggio rebounded to lead the Yankees back to the World Series, where they beat the Brooklyn Dodgers in seven games. The 32-year-old center fielder won his third MVP award, despite Williams winning the Triple Crown and having better numbers across the board.

After leading the American League in home runs (39) and RBIs (155) in 1948, DiMaggio underwent surgery after the season for painful bone spurs in his right heel. DiMaggio missed the first 65 games of the 1949 season and there were rumors that he was going to retire.

The pain in his heel was gone in late June and DiMaggio returned with a bang in a three-game series against the Red Sox at Fenway Park. With Boston trying to close the gap on the first-place Yankees, DiMaggio hit four home runs and drove in nine as the Yankees swept the Red Sox.

DiMaggio suffered another setback in mid-September when he was hospitalized with pneumonia. He missed 12 games and the Yankees went 6-6, while the Red Sox won 12 of 13 to take a one-game lead with a two-game, showdown series scheduled for Yankee Stadium on the final weekend of the season. A weakened DiMaggio returned to play the first game and had two hits in a 5–4 Yankee win that left the teams tied for the pennant. In the winner-take-all game the next day, DiMaggio legged out a triple in the first inning but did not score. The Yankees led 5–0 going to the ninth, but a fatigued DiMaggio failed to run down a drive by Boston's Bobby Doerr in center field that resulted in a two-run triple. DiMaggio removed himself from the game, and the Yankees held on to win, 5–3.

The Yankee Clipper had one more big year in 1950 with 32 home runs and a league-leading .585 slugging percentage. In 1951, the 36-year-old's numbers dropped off drastically. A young phenom named Mickey Mantle, who was being labeled the heir apparent to the great DiMaggio, made his debut in 1951 so the writing was on the wall for the Yankee great.

DiMaggio announced his retirement in December 1951. In 1952, the Yankees retired DiMaggio's #5. He was elected to the Baseball Hall of Fame in 1955.

On June 8, 1969, the Yankees honored all-time great Mickey Mantle with Mickey Mantle Day. The Yankee great announced his retirement three months prior, so the organization decided to retire his number and honor him between games of a doubleheader against the Chicago White Sox. That was the second Mickey Mantle Day at Yankee Stadium. What year did the Yankees hold the first Mickey Mantle Day?

On Saturday, September 18, 1965, the Yankees held the first eponymous Mickey Mantle Day at Yankee Stadium to honor their longtime star, who would be playing in the 2,000th game of his career that day against the Detroit Tigers. Mantle was in the twilight of his career (Mantle was moved from center field to left field in 1965 and then to first base in 1967), so the Yankees wanted to honor him for his milestone game and his career accomplishments.

The day before, New York City mayor Robert Wagner proclaimed Mickey Mantle Day in New York City. Mantle and general manager Ralph Houk were guests of the mayor at City Hall.

The lavish ceremonies began at 1:00 p.m., approximately an hour before the scheduled first pitch. Yankee attendance was down in 1965, but they had over 51,000 fans on hand to honor the all-time great.

Hall of Fame announcer Red Barber was the master of ceremonies and a number of dignitaries were on hand including US senator Robert Kennedy of New York. Mickey's wife, Merlyn, and Mickey Jr., his oldest son.

Hall of Famer and Yankee great Joe DiMaggio was there and he had the honor of introducing Mickey. "I am proud and honored to introduce the man who succeeded me out in center field," DiMaggio said as he addressed the raucous crowd. "He certainly has lived up to his expectations and there's no doubt in my mind, when he calls it a career, he'll be in the Hall of Fame." At this point, the crowd started to roar. "Ladies and gentlemen, Mickey Mantle!"

Mantle opened his remarks by honoring his predecessor. "Thank you very much, Joe. I think just to have the greatest baseball player I ever saw introduce me is tribute enough for me in one day."

Mantle ended his remarks by citing his career. "I just wish I had 15 more years. Thank you very much," he said.

Mantle hit third in the lineup, and when he came to the plate in the bottom of the first inning, the crowd gave him a thunderous ovation. The Tigers' starting pitcher was 23-year-old right-hander Joe Sparma, who took this opportunity to personally introduce himself to Mantle.

Sparma stepped from the mound and walked toward home plate to shake Mantle's hand and tell him how much he admired the switch-hitter. Mantle flied out to left field in that at-bat and was 0-for-3 on his memorable day.

On June 8, 1969, the Yankees honored their switch-hitting slugger with a second more renowned Mickey Mantle Day. Over 60,000 fans showed up to pay tribute in a memorable ceremony between games of a doubleheader against the Chicago White Sox. The Yankees retired Mantle's #7, at the time, only the fourth number retired by the team.

When Mantle was called out onto the field by longtime Yankee broadcaster Mel Allen (who was not with the team anymore but was brought back for this occasion), he called him "The Magnificent Yankee," and the massive crowd gave him a standing ovation that lasted more than six minutes.

On August 4, 1968, the Yankees held their first ever Banner Day, and the theme was Mickey Mantle. Before the game, a reported 2,325 signs were paraded by Mantle, who sat on the top step of the dugout as they went by.

The Hall of Famer was a three-time MVP Award winner, 20-time All-Star, seven-time world champion, and a Triple Crown winner. Mantle possessed prodigious power from either side of the plate and is famous for blasting some of the longest home runs in the history of baseball.

Four Yankees have hit two home runs in one inning. Who was the first Yankee to do it twice?

Alex Rodriguez was the first Yankee to hit two home runs in one inning twice.

The first time was September 5, 2007, when the Yankees hosted the Seattle Mariners at Yankee Stadium. The Yankees trailed 2–1 when Rodriguez led off the bottom of the seventh with a home run off of Mariners left-hander Jarrod Washburn to tie the game at 2. Later in the inning, A-Rod hit a two-run home run off of Mariners pitcher Brandon Morrow to give the Yankees a 9–2 lead, en route to a 10–2 win.

The second time occurred on October 4, 2009, which just happened to be the final day of the regular season. The Yankees were in Tampa Bay playing the Rays. In the top of the sixth inning, Rodriguez hit a three-run home run off of Rays pitcher Wade Davis to give the Yankees a 3–2 lead. Later in the inning, A-Rod hit a grand slam home run off of Rays pitcher Andy Sonnanstine to give him two home runs and seven runs batted in during a 10-run rally.

The Yankees sent Alfonso Soriano to the Texas Rangers in exchange for Rodriguez in February 2004. A-Rod was already an MVP winner and seven-time All-Star as a shortstop, but he moved over to third base to play next to Derek Jeter.

In his first season with the Yankees in 2004, Rodriguez hit .286 with 36 home runs and 118 runs batted in as the Yankees won the AL East with 101 wins. In the American League Division Series against Minnesota, Rodriguez hit .421 with a home run, three RBIs, and three runs scored in four games.

In the 2004 American League Championship Series against the Boston Red Sox, Rodriguez started off fast. In the first three games, A-Rod was 6-for-14 (.429) with a home run, three RBIs, and seven runs scored as the Yankees took a 3–0 lead.

The Red Sox staged an historic rally from being down three games to none as they won the final four games. During that time, Rodriguez was 2-for-17 (.118) as the Yankees failed to finish off their hated rivals and suffered a humiliating defeat. Rodriguez was not the only Yankee who failed to hit in those fateful four games, but a narrative began that he was not a clutch player in the postseason.

In 2005, A-Rod won his second MVP award and first as a Yankee. Rodriguez led the league with 48 home runs, 128 runs scored, a .610 slugging percentage, and an OPS of 1.031. In the ALDS against the Los Angeles Angels of Anaheim, Rodriguez batted .133 in the five-game loss and had no home runs and no runs batted in.

The Yankees won the AL East again in 2006 and were favored against the AL wild card team, the Detroit Tigers, in the American

League Division Series. The Yankees lost in four and Rodriguez was 1-for-14 (.071) while also suffering the indignity of manager Joe Torre batting him eighth in the order in Game 4.

Rodriguez had another monster season in 2007 when he won his third AL MVP Award and second with the Yankees. A-Rod led the major leagues in nearly every prominent offensive category including home runs (54), runs batted in (156), runs scored (143), slugging percentage (.645), and OPS (1.067)

On August 4, Rodriguez became the youngest player (32 years old) to reach 500 home runs. The milestone home run came off of Kansas City Royals pitcher Kyle Davies.

The Yankees made the playoffs as the American League's wild card team. For Rodriguez, it was the same old story in the postseason. In the 2007 ALDS loss to the Cleveland Indians, Rodriguez hit .267 with a home run and one run batted in.

While Rodriguez put together another great season in 2008 with 35 home runs, 103 runs batted in, and a league-leading slugging percentage of .573, the Yankees missed the playoffs.

In March 2009, Rodriguez underwent hip surgery and didn't make his season debut until May 8 in Baltimore. In his first at-bat of the season, Rodriguez hit a three-run home run off of Orioles pitcher Jeremy Guthrie. Despite missing the first five weeks of the season, Rodriguez still hit 30 home runs with 100 RBIs as the Yankees captured the American League East with 103 wins.

The 2009 postseason would provide Rodriguez with his greatest time as a Yankee.

A-Rod hit .455 with two home runs and six RBIs in the three-game American League Division Series sweep of the Minnesota Twins.

In Game 2 of the ALDS against the Twins at Yankee Stadium, the Yankees trailed 3–1 in the bottom of the ninth, but Rodriguez hit a two-run home run off of stud closer Joe Nathan, who had 47 saves that season. The Yankees went on to win the game in 10 innings.

The Yankees trailed Minnesota 1–0 in the seventh inning of Game 3 in Minnesota, but Rodriguez hit a two-run home run to give the Yankees the lead as they went on to finish the Series with a 4–1 win.

In six games against the Los Angeles Angels of Anaheim in the American League Championship Series, Rodriguez slashed .429/.567/.952, with an OPS of 1.519, three home runs, and six runs batted in.

In Game 2 of the ALCS at Yankee Stadium, the Angels took a 3–2 lead in the top of the 11th as they looked to even the Series at a game apiece, but Rodriguez spoiled that idea with a game-tying home run in the bottom of the inning. The Yankees went on to win the game in 13 innings to take a two games to none lead in the Series.

After the Angels won Game 3, Rodriguez again came up big in Game 4 as he had three hits, including a home run, and scored three runs in the Yankees' 10–1 rout that gave them a commanding three games to one lead. The Yankees lost Game 5 but returned home to Yankee Stadium to wrap up the Series with a 5–2 win and Rodriguez was headed to his first World Series.

In the World Series win over the Philadelphia Phillies in six games, Rodriguez had a home run and six more runs batted in. In a total of 15 postseason games, Rodriguez had six home runs and 18 runs batted in.

The Series was tied at a game apiece and the Phillies had a 3–0 lead in the fourth inning of Game 3 when Rodriguez hit a two-run home run off of Phils pitcher Cole Hamels that put the Yankees right back in the game. The ball was hit down the right field line and was initially ruled to be in play. It struck a television camera and caromed back onto the field. For the first time in postseason history, replay was used to determine that it was a home run and the Yankees rallied to win the game.

In Game 4, Rodriguez snapped a 4–4 tie in the ninth with a run-scoring double off of Phillies reliever Brad Lidge, and the Yankees went on to win 8–5 to move within one win of winning the Series.

Rodriguez had two hits and three runs batted in, but the Yankees lost Game 5 to send the Series back to New York for the clinching Game 6.

Hideki Matsui grabbed the headlines in Game 6 and the World Series MVP with his record-setting six-RBI game as the Yankees beat the Phillies 7–3 for their 27th World Series title. Even though he lost out on the Series MVP, Rodriguez was voted the Postseason Most Valuable Player by the New York Chapter of the Baseball Writers Association of America.

On August 4, 2010, at Yankee Stadium, exactly three years to the day after he hit his 500th career home run, Rodriguez hit his 600th career home run. Rodriguez hit the milestone round-tripper in the bottom of the first inning off of Toronto Blue Jays pitcher Shaun Marcum.

Rodriguez had one more season of 100-plus (125) RBIs in 2010, but injuries limited him in the 2011 and 2012 seasons.

In January 2013, A-Rod underwent another hip surgery and did not make his debut until August. On August 5, Rodriguez, who had been linked to performance-enhancing drugs, was suspended by Major League Baseball for violating the drug policy. Rodriguez said he would contest the decision and played the remainder of the season. Before the 2014 season, Rodriguez accepted his fate and was suspended for the entire season.

A-Rod returned in 2015, primarily as a designated hitter, and he finished with over 30 home runs for the final time in his career as he blasted 33 long balls. On June 19, Rodriguez homered off of Detroit Tigers pitcher Justin Verlander for his 3,000th career hit. Rodriguez drove the first pitch from Verlander over the scoreboard in right-center field into the bleachers as he became the third player to reach 3,000 hits with a home run.

Rodriguez was 40 years old in his final season of 2016. Once again, injuries cost him playing time. In early August, Rodriguez had only nine home runs. On August 7, Rodriguez announced that he would retire after the game on August 12.

In his final game, Rodriguez doubled in the first inning for his final hit. As a ceremonial gesture, Yankee manager Joe Girardi took Rodriguez out of the DH spot and inserted him at third base in the top of the ninth for one last time.

Rodriguez hit 351 of his 696 career home runs during his 12 seasons with the Yankees.

Joe DiMaggio, Joe Pepitone, and Cliff Johnson are the other Yankees who have hit two home runs in one inning.

On May 23, 1962, Pepitone hit two home runs in the bottom of the eighth inning of a 13–7 win at Yankee Stadium against the Kansas City Athletics.

Pepitone led off the eighth inning with a home run off of Kansas City right-hander Dan Pfister. That was the beginning of a nine-run inning that was capped off by Pepitone's second home run of the inning, a three-run shot off of A's right-hander John Wyatt.

A local kid from Brooklyn, Pepitone was a slick-fielding first baseman with a left-handed swing that was tailor made for Yankee Stadium. During his eight seasons with the Yankees, Pepitone was a three-time All-Star and three-time Gold Glove Award winner.

As a high schooler, Pepitone played with older players on the "Nathan's Famous" semipro team. The Yankees scouted him and signed him to a contract in August 1958.

Pepitone was promoted to Triple-A Richmond of the International League to start the 1962 season. After batting .315 with eight home runs and 27 runs batted in in 46 games, Pepitone was promoted to the Yankees and never saw the minors again.

The 21-year-old played in 63 games in 1962, but it was mostly in the outfield because he was blocked by the incumbent first baseman, Bill Skowron. The Yankees traded Skowron to the Los Angeles Dodgers after the season, and Pepitone became the starter in 1963. The Yankee first baseman responded well to the starting role as he hit .271 with 27 home runs and 89 RBIs and was named an All-Star for the first time.

In Game 1 of the 1963 World Series against the Dodgers, Pepitone had two hits off of Hall of Famer Sandy Koufax, who in the same game set a then-Series record with 15 strikeouts (Bob Gibson later broke the record with 17 against the Detroit Tigers in Game 1 of the 1968 World Series) in the first of a four-game sweep.

In Game 4 in Los Angeles, the Yankees and Dodgers were tied at 1 in the bottom of the seventh inning at Dodger Stadium. Leadoff batter Jim Gilliam hit a groundball to third baseman Clete Boyer, but his throw got past Pepitone at first and the Dodgers third baseman made it all the way to third. Willie Davis's sacrifice fly to deep center field scored Gilliam with the go-ahead run as the Dodgers went on to a 2–1 win and a four-game sweep. After the game, Pepitone, who was charged with the error, said that he couldn't see the ball because of all the white shirts in the crowd that was occupying the field boxes on the left field side. It was a bright sunny day and Pepitone said, "I just lost it in the crowd."

In 1964, Pepitone drove in 100 runs for the first and only time of his career. In Game 6 of the 1964 World Series against the St. Louis Cardinals, he hit a grand slam home run off of Cardinals pitcher Gordie Richardson.

For the remainder of his Yankee career, Pepitone did not play on winning teams and was a holdover from another era. To his credit, he continued to perform. The Yankees wound up in last place in 1966, but Pepitone was one of the few bright spots with 31 home runs and 83 runs batted in.

After the 1969 season, the Yankees traded Pepitone to the Chicago Cubs for utility player Curt Blefary.

Johnson joined the Yankees' two home runs in one inning club on June 30, 1977, against the Toronto Blue Jays at Exhibition Stadium. Johnson hit a total of three home runs in the game, but two came in an eight-run eighth inning of an 11–5 win.

Johnson's first home run, and second of the game, off of Toronto starter and left-hander Jerry Garvin led off the eighth-inning rally. Johnson's two-run home run with two out off of Blue Jays right-hander Jerry Johnson was his second of the inning and third of the game.

Johnson was a fearsome right-handed hitter who was tough on left-hand pitchers. The 6'4" Johnson was a part of the 1977 and 1978 Yankees' world championship teams, but he was also known in Yankee lore for being involved in an infamous incident.

As a result of some good-natured ribbing, Johnson got into a fight in the shower with Hall of Fame closer Rich "Goose" Gossage. Reggie Jackson was kidding Johnson about his inability to hit the flamethrowing Gossage. Gossage reportedly told Jackson that Johnson never hit him. Jackson told that to Johnson, who became incensed. Gossage tore ligaments in his right thumb and missed three months.

The incident did not sit well with Yankee owner George Steinbrenner. A little over two months after the fight, Johnson was traded to the Cleveland Indians.

Name the first Yankee to hit a home run on the first pitch he ever saw. Bonus: Who was the first Yankee to hit a home run in his first major-league at-bat?

On June 10, 2002, right fielder Marcus Thames made his major-league debut and became the first Yankee to hit a home run on the first pitch that he ever saw in the big leagues.

The Yankees and the Arizona Diamondbacks were scoreless in the bottom of the third inning at Yankee Stadium. Hall of Famer Randy Johnson was on the mound for Arizona in his first appearance at the Stadium since the 2001 World Series. With Shane Spencer on second and nobody out, Thames took the first pitch from Johnson and drove it over the left-center field wall. The fans were in a frenzy and gave him a curtain call after he returned to the dugout.

Thames played only seven games for the Yankees in 2002. In June 2003, the Yankees traded Thames to the Texas Rangers for outfielder Rubén Sierra.

Thames came back to the Yankees as a free agent for the 2010 season. Thames hit .288 in 82 games with 12 home runs and 33 runs batted in and had a couple of memorable moments.

On May 17, Thames capped off a three-run rally in the bottom of the ninth inning with a two-run walkoff home run off of Boston Red Sox pitcher Jonathan Papelbon to give the Yankees a thrilling 9–7 win.

Thames came up as a pinch-hitter in the bottom of the 10th inning against Toronto and delivered a walkoff RBI single to give the Yankees a 7–6 win on July 4, which just happened to be owner George Steinbrenner's 80th birthday. (Unfortunately, Steinbrenner passed away nine days later.)

Following his playing career, Thames served as the Yankees' hitting coach from 2018 to 2021.

In 1966, outfielder John Miller was the first Yankee to hit a home run in his first major-league at-bat.

Miller was a September callup who made his debut on September 11, 1966 against the Boston Red Sox at Fenway Park. The game was scoreless in the top of the second when Miller, who was batting seventh, hit a solo home run off of Red Sox pitcher Lee Stange.

Miller played a total of six games for the Yankees.

Players who hit at least 30 home runs and steal at least 30 bases in the same season are known as members of the "30-30 Club." Who was the first Yankee to become a member of the 30-30 Club? Bonus: There is only one other Yankee who was a 30-30 player. Name him.

In 1975, Bobby Bonds became the first Yankee to join the 30-30 Club when he hit 32 home runs and stole 30 bases.

The talented outfielder was acquired by the Yankees in a controversial trade with the San Francisco Giants. On October 22, 1974, the Yankees sent fan favorite Bobby Murcer to the Giants for Bonds in a one-for-one swap. Bonds's Yankee tenure lasted only one season, but he was an All-Star with a slash line of .270/.375/.512 and an OPS of .888.

Bonds got off to a slow start in 1975, which didn't sit well with the Yankee fans because he was acquired for Murcer, the homegrown Yankee who was portrayed as the heir to Mickey Mantle. Like Murcer, Bonds had trouble hitting home runs at Shea Stadium as he had only nine home runs at home and 23 on the road.

Bobby Bonds
WIKIMEDIA COMMONS

In mid-May, Bonds had five home runs and was hitting .194, but he began to turn things around. Injuries limited Bonds in June, but after posting a first-half slash line of .238/.332/.509 with an OPS of .842, Bonds improved to .304/.418/.515 with an OPS of .933 in the second half of the season.

Bonds was at his best in the final two months of the season, but the Yankees fell 10 games back of the front-running Boston Red Sox in early August and never recovered.

In December 1975, the Yankees traded Bonds to the California Angels for pitcher Ed Figueroa and outfielder Mickey Rivers. Those two players were contributors in helping the Yankees win the 1976 American League pennant.

Alfonso Soriano is the only other Yankee to have at least 30 home runs and 30 stolen bases in the same season. Soriano reached the mark twice in 2002 and 2003.

Soriano grew up in San Pedro de Macorís in the Dominican Republic. A number of major-league players came out of that city including Robinson Canó and Hall of Famers Pedro Martínez, David Ortiz, Vladimir Guerrero, and Juan Marichal.

Soriano, who began his professional career in Japan with the Hiroshima Toyo Carp, signed with the Yankees as a free agent in 1998. The 23-year-old rapidly moved through the Yankees' minor-league system in 1999. Soriano hit two home runs in the inaugural Futures Game at Fenway Park, and won the Larry Doby Award as the game's Most Valuable Player. Later in the year, Soriano was a September callup. On September 24, 1999, Soriano's first major-league hit was an 11th-inning, pinch-hit, walkoff home run to beat Tampa Bay, 4–3.

After Soriano split the 2000 season between the Yankees and their Triple-A affiliate at Columbus, he was anointed the starting second baseman for the 2001 season. Soriano had a breakout season in 2001 with 18 home runs, 73 runs batted in, and 43 stolen bases. He finished third in the Rookie of the Year voting behind Seattle's Ichiro Suzuki and Cleveland's C. C. Sabathia.

In the postseason, Soriano hit a two-run walkoff home run to win Game 4 of the 2001 American League Championship Series against

Seattle. Then in the eighth inning of Game 7 of the 2001 World Series against the Arizona Diamondbacks, Soriano hit a solo home run off of pitcher Curt Schilling to give the Yankees a 2–1 lead. Soriano was in line to possibly win the Series MVP award, but Arizona scored twice in the bottom of the ninth off of Yankees closer Mariano Rivera to win the game, 3–2, and the Series.

Soriano played to his potential in 2002 when he led the league with 696 at-bats, 128 runs scored, 209 hits, and 41 stolen bases. Soriano posted a slash line of .300/.332/.547 with an OPS of .880. He was an All-Star for the first time and finished third in the voting for the AL MVP Award.

After another solid season in 2003, Soriano struggled mightily in the postseason. In 17 postseason games, including the World Series loss to the Florida Marlins, Soriano hit .225 with one home run, while he struck out 26 times in 71 at-bats. Pitchers were feeding Soriano a steady diet of offspeed stuff that he was having trouble handling.

In February 2004, the Yankees traded Soriano to the Texas Rangers for Alex Rodriguez.

In 1977, the Yankees played the expansion Seattle Mariners at the Kingdome for the first time. It was the first ever game for the Yankees in a domed stadium. Who was the first Yankee to hit a home run in a domed stadium?

On May 11, 1977, Hall of Famer Reggie Jackson hit a two-run home run in the top of the first off of Mariners pitcher Glenn Abbott, the first Yankee home run in a domed stadium. (Mickey Mantle hit the first home run at the Houston Astrodome in an exhibition game in 1965.)

Jackson was one of the most enigmatic and colorful players to ever wear the Yankee uniform. In November 1976, the Yankees signed Jackson to a five-year contract. The Yankees needed one more power bat to balance out their lineup, and Jackson seemed to be a perfect fit, but it took some time.

Before Jackson even donned the uniform he was mired in controversy when he made disparaging remarks about Thurman Munson in a national publication. That immediately created a rift between the two top stars.

Jackson also had a difficult relationship with manager Billy Martin. That came to a head on June 18, 1977, at Fenway Park. In the bottom of the sixth inning, Martin felt Jackson didn't hustle on a ball hit by Red Sox outfielder Jim Rice that ended up being a double instead of a single.

Martin sent Paul Blair out to right field and Jackson was removed from the game in the middle of the inning. When he got back to the dugout, Jackson confronted Martin. The men came perilously close to a fistfight, but coaches Yogi Berra and Elston Howard stepped in to deescalate the incident. Jackson went back to the clubhouse and was advised by teammate Lou Piniella to go back to the hotel before the game ended.

In a show of his authority as the manager, Martin began hitting Jackson in the sixth spot in the batting order until mid-August, when he was urged to move his best power hitter to the cleanup spot. Once Jackson was moved to the cleanup spot, the Yankees won 40 of their last 53. In that stretch, Jackson hit .288 with 13 home runs with 49 runs batted in as the Yankees came from five games behind to win their second consecutive American League East division championship.

In the 1977 American League Championship Series against Kansas City, the relationship between Martin and Jackson became a story before the deciding Game 5. Jackson was 1-for-14 in the first four games and the Royals were starting left-hander Paul Splittorff, who was tough on left-handed batters. Jackson was 0-for-4 against Splittorff in the Yankees' Game 1 loss, so he was not in the starting lineup. It was a stunning gamble by Martin to bench one of his best hitters, and it gave the national media a pregame storyline.

Jackson would make his presence felt off the bench. The Yankees trailed the Royals 3–1 in the eighth inning and had runners on first and third with one out. Jackson pinch-hit for DH Cliff Johnson and singled to center to score Willie Randolph and cut the lead to 3–2. The hit became even more significant when the Yankees scored three in the ninth to win 5–3. The win gave the Yankees their second consecutive Game 5 win against the Royals and their second straight American League pennant.

Jackson made history in Game 6 of the 1977 World Series and earned the nickname "Mr. October" when he hit three home runs to lead the Yankees past the Los Angeles Dodgers for their first world championship in 15 years. Jackson had homered in Games 4 and 5, which gave him a record five home runs total for the Series. After a tumultuous season for the Yankees, Jackson ended it with a championship and his second World Series MVP (1973) award.

The year 1978 would provide even more storylines for the Yankees. In mid-July, the defending champion Yankees were in fourth place, 14 games behind the front-running Boston Red Sox in the AL East. The Yankees were over .500 (47-42), but Boston was playing at an incredible .685 pace (61-28) and it didn't appear is if they would ever slow down.

The Yankees fired Martin as their manager in late July and brought in Bob Lemon to replace him. That seemed to settle the team down, and they began to play much better.

The Red Sox finally started to slow down as the Yankees pulled to within 6½ games of Boston, who had lost 11 of 14, with a huge two-game showdown series in early August, scheduled for Yankee Stadium.

The Red Sox swept the two-game series to leave the Yankees 8½ games behind. The first game was interrupted by a 1:00 a.m. league curfew and was resumed the next day. The Yankees lost that game in 17 innings, 7–5, and the regularly scheduled game, 8–1.

It was a rough 24 hours for the Yankees, but they went on to win 23 of their next 31 games to pull within four games of Boston. In what became known as the "Boston Massacre," the Yankees swept a four-game series from the Red Sox at Fenway Park to pull into a tie atop the AL East at 86-56.

When the regular season ended, the Yankees and Red Sox were tied at 99-63, so a one-game playoff at Fenway Park was needed to decide the division title. Bucky Dent's famous three-run home run was the key blow in the game, but Jackson had a huge hand in the win.

In the top of the eighth, Jackson hit a majestic solo home run to dead center field off Red Sox reliever Bob Stanley to give the Yankees a 5–2 lead. That run proved to be pivotal as the Red Sox rallied in the ninth but came up short as the Yankees won 5–4 to clinch their third straight division title.

The Yankees had to fly to Kansas City for Game 1 of the American League Championship Series, where Jackson produced another memorable moment.

In the top of the eighth inning, the Yankees were leading 4–1 and had two on and two out with Jackson due up. The Hall of Famer was already 2-for-2 with two walks in the game, so Kansas City elected to bring in their closer, left-hander Al Hrabosky.

Hrabosky, aka "The Mad Hungarian," would psyche himself up by stepping behind the mound and, while facing the center field wall, violently pounding the ball into his glove. Hrabosky vs. Jackson made for great theater.

On an 0-1 pitch, Jackson crushed a belt-high fastball from Hrabosky over the right-center field wall for a game-breaking three-run homer. Knowing that he had squared up a perfect pitch to drive, Jackson flipped his bat and began his trot around the bases.

Another theatrical moment took place in the 1978 World Series against the Los Angeles Dodgers. The Yankees lost Game 1 and were trailing 4–3 in the ninth inning of Game 2 in Los Angeles. Bucky Dent led off with a single and with one out, Paul Blair walked to put the tying run in scoring position.

The Dodgers brought in their hard-throwing, dynamic young closer Bob Welch to face Thurman Munson with Jackson in the hole. Welch got Munson on a line drive to right for the second out, bringing up Jackson to face the young phenom.

It was an epic one-on-one, baseball showdown. Pitcher vs. hitter.

The first pitch was a blazing fastball right down the middle and Jackson swung through it for strike one. Welch knocked Jackson down on the next pitch to even the count at 1-1.

On the seventh pitch of the at-bat, Jackson missed a pitch that he thought he should have drove, but he fouled it off. The eighth pitch was ball three, so it came down to one more pitch. Welch threw a fastball that Jackson swung and missed for strike three as the Dodgers won Game 2, but Reggie would have his revenge.

The Yankees won the next three games at Yankee Stadium and were back at Dodger Stadium in Game 6 with a chance to wrap up the Series. In the top of the sixth, Welch faced Jackson once again.

The Yankees had a 5–2 lead and had a man on with one out when Jackson hammered Welch's first pitch deep into right-center field. The Yankees went on to win the game and their second consecutive World Series championship.

The year 1979 was a tough one for the two-time defending champion Yankees, who lost captain Thurman Munson in a tragic plane crash in August. Jackson had 29 home runs and hit a career high .297, but the Yankees missed the postseason for the first time in four seasons.

Jackson's best season with the Yankees was 1980. He slashed .300/.398/.597 and tied for the American League lead in home runs with 41. Jackson finished second in the AL MVP vote to Kansas City's George Brett, but the Yankees were eliminated by the Royals in three straight in the ALCS.

In his final Yankee season, Jackson provided one more postseason highlight in the fifth and deciding game of the 1981 American League Divisional Series against the Milwaukee Brewers. Trailing 2–0, Jackson tied the game in the fourth with a home run off of the Brewers' Moose Haas that reached the upper deck in right field.

The Yankees won that series and beat the Oakland Athletics in the ALCS, but they lost the World Series to the Dodgers in six games. Jackson was injured and missed some of the Series, but he did hit one more World Series home run for the Yankees in Game 4.

After the season, Jackson left the Yankees as a free agent and signed with the California Angels.

Throughout the history of baseball, an inside the park, grand slam home run has happened fewer times than a no-hitter or hitting for the cycle. Name the first Yankee pitcher to hit an inside the park, grand slam home run.

Mel Stottlemyre was the first Yankee pitcher and only the second pitcher all time to hit an inside the park, grand slam home run. (In 1910, Pittsburgh Pirates pitcher Deacon Phillippe became the first pitcher to hit an inside the park grand slam.)

On July 20, 1965, at Yankee Stadium, the Yankees were leading the Boston Red Sox 2–1 in the bottom of the fifth inning. Stottlemyre, who had already proven he could swing the bat, faced Red Sox pitcher Bill Monbouquette with the bases loaded and no one out.

Red Sox left fielder Carl Yastrzemski and center fielder Jim Gosger were playing shallow in the spacious Yankee Stadium outfield. Stottlemyre lined a ball to the gap between the two outfielders that rolled to the bleacher wall in deep left-center field to clear the bases. Yastrzemski got to the ball as Stottlemyre rounded third base and headed home. The Yankee pitcher slid into home plate as the throw got past Red Sox catcher Bob Tillman.

The Yankees had a 6–1 lead, but there was some concern if Stottlemyre could go on and finish the game. In those days, teams didn't rely on the bullpen as much, but Stottlemyre finished the game by retiring the Red Sox in order in the ninth.

In 1964, the Yankees were locked in a tight pennant race in early August when Hall of Famer Whitey Ford suffered a hip injury. The Yankees had lost a doubleheader at home to the White Sox and were in third place, 2½ games behind Chicago in second and 3½ behind the first-place Orioles, when Stottlemyre was called up to make his major-league debut against the White Sox.

Stottlemyre was dominating the International League with a 13-3 record and a 1.42 ERA, so it was an easy decision for GM Ralph Houk to call him up. The 22-year-old gave the Yankees a boost as he tossed a complete-game win that snapped a three-game losing streak and sent the Yankees on their way.

The Yankees won 34 of their final 52 games from the time Stottlemyre was promoted. The young right-hander went 9-3 with a 2.06 ERA. On September 26, Stottlemyre did it all as he beat the Washington Senators at D.C. Stadium with a two-hit shutout and was 5-for-5 at the plate, becoming the last pitcher to accomplish that batting feat.

In the 1964 World Series against the St. Louis Cardinals, Stottlemyre won Game 2 with a complete-game effort to even the Series at a game apiece. He lost Game 5 but pitched well, giving up two runs, one earned, in seven innings pitched.

Yankee manager Yogi Berra called on Stottlemyre to start Game 7 against Hall of Famer Bob Gibson, but his young pitcher came up short as he gave up three runs in four innings and took the loss in what was his final World Series appearance.

Stottlemyre had the misfortune of pitching for the Yankees at a time when they were entering a down period of their history. From 1965 to 1969, Stottlemyre was a four-time All-Star, won 20 or more games three times, and averaged a little over 17 wins per season while the Yankees never finished higher than fifth during that span.

In 1966, Stottlemyre lost 20 games for a Yankee team that finished in last place in the American League for the first time since they were the New York Highlanders in 1912. In 1969, Stottlemyre won 20 games for the third and final time in his career. He also led the American League with 24 complete games.

The Yankees made Stottlemyre the highest paid pitcher in club history when they signed him to a $70,000 contract in 1970. Despite pitching with chronic shoulder pain, he went on to win 15 games and pitch in the All-Star Game.

In his final season of 1974, Stottlemyre made 15 starts but was diagnosed with a torn rotator cuff. The 32-year-old came back to pitch one more time in August, but that would be the final game of his career. Stottlemyre was released by the Yankees in late March 1975.

From 1996 to 2005, Stottlemyre was Yankee manager Joe Torre's pitching coach and won four championship rings.

Who is the first Yankee to hit two pinch-hit, grand slams in the same season? Bonus: Who was the first Yankee to hit two career pinch-hit grand slams in franchise history?

Darryl Strawberry is the first and only Yankee to hit two pinch-hit grand slams in the same season.

On May 2, 1998, Strawberry pinch-hit for catcher Joe Girardi with two out and the bases loaded and the Yankees leading the Royals in Kansas City, 8–6. Strawberry unloaded on a 1-0 pitch from Royals reliever Scott Service to blow the game open. The ball went over the 400-foot mark in dead center field where it landed on the grassy knoll at Kauffman Stadium.

Strawberry duplicated the feat in early August at the Oakland Coliseum. The Yankees were trailing 5–1 in the top of ninth and had the bases loaded with no one out. Once again, Strawberry pinch-hit for Girardi, and once again, the left-handed slugger delivered.

Facing A's reliever Billy Taylor, Strawberry drove a 2-2 pitch over the 400-foot mark in dead center field. It was like déjà vu as Strawberry's second pinch-hit grand slam of the season landed in the same spot as it did at Kansas City's Kauffman Stadium earlier in the season.

Strawberry was the number one overall pick of the New York Mets in the 1980 MLB June Amateur Draft. He made his major-league debut in May 1983 and hit 26 home runs to capture the National League Rookie of the Year Award.

After eight years with the Mets, Strawberry, a native of Los Angeles, signed with the Dodgers as a free agent, but his career fizzled due to off the field issues such as drug and alcohol addictions. After a stint at the Betty Ford Clinic in 1993 for alcohol addiction, Strawberry was released by the Dodgers in June.

The San Francisco Giants took a chance on Strawberry and signed him in June 1994. The 32-year-old outfielder was playing well before the players strike abruptly ended the season. San Francisco was willing to take him back in 1995, but more off the field troubles prevented Strawberry from returning to the Bay Area.

Yankee owner George Steinbrenner had always admired Strawberry from afar and was not averse to trying to help rehabilitate him. In June 1995, the Yankees signed the former Met to a one-year deal and sent him to the minor leagues where he played 31 games at three levels. He was promoted in August and played in 32 games and two games in the 1995 American League Division Series loss to Seattle.

The Yankees did not re-sign Strawberry to start the 1996 season. To try and keep his career going, the 34-year-old signed with the St. Paul Saints, a team that played in the Northern League, an independent league that was not affiliated with any major-league teams.

The Yankees signed Strawberry to join them in early July. Down the stretch, he made a strong contribution to help the Yankees win the American League East Division title. In August, Strawberry slashed a blistering .315/.400/.618 with an OPS of 1.018. On August 6, Strawberry had the second three-home-run game of his career to key a 9–2 win over the Chicago White Sox at Yankee Stadium.

In Game 4 of the 1996 American League Championship Series against the Baltimore Orioles at Camden Yards, Strawberry slammed two home runs and drove in three in the Yankees' 8–4 win that gave them a three games to one lead.

Strawberry was plagued by injuries in 1997 and played only 11 games, but he bounced back in 1998 to hit 24 home runs. Unfortunately, Strawberry was diagnosed with colon cancer in late September and missed the postseason.

After undergoing treatment and serving a mandated suspension for possession of cocaine that forced him to miss most of the 1999 season, Strawberry rejoined the Yankees in early September. In Game 3 of the 1999 American League Division Series against the Texas Rangers at the Ballpark in Arlington, Strawberry hit a three-run home run that propelled the Yankees to a series-sweeping 3–0 win.

The 37-year-old retired after the season, having the distinction of being one of two players (Dwight Gooden) who have won a World Series with the Yankees and the Mets (Yogi Berra was a Mets coach in 1969).

First baseman Bill "Moose" Skowron was the first in franchise history to hit two career pinch-hit grand slams.

Skowron's first pinch-hit grand slam was in August 1954 at Philadelphia's Connie Mack Stadium off of Athletics pitcher Al Sima in the ninth inning of an 11–1 blowout. The second carried a little more importance.

The Yankees were trailing the Chicago White Sox, 4–1 in the ninth inning at Comiskey Park. With bases loaded and one out, Skowron was sent up to pinch-hit for Jerry Coleman and he delivered with a home run, deep into the left field seats off of pitcher Jim Wilson to clear the bases and give the Yankees a 5–4 lead in a game they went on to win 6–4.

Skowron first drew the Yankees' interest because of his power. During a tryout at Comiskey Park in 1950, Skowron showed off his power stroke by driving a number of balls deep into the stands, including a couple that reportedly went into the upper deck. The Yankees signed Skowron for $22,000. Skowron was primarily a third baseman before he turned pro, but the Yankees wanted Skowron to learn how to play the outfield in the minors. But there were some in the organization who didn't feel the slugger was in his best position. Skowron lacked speed and a strong arm, two skills that are needed in major-league outfields. Skowron was still able to produce at the plate, as he led the Class B Piedmont League with a .334 average with 18 home runs and 76 runs batted in. In 1952, Skowron was promoted to the Yankees' top farm team at Kansas City, where he hit .341 with 31 home runs and 134 RBIs.

Yankee manager Casey Stengel had Skowron in spring training in 1953 and made the decision to convert Skowron to a first baseman. He was sent to Kansas City to work with Johnny Neun, who had been a pretty good defensive first baseman with the Detroit Tigers and Boston Braves.

Skowron made the team in 1954 and didn't get his first hit until his third game when he tripled against Philadelphia Athletics pitcher Alex Kellner at Yankee Stadium. Later in the game, Skowron also hit his first home run off of Kellner.

In his first season, Skowron was part of a platoon with Joe Collins and Eddie Robinson. He played in 87 games and batted .340 with seven home runs and 41 runs batted in. The Yankees failed to win the American League pennant, but Skowron would go on to play in seven World Series with the Yankees.

The first three times that Skowron played in a World Series in 1955, 1956, and 1957, he was still platooning at first base and appeared in 10 of 21 games. In Game 7 of the 1956 World Series at Ebbets Field against the Brooklyn Dodgers, Skowron hit a grand slam off of Dodgers pitcher Roger Craig in the top of the seventh to give the Yankees an insurmountable 9–0 lead.

Skowron had a clutch gene, and it showed in the 1958 World Series rematch against the Milwaukee Braves. Milwaukee won Game 7 at Yankee Stadium in the previous season and the Yankees had rallied from a three games to one series deficit to force Game 7 at Milwaukee's County Stadium.

The Yankees took a 3–2 lead in the top of the eighth and had men on first and third with two out. Skowron connected for a clutch three-run home run off of Braves pitcher Lew Burdette, a 20-game winner that season. The Yankees avenged their loss from the previous season as they beat the Braves on their home field, 6–2.

A broken wrist in July limited Skowron to 74 games in the 1959 season, but he still had 15 home runs and 59 runs batted in. In 1960, Moose bounced back to hit 26 home runs with a career-high 91 RBIs. In the 1960 World Series loss to the Pittsburgh Pirates, Skowron had 12 hits in seven games with two home runs and six RBIs.

Skowron was a part of two more World Series winning teams in 1961 and 1962, but the Yankees were grooming a young first baseman in the minors named Joe Pepitone, a local product with a sweet left-handed swing. After the 1962 season, the Yankees traded the popular Skowron to the Los Angeles Dodgers for right-handed pitcher Stan Williams.

Skowron got a measure of revenge in the 1963 World Series when the Dodgers swept the Yankees in four straight games. The former Yankee drove in the first run of the Series in Game 1 with an RBI single off of his former teammate Whitey Ford. He added another RBI as the Dodgers won Game 1 behind Sandy Koufax's record-setting 15-strikeout performance.

In Game 2, Skowron hit a solo home run off of Al Downing as the Dodgers took a 2–0 lead in the Series with a 4–1 win. Los Angeles won Game 4, 2–1 to cap off the sweep. Skowron admitted afterward that he "wanted to come back and beat the club that traded me."

Striking out four batters in one inning is a rare and notable achievement. Who was the first Yankee pitcher to strike out four batters in a single inning?

A. J. Burnett was the first Yankee to strike out four batters in a single inning.

Burnett fanned four Colorado Rockies hitters in a game at Yankee Stadium on June 24, 2011. In the top of the sixth inning, Burnett got Chris Iannetta and Carlos González on a called third strike. Chris

Nelson struck out swinging but reached first on a wild pitch. Burnett fanned Todd Helton for his fourth strikeout of the inning.

Burnett spent three seasons with the Yankees from 2009 to 2011. The free agent right-hander signed a five-year, $82.5 million contract before the 2009 season and played a role in helping the Yankees win their 27th world championship.

Burnett began his major-league career with the Florida Marlins in 1991. Burnett was an enigmatic right-handed pitcher who had great stuff but could never fully harness his ability.

On May 12, 2001, Burnett pitched a no-hitter against the San Diego Padres at Qualcomm Stadium. Burnett walked nine and struck out seven as he tossed the second no-hitter in Marlins franchise history.

Burnett was on the Marlins' roster in 2003 when they won their first World Series. Burnett underwent Tommy John surgery early that season, but he still received a World Series ring. From 2006 to 2008, Burnett was with the Toronto Blue Jays. In 2008, Burnett won a career-high 18 games and led the American League with 231 strikeouts.

In Burnett's final start of 2008, he tossed eight strong innings against the Yankees who certainly took notice. The right-hander signed a five-year deal with Toronto, but he exercised an opt out after three years and signed with the Yankees.

Burnett had an up and down regular season and finished 13-9 with a 4.04 ERA, but he had his "Yankee moment" in the postseason.

The Yankees lost Game 1 of the 2009 World Series against the Philadelphia Phillies at Yankee Stadium. There was already pressure on Burnett to perform in Game 2, but now the Yankees needed to avoid falling behind, two games to none. Adding to the drama, the Yankees were facing their ol' nemesis, Pedro Martínez, who pitched for the Phillies in what was his final season.

Burnett outpitched the Hall of Famer as he gave up one run in seven innings, with two walks and nine strikeouts in earning his first and only World Series win. Burnett was able to get the ball to Hall of Fame closer Mariano Rivera, who finished the game with two scoreless innings.

Burnett could never match his first year with the Yankees. In 2010, the right-hander was 10-15 with a 5.26 ERA. In his final two seasons of 2010 and 2011, Burnett was a combined 21-26 with a 5.20 ERA. In February 2012, Burnett was traded to the Pittsburgh Pirates.

Three other Yankee pitchers recorded four strikeouts in one inning.

On September 20, 2012, right-hander Phil Hughes struck out four batters in one inning. Hughes accomplished the unique feat at Yankee Stadium against the Toronto Blue Jays in the top of the fourth inning.

The 26-year-old struck out Toronto's J. P. Arencibia to begin the inning. Adeiny Hechavarría struck out but reached on a passed ball by Yankees catcher Russell Martin. Hughes struck out Anthony Gose and got Brett Lawrie for his fourth "K" of the inning.

The Yankees had high hopes for Hughes after they drafted him with their first-round pick, 23rd overall, in the 2004 MLB June Amateur Draft. Hughes worked his way through the Yankees' minor-league system and was promoted to make his major-league debut in April 2007.

In his second major-league start, Hughes flirted with a no-hitter into the seventh inning against the Texas Rangers, but he suffered a hamstring pull and left the game. Hughes earned his first major-league win, but he went on the disabled list and did not return until August.

After starting the 2008 season with an 0-4 record, Hughes sustained a strained oblique and cracked rib that set him back. After rehabbing, Hughes was sent to the minors but returned in September.

Hughes began the 2009 season in the rotation, but he was struggling as a starter. Hughes was moved to the bullpen in early June, and he thrived as the setup man for Mariano Rivera.

As a reliever, Hughes made 44 appearances and posted an ERA of 1.40 with three saves. One of his highlights was a scoreless streak that lasted just over 25 innings. Despite his success as a reliever, the Yankees were insistent on using Hughes as a starter.

Hughes was an All-Star for the first time in 2010. Hughes made 29 starts and finished the season with a career-high 18 wins. In the 2010 American League Division Series against the Minnesota Twins, Hughes tossed seven shutout innings and got the win in the series-clinching Game 3 at Yankee Stadium.

Injuries plagued Hughes in 2011 and limited him to 17 appearances, but he rebounded in 2012 to make 32 starts and win 16 games. Hughes began the 2013 season on the disabled list with a bulging disc in his back. In what turned out to be Hughes's final season with the Yankees, he finished with a 4-14 record and a 5.19 ERA.

Hughes played parts of seven seasons with the Yankees. He was 56-50 with a 4.53 ERA in New York.

On June 25, 2021, at Fenway Park, Yankee pitcher Jonathan Loáisiga struck out four Boston Red Sox hitters in the seventh inning including Michael Chavis, who reached on a wild pitch, Alex Verdugo, J. D. Martinez, and Xander Bogaerts.

A month later on July 25, 2021, Yankee pitcher Domingo Germán duplicated the feat at the same venue. German struck out Red Sox hitters Jarren Duran, Xander Bogaerts, who reached on a passed ball by Yankee catcher Gary Sánchez, Rafael Devers, and J. D. Martinez.

Yankee pitchers have tossed 12 no-hitters (including Don Larsen's perfect game in the 1956 World Series) in the team's glorious history. Who was the first Yankee pitcher to throw two no-hitters in the same season?

Right-handed pitcher Allie Reynolds was the first, and still the only Yankee pitcher to throw two no-hitters in the same season.

Reynolds accomplished the feat during the 1951 season.

On July 12, 1951, Reynolds no-hit the Cleveland Indians, his former team, in a 1–0 win at Municipal Stadium. On September 28, 1951, Reynolds tossed his second no-hitter of the season as he beat the Boston Red Sox 8–0 at Yankee Stadium in the first game of a doubleheader. In the ninth inning, catcher Yogi Berra had a miscue that nearly prevented Reynolds from pitching that second no-hitter.

Reynolds was one out away from the no-hitter when he faced Boston outfielder and Hall of Famer Ted Williams. The Boston legend hit a foul pop that Berra dropped for an error, giving Williams another chance to hit. Williams lifted another foul pop that Berra caught to preserve the no-hit game. The Yankees won the second game and clinched their third straight American League pennant.

In October 1946, the Yankees sent Hall of Fame second baseman Joe Gordon to the Cleveland Indians in exchange for Reynolds. Cleveland needed a second baseman and offered any pitcher on the staff, except

Allie Reynolds, left, with Vic Raschi and Eddie Lopat
COURTESY OF THE BOSTON PUBLIC LIBRARY, LESLIE JONES COLLECTION

for Bob Feller, in return. Reportedly, the Yankees chose Reynolds on the recommendation of Joe DiMaggio.

The 6-foot right-hander was nicknamed "Superchief" for his Creek Indian heritage. Reportedly, Yankee broadcaster Mel Allen coined that nickname after Reynolds threw his second no-hitter.

Reynolds pitched eight seasons for the Yankees and posted an outstanding 131-60 record with a 3.30 ERA. With the Yankees, Reynolds was a five-time All-Star and six-time world champion. Reynolds finished second in the voting for the 1952 American League MVP Award after he posted a 20-8 record with a major-league-leading 2.06 ERA.

"Superchief" was even better in the World Series. Reynolds had a 7-2 record in Series play with a 2.79 ERA overall that included four saves. In the 1952 World Series, Reynolds got a huge save in Game 6 to even the Series at three games apiece. The Yankees had a 3–2 lead in the eighth, but the Dodgers had the tying run on second with two out. Reynolds struck out Dodgers catcher and Hall of Famer Roy Campanella to end the eighth and then retired the Dodgers in the ninth to preserve a 3–2 win. The Yankees went on to win the Series in seven games.

In his final season of 1954, Reynolds had a 13-8 record with seven saves. The Yankees missed the World Series for the first time since 1948, and Reynolds retired after the season.

Which two Yankees hit back-to-back home runs to start a game for the first time in franchise history?

Yankees right fielder Hank Bauer and third baseman Andy Carey were the first players in franchise history to hit back-to-back home runs to start a game.

The duo accomplished the feat on April 27, 1955, against the Chicago White Sox at Comiskey Park. Bauer opened the game with a home run to deep left field against White Sox starter Virgil Trucks. Carey followed with another shot to deep left field and the Yankees had a 2–0 lead after two batters, although they ended up on the short end of a 13–4 score.

Bauer played 12 of his 14 major-league seasons with the Yankees.

Bauer was a war hero when he signed with the Yankees in 1946. Bauer served in the US Marine Corps and earned 11 campaign ribbons, two Bronze Stars, and two Purple Hearts for twice being wounded in battle. The second time was during the Battle of Okinawa when he was wounded by shrapnel in his thigh, after which he was sent back to the United States.

After playing in 19 games as a September callup in 1948, Bauer hit 10 home runs with 45 RBIs in 1949 as a platoon player for first-year manager Casey Stengel.

The Yankees won the 1949 American League pennant by beating the Boston Red Sox on the final day of the regular season. Bauer pinch-ran and scored an important run in the Yanks' 5–3 victory.

From 1952 to 1954, Bauer was the American League's starting right fielder in the All-Star Game. In 1953, Stengel began using Bauer in the leadoff spot, and he posted a career high .394 on-base percentage.

From 1949 to 1958, Bauer was part of nine American League pennant winners and seven World Series championships. Bauer is tied for fourth all time with 53 World Series games played and tied for sixth in hits with 46.

The former Marine had some memorable moments in World Series play. In Game 6 of the 1957 Series against the Milwaukee Braves, Bauer hit a solo home run to snap a 2–2 tie in the seventh and the Yankees went on to a 3–2 win to force Game 7.

In the rematch a year later, Bauer could have won the Series MVP award with his performance. In the come-from-behind, seven-game win, Bauer slashed .323/.323/.710 with an OPS of 1.032 with four home runs and eight runs batted in. Bauer was 0-for-5 in Game 7 and lost out on the award to pitcher Bob Turley, who won Games 5 and 7 as the Yankees rebounded from a three games to one deficit to beat the Braves.

Bauer batted .238 in 1959, his lowest average since he became a regular player. After the season, he was traded to the Kansas City Athletics as part of the deal that brought Roger Maris to the Yankees.

Andy Carey was a confident and cocky third baseman who played parts of nine seasons with the Yankees.

Carey had a contentious relationship with Stengel throughout his Yankee career. Carey wasn't afraid to speak his mind, and Stengel knew how to push his buttons to make him a better player.

After appearing in 67 games in 1952 and 1953, Carey got his chance in 1954 to be the starting third baseman. Billy Martin was doing military service so Gil McDougald moved from third base to second base, opening a spot for Carey to start. Carey suffered an injury in spring training, but in his first start of the season, he had two hits in one inning in a win against the Detroit Tigers. Carey hit .303 with eight home runs and 65 RBIs. The Yankees were out of the race, but Carey hit in 13 of his last 14 games to finish over .300.

The native of Oakland, California, played a significant role in Don Larsen's perfect game in the 1956 World Series.

In the top of the second, Brooklyn Dodgers third baseman and Hall of Famer Jackie Robinson hit a line drive toward Carey at third base.

The ball deflected off of Carey's glove to shortstop Gil McDougald, who threw the speedy Robinson out at first.

Carey singled to lead off the sixth inning and scored on Hank Bauer's RBI single. In the eighth, Carey made a nice play to snag Gil Hodges's line drive for the second out of the inning to preserve Larsen's gem. Four outs later, Larsen made history.

During his final three seasons with the Yankees, Carey was not a starting player anymore. In 1957, Carey, Jerry Coleman, and rookie Tony Kubek manned third base. In 1958, Carey, a right-handed batter, platooned with left-handed hitting Jerry Lumpe.

In 1957, the Yankees acquired 20-year-old slick-fielding infielder Clete Boyer from Kansas City. Boyer was a defensive stalwart at shortstop, but the Yankees pictured him as their third baseman of the future. Boyer was tabbed the starting third baseman in 1960, and Carey was traded to the Kansas City Athletics in May.

Who was the first Yankee pitcher to throw an immaculate inning?

An immaculate inning is when a pitcher strikes out the side on nine pitches. On August 11, 1967, left-hander Al Downing became the first Yankee pitcher to achieve that feat.

The Yankees were playing the Cleveland Indians at Cleveland Stadium. In the bottom of the second, Downing struck out Indians first baseman Tony Horton, left fielder Don Demeter, and catcher Duke Sims on nine pitches.

Downing was the first African-American pitcher in Yankee franchise history. The Trenton, New Jersey, native was a two-sport star in baseball and basketball at Trenton Central High School.

After signing with the Yankees as an amateur free agent in 1961, Downing was outstanding for the Yankees' Class A affiliate at Binghamton in the Eastern League. The left-hander was 9-1 with a 1.84 ERA in 12 starts with eight complete games and three shutouts. Downing was promoted in July, but his major-league debut did not go well as he gave up five runs in just one inning of work.

Downing's breakout season was 1963. He began the season at Richmond, the Yankees' Triple-A affiliate in the International League, but was promoted to the big club in June.

The left-hander made 22 starts in 1963 and finished 13-5 with a 2.56 ERA with four shutouts. In his second start of the season, Downing pitched a complete-game, two-hit shutout against the Washington Senators.

On July 2, Downing took a no-hitter into the seventh inning against the Chicago White Sox at Yankee Stadium, but with two out, catcher Cam Carreón singled to center to spoil the bid. Downing went the distance on a one-hitter with 10 strikeouts.

In the 1963 World Series loss to the Los Angeles Dodgers, Downing started Game 2 and took the loss as he gave up three runs in five innings pitched.

Downing won 13 games in 1964 and led the American League with 217 strikeouts. In the 1964 World Series loss to the St. Louis Cardinals, Downing did not fare well. He appeared in three games and was 0-1 with an 8.22 ERA.

Downing was named to the American League All-Star team in 1967 and pitched two scoreless innings in the game. Downing began the ninth with the game tied at 1, and he gave up a leadoff single to Jimmy Wynn, but then retired three Hall of Famers: Willie Mays on a flyout, Roberto Clemente on a strikeout, and Hank Aaron on a groundout to third to end the inning.

In Downing's second inning of work in the 10th, he retired Hall of Famer Orlando Cepeda and Dick Allen. Hall of Famer Ernie Banks singled with two out, but Downing retired yet another Hall of Famer, Bill Mazeroski, to keep the game tied at 1.

Downing had an injury-plagued season in 1968 and only made 12 starts. Yankee manager Ralph Houk used Downing in the bullpen in his final Yankee season of 1969.

The Yankees traded Downing and catcher Frank Fernández to the Oakland Athletics for infielder Danny Cater, who was a .300 hitter in his first season with the team in 1970.

Downing became famous in 1974 when he was pitching for the Los Angeles Dodgers. The left-hander gave up Hank Aaron's record-setting 715th home run that broke Babe Ruth's all-time record.

Left-hander Ron Guidry is the only Yankee to toss an immaculate inning in the ninth inning.

On August 7, 1984, Guidry faced the Chicago White Sox at Yankee Stadium and was working on a four-hit shutout, entering the ninth inning. Guidry struck out Hall of Famer and White Sox catcher Carlton Fisk to start the inning and then fanned right fielder Tom Paciorek and DH Greg Luzinski on a total of nine pitches.

In 1978, Guidry had one of the greatest pitching seasons in Yankee history. He had a 25-3 record that included a win in the one-game playoff against Boston, with a major-league-leading 1.74 ERA. Guidry won the American League Cy Young Award and is the only unanimous winner in Yankee history.

Other Yankees who have thrown an immaculate inning include:

- A. J. Burnett (2009)
- Iván Nova (2013)
- Brandon McCarthy (2014)
- Dellin Betances (2017)
- Michael King (2021)
- Chad Green (2021)
- Nestor Cortés (2022)

Who was the first Yankee to set an American League record for sacrifice flies in one season?

In 1971, outfielder Roy White became the first Yankee to set an American League record for the most sacrifice flies in one season. White had 17 sacrifice flies to set a new American League record. (Orioles switch-hitter Bobby Bonilla tied the mark in 1996. Brooklyn Dodgers first baseman and Hall of Famer Gil Hodges holds the all-time record with 19 in 1954.)

White joined the Yankees in the mid-1960s. The team was about to enter a championship drought, but the switch-hitter played his entire 15-year career with the Yankees and was able to be a contributor to two World Series winning teams.

White is one of the most underrated players in Yankee history. He was a fundamentally sound player who did not light up the box score with impressive offensive numbers but did a number of little things to help the Yankees win ballgames. White's record for sacrifice flies is a prime example of his ability to impact a game in other ways than hitting a home run.

White signed with the Yankees as a 17-year-old out of Centennial High School in Compton, California. The Los Angeles native was a speedy, switch-hitting infielder who had modest power and hit over .400 in high school. White started his minor-league career in 1962, but it took until 1965 for him to show the Yankees that he was ready for the big leagues.

White played the 1965 season with the Yankees' Double-A affiliate at Columbus and had a breakout season. White scored 103 runs with 19 home runs and 56 runs batted in while posting an OBP of .391 and a .300 batting average and was named the Southern League's Most Valuable Player.

The Yankees ran into hard times in 1965. The team was under .500 and out of the pennant race heading into September so changes were in order. The Yankees were counting on players like White and the much heralded Bobby Murcer to lead them into a new era of winning. White was primarily a second baseman in the minors and had not played any outfield, but when he was promoted in September, the Yankees began to groom him as an outfielder.

On September 7, 1965, the Yankees hosted the Baltimore Orioles in the first game of a doubleheader. White made his major-league debut as a pinch-hitter for pitcher Al Downing and he singled off Orioles pitcher Dave McNally.

White started the second game at second base, the only time that he played there for the remainder of the season. In 14 games, White hit .333 (14-for-42) and posted a .404 OBP.

Like the rest of the Yankees, White struggled in 1966. The team finished in last place while the switch-hitter slashed .225/.308/.345 with a .633 OPS. Reportedly, White was lured by the short right field porch in Yankee Stadium and got home run happy.

White split the 1967 season between the minor leagues and the big team so he appeared in only 70 games, but he rebounded in 1968 to lead the team in games played (159) hits (154), and RBIs (62).

White became a steady presence in the Yankee lineup. The switch-hitter was an All-Star in 1969 and 1970, when he established career highs with 22 home runs and 94 runs batted in.

Through some down years and a two-year run at Shea Stadium in 1974 and 1975 while Yankee Stadium was being refurbished, White had seen it all and finally got a taste of winning in 1976. George Steinbrenner led a group that bought the team in January 1973, and by 1976, the Yankees were winners once again as they won their first ever American League Eastern Division title.

White was a major contributor to the Yankees' success in 1976. Yankee manager Billy Martin slotted the switch-hitter into the number two hole, behind dynamic leadoff hitter Mickey Rivers and before Thurman Munson, the American League's Most Valuable Player in 1976. The switch-hitting left fielder played in 156 games and led the American League with 104 runs scored, many of those driven in by Munson, who had 105 RBIs.

In Game 1 of the 1976 American League Championship Series vs. Kansas City at Royals Stadium, White's first postseason hit was an important two-out, two-run double in the top of the ninth to give the Yankees some breathing room in a 4–1 win over the Royals. In the five-game series win, White had five hits, three doubles, four runs scored, three runs batted in, and slashed .294/.455/.471 with an OPS of .925.

In 1977, White was finally part of a World Series winning team, but he got little playing time during the postseason. Martin elected to go with Lou Piniella as his starting left fielder, so White was relegated to being a bench player as the Yankees captured their first world championship in 15 years.

White's role did not change in the first half of the 1978 season, but after Martin was fired in July and replaced by Bob Lemon, the switch-hitter began to play a significant role in the Yankees' heralded comeback against the Boston Red Sox.

In the final 32 games of the regular season, (including the one-game playoff in Boston which counted as a regular-season game), White slashed .337/.417/.410 with 28 hits and 12 runs scored.

In the one-game playoff at Fenway Park, the Yankees trailed 2–0 in the top of the seventh inning, but White helped key the rally that turned the game around. The left fielder singled with one out and one on and scored on Bucky Dent's famous three-run home run that gave the Yankees the lead as they went on to win the American League Eastern Division with a 5–4 win.

White kept it going in the postseason as the Yankees went on to win their second consecutive World Series title. The switch-hitter batted .313 against Kansas City in the American League Championship Series. In the sixth inning of the clinching Game 4 at Yankee Stadium, White's solo home run off of Royals pitcher Dennis Leonard snapped a 1–1 tie and proved to be the series- and game-winning run in a 2–1 win. In the 1978 World Series against the Los Angeles Dodgers, White hit in every game and was 8-for-24 (.333) with nine runs scored and four runs batted in.

White played one more season with the Yankees before he signed to play with the Yomiuri Giants of Japan's Central Professional League.

Hall of Famer Reggie Jackson astutely described what White brought to the ballclub. "Here's a guy who's going to do his job and not make mental mistakes," Jackson said. "A guy who will bunt, hit a grounder to the other side to advance a runner, hit a sacrifice fly, get you a quiet single and get on base."

Today's players rarely appear in all 162 games. Who was the first Yankee to appear in 163 games in a season?

In 2003, Hideki Matsui was the first Yankee to play in 163 games.

In mid-September, the Yankees played a five inning, 1–1 tie against the Baltimore Orioles. In a game that is tied after five innings, all the statistics up to that point count, but the game is replayed from the start in its entirety. (That rule has since been changed. A tie game that is tied after five innings is suspended and picked up from the point from where it was stopped.)

Hideki Matsui
KEITH ALLISON VIA WIKIMEDIA COMMONS

Matsui played the entire 162-game schedule and he also played in the tie game, so he was credited with having played in 163 games. Matsui also played in 162 games in 2004 and 2005.

Matsui's rookie season with the Yankees was 2003. After a successful 10-year career with the Yomiuri Giants of Japan's Professional Baseball League where he won three Central League Most Valuable Player awards and was a nine-time All-Star and three-time Japan Series champion, Matsui signed a three-year, $21 million contract to join the Yankees beginning with the 2003 season.

Matsui (whose nickname was "Godzilla" in honor of the famous Japanese movie monster) was idolized in Japan, but there was much joy over his signing with the world famous New York Yankees. A parade was staged in Matsui's honor in the city of Tokyo, and he brought along a large following of Japanese media to document his every move.

The Yankees were intrigued by Matsui's left-handed power bat, which produced 170 home runs in his final four seasons in Japan, including 50 home runs in 2002.

Matsui's career in the American major leagues began on March 31, 2003 when the Yankees opened the season against the Blue Jays in Toronto, Canada. In his very first at-bat, Matsui's RBI single brought in the first run of the season as the Yankees went on to a season opening, 8–4 win.

The Japanese star's first taste of Yankee Stadium came with much fanfare, and he did not disappoint. On April 8, the Yankees hosted the Minnesota Twins in the home opener and Matsui became the first Yankee to hit a grand slam in his first game at Yankee Stadium.

In the bottom of the fifth inning, the Yankees had a 3–1 lead and the bases loaded with one out, when Matsui drove a 3–2 slider from Twins pitcher Joe Mays into the right-center field bleachers for a grand slam that sent the crowd of over 33,000 into a frenzy.

Matsui had a terrific rookie season. He played 163 games and slashed .287/.353/.435 with an OPS of .788 with 16 home runs and 106 runs batted in. Matsui was an All-Star and finished second to Kansas City's Ángel Berroa in the voting for the American League Rookie of the Year Award.

Matsui became the first Japanese player to hit a home run in the World Series when he went deep in Game 2 of the 2003 series against the Florida Marlins. The Yankees had already lost Game 1, but in the bottom of the first inning of Game 2, Matsui hit a three-run home run off of Florida's Mark Redman to get the Yankees an early lead as they went on to a 6–1 win.

Matsui followed up his rookie season with another All-Star appearance in 2004, after he hit a career-high 31 home runs with 108 RBIs while slashing .298/.390/.522 with an OPS of .912. In 2005, Matsui had a career high with 116 RBIs and put together a third straight season of playing in every game.

That streak came to an end in 2006. On May 11, the Yankees were hosting the Boston Red Sox. In the top of the first, Boston's Mark Loretta, the second batter of the game, hit a ball into short left field. Matsui charged in and tried to make a diving catch, but he ended up breaking his left wrist. Matsui missed the next four months and played only 51 games.

Matsui bounced back nicely in 2007. He played in 143 games and hit .285 with 25 home runs and 103 runs batted in, while also scoring 100 runs.

Matsui was in the World Series in his rookie season but would not return until 2009 when he would experience his greatest postseason moment.

The Yankees played the National League champion Philadelphia Phillies and lost Game 1 at Yankee Stadium. In Game 2, Matsui homered off of Phillies pitcher, Hall of Famer, and longtime Yankee nemesis Pedro Martínez to snap a 1–1 tie in the sixth inning as the Yankees evened the Series with a 3–1 win.

The Yankees had a three games to two series lead with Game 6 set for Yankee Stadium. Matsui put on a memorable performance as the Yankees won their first World Series since 2000.

In Game 6, Matsui was 3-for-4 with a Series record tying six runs batted in as the Yankees won 7–3. For the Series, Matsui hit .615 with three home runs and eight runs batted in, but his Game 6 performance earned him the World Series Most Valuable Player Award. Matsui became the first Japanese-born player to win the award and the first to win as a full-time designated hitter.

Despite his spectacular World Series performance, the 38-year-old Matsui was not tendered a contract. He went on to play with the Los Angeles Angels, Oakland A's, and Tampa Bay Rays. During his seven-year Yankee career, Matsui slashed .292/.370/.482 with an .852 OPS, 140 home runs, and 597 runs batted in.

Roy White is the only other Yankee to play in 162 games more than once. In 1970, White played 162 of the team's 163 games played. The switch-hitting outfielder played in all 162 games in the 1973 season.

In 1961, second baseman Bobby Richardson was the first Yankee to play in 162 games. It was also the first season that a 162-game schedule was played in the American League. The league expanded to 10 by adding two teams, the Los Angeles Angels and the Washington Senators. (The National League stuck to a 154-game schedule and went to 162 in the 1962 season when they added the New York Mets and Houston Colt .45s.)

Hitting a home run in your first major-league game is a memorable experience, but hitting one in each of your first two games is a rare feat. Who was the first Yankee to hit a home run in each of his first two major-league games?

Left-handed-hitting outfielder Joe Lefebvre played one season with the Yankees, but he was the first in franchise history to hit a home run in each of his first two major-league games.

Lefebvre made his major-league debut on May 22, 1980, against the Toronto Blue Jays at Exhibition Stadium. In the top of the seventh, he hit a solo home run in his third major-league at-bat, off of Toronto pitcher Dave Stieb. The next day, Lefebvre pinch-hit for Lou Piniella in the sixth inning and slammed a solo home run off of Blue Jays pitcher Dave Lemanczyk, to become the first Yankee to homer in each of his first two big-league games.

During his only season with the Yankees, Lefebvre played in 74 games and had eight home runs. The highlight of Lefebvre's 1980 campaign came on June 29, when the Yankees hosted the Cleveland Indians. Lefebvre snapped a 2–2 tie in the sixth inning with a three-run home run off of Indians starter Len Barker as the Yankees went on to a 7–2 win.

Right before the 1981 season, Lefebvre was sent to the San Diego Padres as part of a six-player trade that brought outfielder Jerry Mumphrey and pitcher John Pacella to the Yankees.

The only other Yankee to hit a home run in each of his first two major-league games was Aaron Judge in 2016.

Judge made his major-league debut on August 13, 2016 at Yankee Stadium against the Tampa Bay Rays. In the bottom of the second inning, rookies Tyler Austin and Judge hit back-to-back home runs. The duo became the first pair of rookies to hit home runs in their first major-league at-bats in the same game.

After Austin homered into the right field stands against Rays pitcher Matt Andriese, Judge, who was batting eighth, followed that with a blast that easily cleared the center field wall.

The next day, Judge hit a solo home run off of Rays pitcher Jake Odorizzi and joined Lefebvre as the only Yankees in franchise history to hit a home run in each of their first two major-league games.

In 2017, Judge set a rookie record with 52 home runs (later broken by New York Mets first baseman Pete Alonso) and was a unanimous winner of the American League Rookie of the Year Award.

Judge set an American League and Yankee franchise record when he slammed 62 home runs in 2022. On October 4 at Globe Life Field, Judge broke Roger Maris's record when he led off the game with his 62nd home run off of Texas Rangers pitcher Jesús Tinoco. In 2022, Judge put together one of the greatest offensive seasons in baseball history. Judge slashed .311/.425/.686 with an OPS of 1.111 and 131 RBIs and became the 14th different Yankee to be named the American League's Most Valuable Player.

Name the first Yankee pitcher to get a hit in a regular-season game after the DH rule began in 1973.

Hideki Irabu was the first Yankee pitcher to get a base hit after the DH rule began in 1973.

When interleague play began in 1997, American League pitchers came to bat in the games that were played at National League ballparks.

On June 10, 1998, at Montreal's Olympic Stadium, Irabu had an infield single against Expos pitcher Dustin Hermanson. Before Irabu's hit, the last Yankee pitcher to get a hit was Larry Gowell, who appeared in a total of two major-league games for the Yankees. Gowell singled in the final game of the 1972 season.

Irabu came to the Yankees in a January 1997 trade with the San Diego Padres, who held his rights thanks to a prior agreement with the Chiba Lotte Marines of the Japan Pacific League. The Yankees sent highly touted prospect Rubén Rivera to San Diego while also getting back a useful player in utility infielder Homer Bush in the same deal.

Irabu was a power pitcher who was labeled the "Nolan Ryan of Japan," thanks to a 99 mph fastball and a biting slider. On July 10, 1997, Irabu made his highly publicized major-league debut against the Detroit Tigers at Yankee Stadium.

Before over 51,000 fans, who were on hand to see what all the fuss was about, Irabu dazzled the Tigers for 6⅔ innings with nine strikeouts. The Japanese right-hander gave up five hits and two runs and left the field in the seventh inning to a thunderous standing ovation.

Unfortunately, Irabu's success in the first game never translated for the remainder of his first season. In his following seven starts, totaling 32 innings (sandwiched around a two-week stint in the minors), Irabu gave up 31 earned runs. He finished the season with a ghastly 7.09 ERA.

Irabu's best season with the Yankees was 1998 when he had a career-best 13 wins and was named American League Pitcher of the Month in May when he was 4-1 with a 1.44 ERA. However, Irabu did not make an appearance in the postseason as the Yankees went on to win the World Series.

The following spring training, Irabu was late in covering first base during an exhibition game in Fort Lauderdale. It was the second time that happened, which prompted Yankee owner George Steinbrenner to call his pitcher a "fat toad," a remark that became a national story.

Irabu was not just having problems with his weight. He was smoking and drinking and was feuding with the large Japanese media contingent that was recording his every move.

Irabu did not pitch badly in 1999 as he made 27 starts and posted an 11-7 record with a 4.84 ERA. He also made his first and only career postseason appearance in Game 3 of the 1999 American League Championship Series against the Boston Red Sox.

The Yankees had won the first two games at Yankee Stadium, but Game 3 starter Roger Clemens did not pitch well and lasted only two innings at his ol' stomping grounds, Fenway Park. Irabu entered the game in the third inning with a man on and no one out and the Yankees already trailing 4–0. When Irabu's outing was done, he had given up eight runs, seven earned, on 13 hits in 4⅔ innings as the Yankees ended up on the short end of an embarrassing 13–1 loss.

It was Irabu's final appearance as a Yankee. After the season, Irabu was dealt to the Montreal Expos as part of a deal for left-handed pitcher Ted Lilly.

Who was the first Yankee to get six hits in a nine-inning game?

On June 6, 1934, Myril Hoag became the first Yankee to get six hits in a nine-inning game. Hoag was 6-for-6 with three runs scored and an RBI as the Yankees had 25 hits en route to a 15–3 thrashing of the Red Sox at Fenway Park.

Hoag, hitting seventh in the lineup, singled in the second, third, and fourth inning off of Red Sox pitcher and Hall of Famer Lefty Grove. In the fourth, Hoag's single drove in a run as the Yankees took an 8–0 lead. Hoag's final three hits came off Red Sox reliever Hank Johnson in the fifth, seventh, and eighth innings.

In 1930 the Yankees had watched Hoag put up some impressive numbers in the minors. While playing with the Sacramento Senators of the Pacific Coast League, the 22-year-old hit .337 with 17 home runs and 127 runs batted in.

Hoag did not develop as anticipated and after two seasons with the big club as a utility player, he played the entire 1933 season with the Yankees' Triple-A affiliate in Newark, New Jersey.

In the 1936 season, Hoag had a collision with Joe DiMaggio during a game in Detroit. In the bottom of the sixth inning, Detroit's Goose Goslin hit a ball into the right-center field gap. Hoag and DiMaggio converged and ran into one another. Goslin came all the way around to score on an inside the park home run. DiMaggio stayed in the game while Hoag was removed for precautionary reasons.

Hoag played the next day and got a hit, but two days later, he collapsed at his hotel and was rushed to a local hospital in Detroit and was diagnosed with a blood clot. Hoag had surgery but missed the remainder of the season.

Hoag totaled seven seasons for the Yankees before being traded to the St. Louis Browns after the 1938 season.

On May 1, 1996, Gerald Williams had six hits in a 15-inning game against the Baltimore Orioles.

Johnny Damon was the only other Yankee to have six hits in a nine-inning game when he recorded this notable achievement on June 7, 2008.

On June 13, 1997, the Yankees played the National League's Florida Marlins at Pro Player Stadium in their first ever interleague game. Who had the first Yankee hit in an interleague game? Bonus: What two players had the first Yankee RBI and first Yankee home run in an interleague game?

Third baseman Charlie Hayes was the first Yankee to get a hit in an interleague game.

Hayes singled off of Florida Marlins pitcher Al Leiter in the top of the second inning. Florida won the game in 12 innings, 2–1.

Hayes had two different stints in a Yankee uniform. In February 1992, the Yankees acquired Hayes from the Philadelphia Phillies.

As the Yankees starting third baseman in 1992, Hayes had a solid season. The 27-year-old played 139 games at third and hit 18 home runs with 66 RBIs. In November 1992, the Yankees gambled and left Hayes unprotected in the expansion draft, and he was selected by the Colorado Rockies with the third overall pick.

Hayes spent the next two years in Colorado. In 1995, Hayes signed a one-year deal with the Philadelphia Phillies and then joined the Pittsburgh Pirates for the 1996 season.

After Hayes went to Colorado, the Yankees signed Hall of Famer Wade Boggs, who was the starting third baseman in 1996. By that time, Boggs was 38 years old and was struggling against left-handed pitching, so Hayes, a right-handed bat, who hit with more power, was reacquired to serve as part of a platoon.

Hayes played 20 games down the stretch and hit .284 with two home runs and 13 RBIs as the Yankees captured their first American League Eastern Division title in 15 years.

In the postseason, Hayes played in 12 of the Yankees' 15 games. In Game 4 of the 1996 World Series vs. Atlanta, Hayes had three hits and played a big role as the Yankees rallied from a 6–0 deficit to even the

Series at two games apiece. In Game 5, Hayes reached on an error and scored the only run of the game on Cecil Fielder's double as the Yankees took a 3–2 lead in the Series with a 1–0 win.

Hayes caught the final out of the 1996 World Series but not without a little adventure.

The Yankees were leading the Braves 3–2 in the top of the ninth inning of Game 6. Atlanta had just scored a run off of Yankee closer John Wetteland to make it a one-run game and had two on and two out with Mark Lemke at the plate.

On a 3-2 pitch, Lemke lifted a foul fly toward the third base dugout. Hayes went over and tried to make a play but ended up falling into the Braves dugout. A few moments later, Lemke hit another foul popup toward the third base side. This time, Hayes had room and he made the catch to seal the win and the Yankees' first World Series title in 18 years.

Hayes and Boggs made up the third base platoon in 1997. Hayes played in 100 games and hit 11 home runs with 53 runs batted in. Following the 1997 season, the Yankees traded Hayes to the San Francisco Giants for pitcher Alberto Castillo and outfielder Chris Singleton.

Switch-hitting center fielder Bernie Williams had the first Yankee RBI in an interleague game. Williams's RBI single came in the sixth inning of the Yankees' first ever interleague game.

Williams put together a fabulous 16-year career with the Yankees and was an integral part of the dynasty that won four of five World Series titles from 1996 to 2000. The talented switch-hitter finished in the top 10 in franchise history in a number of offensive categories including games played (2,076), runs scored (1,366), hits (2,336), walks (1,069), home runs (287), and runs batted in (1,257) Williams was a five-time All-Star, four-time Gold Glove Award winner, and was the American League batting champion in 1998 with a .339 average.

The Yankees signed Williams as a 17-year-old out of Puerto Rico in September 1985. It took some time to develop his raw talent, but Williams began to show his stuff in 1988 when he hit .335 and won the Carolina League batting title while playing for the Yankees A-affiliate at Prince William.

Williams made his major-league debut in 1991 as a 22-year-old. Center fielder Roberto Kelly was injured, so Williams was promoted from Triple-A Columbus and started in center field against the Baltimore Orioles at Yankee Stadium on July 7, 1991. In his second at-bat in the fifth inning, Williams got his first major-league RBI with a sacrifice fly. His first hit was an RBI single in the ninth inning off of Orioles pitcher Gregg Olson.

Williams spent time with the big club and Columbus during the 1992 season, but he was tabbed the Yankees starting center fielder for the 1993 season.

Beginning with the 1995 season, Williams posted eight consecutive seasons of hitting .300 or better. In 1998, he not only won a batting title, but also a Gold Glove and a World Series ring, making him the first player to accomplish that baseball trifecta in the same season. It was also his walk year, and the switch-hitter nearly left the Yankees to sign with the rival Boston Red Sox.

The Yankees were rumored to be negotiating with free agent slugging outfielder Albert Belle. At the last minute, Williams and the Yankees came to an agreement for a seven-year, $87.5 million contract to remain with the team for the remainder of his career.

Williams had an up and down postseason career with the Yankees, although he did hit two postseason walkoff home runs.

In Game 1 of the 1996 American League Championship Series against the Baltimore Orioles, Williams, batting from the right side, homered off of Orioles' left-handed reliever Randy Myers to lead off the bottom of the 11th inning to give the Yankees a 5–4 win.

Williams duplicated the feat in Game 1 of the 1999 American League Championship Series against the Red Sox. Like three years previous, the walkoff homer came in extra innings. This time, however, Williams was hitting left-handed against Red Sox righty Rod Beck. The Yankee center fielder drove an 0-1 pitch over the center field wall to lead off the bottom of the 10th inning as the Yankees won Game 1, 4–3.

The switch-hitter had not had much success in World Series play until 2003 when the Yankees were beaten by the Florida Marlins in six games. Williams was the Yankees' best hitter in that series with a slash line of .400/.429/.720 with an OPS of 1.149. In six games, Williams had two home runs, five runs scored, and five runs batted in.

Williams's last big year was 2002 when he batted .333 with a career-high 204 hits. Williams had 58 extra-base hits, including 19 home runs, with 102 RBIs and won his only Silver Slugger Award.

Williams's career ended after the 2006 season. On May 24, 2014, the Yankees retired Williams's #51 and also honored him with a plaque in Monument Park in center field at Yankee Stadium.

On June 18, 1997, at Yankee Stadium, outfielder Chad Curtis became the first Yankee to hit a home run in an interleague game. Curtis hit a 1-1 pitch into the left field seats off of New York Mets pitcher Rick Reed to give the Yankees a 1–0 lead in the third inning. The Yankees beat the Mets in 10 innings, 3–2.

Curtis played three seasons with the Yankees from 1997 to 1999. The 30-year-old had a "Yankee moment" in the four-game sweep of the Atlanta Braves in the 1999 World Series.

Curtis hit two home runs in Game 3 at Yankee Stadium, including a walkoff solo home run in the bottom of the 10th to give the Yankees a 6–5 win and a three games to none lead in the Series.

The Yankees were down 5–1 in the fifth inning when Curtis hit the first of his two home runs, a solo shot off of Hall of Famer and Braves pitcher Tom Glavine to begin the comeback. The Yankees eventually rallied to tie the game at 5 and Curtis led off the bottom of the 10th with the game-winning blow off of Braves pitcher Mike Remlinger.

Following the 1999 season, the Yankees traded Curtis to the Texas Rangers.

Who was the first Yankee winning pitcher in an interleague game?

Left-handed reliever Mike Stanton was the Yankees' first winning pitcher in an interleague game.

Interleague play debuted during the 1997 season. The Yankees' first ever interleague series was scheduled against the National League's Florida Marlins in Miami. The Yankees lost their first interleague game and after the second game was rained out, the teams were forced to play a doubleheader on the final day of the series.

On June 15, 1997, the Yankees beat the Marlins 8–5 in the first game of a doubleheader at Pro Player Stadium for their first ever win in their second interleague game. With the Yankees trailing 5–4, Stanton pitched a scoreless eighth inning. In the ninth, the Yankees scored four runs to take the lead. Stanton was the pitcher of record, so he was awarded the win.

Stanton pitched six full seasons and parts of another (1997–2002, 2005) for the Yankees. He became a valuable member of a bullpen that played a key role in winning three straight World Series championships from 1998 to 2000.

The Houston, Texas, native signed with the Yankees in December 1996 as a free agent. The Yankees were the defending World Series champions and wanted to upgrade the bullpen with a veteran left-handed arm so Stanton, who had already pitched in two World Series with the Atlanta Braves, was a fit. Stanton was hoping to claim the closer role when he signed, but Hall of Famer Mariano Rivera was beginning his fabulous career in that role.

Stanton got off to a great start in his first season. He did not give up a run in his first 10 appearances and finished the season with a 6-1 record, three saves, and a 2.57 ERA in 64 games.

In Game 5 of the 1997 American League Division Series against Cleveland, the Indians had a one-run lead and two runners on with two out. Stanton came on to strike out David Justice to keep the deficit at one; however the Yankees ended up on the short end of a 4–3 score.

In the 1998 season, Stanton got off to a good start, but he seemed to be a different pitcher after he was suspended in June. Stanton was facing the Baltimore Orioles in a mid-June game and after Rafael Palmeiro homered, Stanton hit Orioles center fielder Eric Davis with a pitch. The Orioles felt it was intentional and so did American League president Gene Budig. A few days later, Budig suspended Stanton for five games.

From there, Stanton's season took a downturn. In July and August, Stanton gave up 22 earned runs in 28 innings pitched. The Yankees were running away with the American League East, so they were patient that Stanton would come around. He recovered to pitch better in September and was sharp in the American League Championship Series vs. Cleveland as he tossed scoreless ball in three appearances.

On May 9, 1999, Stanton made the only start of his 19-year major-league career against the Seattle Mariners at Yankee Stadium and tossed four scoreless innings. Stanton gave up two hits, walked one, and struck out three and left the game with a 4–0 lead but did not qualify for a win because he did not pitch the required five innings.

In 2001, Stanton made his one and only All-Star team. That year he went 9-4 in relief with a 2.58 ERA in 76 appearances. Stanton got into the All-Star Game in Seattle and faced two batters and retired them both, including Hall of Famer Vladimir Guerrero on a flyout to left field to end the sixth inning.

After the 2002 season, Stanton signed as a free agent with the New York Mets, but he was traded back to the Yankees in December 2004. Left-handed reliever Félix Heredia went back to the Mets in a rare deal between the New York City rivals.

Stanton made 28 appearances in 2005, but he gave up 11 earned runs in 14 innings pitched and was released in July with a 7.07 ERA.

Who was the first Yankee to hit into an unassisted triple play?

On May 29, 2000, DH Shane Spencer became the first Yankee to hit into an unassisted triple play in a game against the Oakland A's at Yankee Stadium.

A's second baseman and former Yankee Randy Velarde was the beneficiary of such a rare play. (Coming into the 2023 season, there have only been 15 unassisted triple plays in Major League Baseball history.)

With Jorge Posada on first and Tino Martinez on second and no one out, the runners were going on a 3-2 pitch when Spencer hit a line drive just to the right of the second base bag. Velarde caught the liner for the first out, tagged Posada who was right within his reach, and then stepped on the bag to complete the unassisted triple play.

Spencer made his major-league debut with the Yankees during the historic 1998 season. In September, Spencer made some history himself.

The native of Key West, Florida, hit three grand slams in the final month of the season. At the time, it was a major-league record for most in a season by a rookie. (In 2008, Chicago White Sox rookie Alexei Ramírez hit four grand slams to set a new record, but he did that over the course of the entire season.)

Spencer quickly became a fan favorite. The Yankees were running away with the American League East, so the games became a subplot to what this rookie was doing.

In the postseason, Spencer homered in Games 2 and 3 of the American League Division Series against the Texas Rangers. In Game 3 in Arlington, Texas, Spencer hit a three-run homer in the sixth inning that blew open a close game as the Yankees cruised to a 4–0 win and a sweep of the three-game series.

During parts of five seasons with the Yankees, Spencer won three World Series and four American League pennants. In Game 4 of the 2001 World Series against the Arizona Diamondbacks, Spencer broke up a scoreless tie in the third inning with his only World Series home run, a solo shot off of Arizona pitcher Curt Schilling.

Who was the first Yankee manager to win 100 games in a season?

In 1927, Miller Huggins became the first Yankee manager to win 100 games. Huggins's 1927 Yankees won 110 games and swept the Pittsburgh Pirates in four straight to win the World Series. The Hall of Fame manager piloted a team that is deemed one of the best in baseball history and featured six Hall of Fame players: Babe Ruth, Lou Gehrig, Waite Hoyt, Tony Lazzeri, Earle Combs, and Herb Pennock.

From 1921 to 1928, Huggins's Yankees won six AL pennants and three World Series championships.

Huggins began his managerial career with the St. Louis Cardinals in 1913. After five seasons with St. Louis, Huggins's contract was not retained, so he was hired by co-owner Jacob Ruppert to manage the Yankees, beginning with the 1918 season.

Huggins did not win in his first two seasons and was already feeling the heat from the New York media, as well as the front office. After the 1919 season, Huggins reportedly urged Yankee owner Jacob Ruppert to acquire Babe Ruth, despite the slugger's reputation as being a partier and a tough player to handle.

Miller Huggins

The 6'2" Ruth did not respect the 5'6" Huggins. Co-owner Til Huston never wanted Huggins in the first place, so he did not support the Yankee manager when he tried to discipline Ruth.

The Yankees did not win in Ruth's first season in 1920, but in 1921, Huggins led the Yankees to what would be the first of three straight American League pennants. The Yankees lost the World Series in 1921 and 1922 to their crosstown rival, the New York Giants, but in 1923, they beat the Giants in six games to win the first world championship in franchise history.

Ruppert, who was more supportive of Huggins than his partner, became the sole owner of the team after he bought out Huston in May 1923. Ruppert came around and began to back Huggins when it came to disciplining Ruth.

In 1925, things came to a head between the manager and his star player.

On August 27, the Yankees were trailing the Chicago White Sox 6–5 at Comiskey Park. With first and second and no one out, Huggins ordered Ruth to bunt the runners over. Ruth ignored the sign and hit into a double play and the Yankees lost.

The next day, the Yankees were in St. Louis to play the Browns and Ruth was late to the game. The Yankees lost 1–0 as they fell to 49-71, 27 games out of first place.

For the good of his own, and the team's, future, Huggins had to discipline Ruth for his behavior. General manager Ed Barrow and Ruppert were fully behind Huggins, who suspended Ruth on August 29 and fined him.

Ruth came to the ballpark and was told he was fined and suspended. Ruth did not take the news very well and thought he would have the owner's backing to reverse the decision. Ruth went back to New York and met with Ruppert, who totally supported his manager's decision. Ruth was humbled and eventually apologized to Huggins and Ruppert. Ruth ended up missing six games and never challenged Huggins's authority again.

Huggins's final season was 1929 and he was ailing physically. In mid-September, the Yankee manager developed a carbuncle on his cheek. Huggins left the team and was admitted to a hospital with a bacterial skin infection on his cheek that spread throughout his body. Despite the doctors' best efforts, Huggins died on September 25.

Huggins finished his 12-season, Yankee tenure with a 1,067-719 record and a .597 winning percentage.

In 1932, Huggins became the first Yankee who was honored with a monument in center field at Yankee Stadium. Huggins was inducted into the Baseball Hall of Fame in 1964.

Other Yankee managers who won 100 or more games in a season: Joe McCarthy, Casey Stengel, Ralph Houk, Billy Martin, Dick Howser, Joe Torre, Joe Girardi, and Aaron Boone. (Martin and Bob Lemon combined for a 100-win season in 1978.)

Match up these Yankees to the uniform numbers they were first to wear:

Jim Bouton	#99
Charlie Keller	#42
Steve Balboni	#60
Gary Sánchez	#56
Stan Bahnsen	#73
Vic Raschi	#66

Pitcher Jim Bouton was the first Yankee to wear #56.

Bouton reportedly kept the high number to remind him of how close he came to not making it to the Yankees. The tenacious right-hander who was nicknamed "Bulldog" would often have his cap fly off his head after he threw a pitch.

Bouton made his major-league debut in late April 1962 by tossing three scoreless innings in relief against the Cleveland Indians. On May 6, Bouton made his first major-league start against the Washington Senators at Yankee Stadium. The 23-year-old right-hander tossed a complete-game shutout, but he walked seven and had men on base in eight of the nine innings.

Bouton did not pitch in the 1962 World Series win over the San Francisco Giants, but he had a breakout season in 1963, winning a career-high 21 games with an ERA of 2.53. He was named an All-Star for the first time.

On September 13, Bouton pitched a complete-game shutout to beat the Minnesota Twins 2–0 at Metropolitan Stadium, as the Yankees clinched the American League pennant. In Game 3 of the 1963 World Series, Bouton gave up a run in seven innings as the Yankees dropped a 1–0 decision to Hall of Famer Don Drysdale and the Dodgers in Los Angeles.

In 1964, Bouton was 18-13 with a 3.02 ERA and was a factor down the stretch. The Yankees were in a dogfight with the Baltimore Orioles and Chicago White Sox for the American League pennant. On September 20, Bouton tossed a complete-game shutout to beat the Kansas City Athletics that extended the Yankees lead to a full game over the Orioles with 12 games to play.

Bouton went on to win two games in the 1964 World Series loss to the St. Louis Cardinals, going the distance in a 2–1 win in Game 3 that ended with Mickey Mantle's walkoff home run in the bottom of the ninth. Bouton gave up three runs in 8⅓ innings pitched to win Game 6 and force Game 7 that the Yankees lost.

Bouton went on to pitch in parts of four more seasons with the Yankees. In June 1968, Bouton's contract was sold to the expansion Seattle Pilots, who would not begin play until the 1969 season.

Bouton wrote about his experience with the Pilots in the controversial book, *Ball Four*, in 1970. *Ball Four* gave readers a peek into the life of a baseball player, both on and off the field.

When Charlie "King Kong" Keller debuted for the Yankees in 1939, he became the first Yankee to wear #99. A writer coined the nickname because of Keller's strength and massive physique.

The 5'10", 185-pound left-handed-hitting Keller played college baseball at Maryland where he was a fearsome slugger who caught the eye of Yankees scout Gene McCann. The Yankees felt Keller's swing played well for Yankee Stadium.

In his rookie season of 1939, Keller slashed .334/.447/.500 and had 83 RBIs in 111 games. In the four-game sweep of the Cincinnati Reds in the 1939 World Series, Keller's numbers were off the charts. Keller was 8-for-17 with three home runs, six RBIs, and eight runs scored. His slugging percentage was 1.188 and his OPS was an eye-opening 1.658.

Keller's best season was 1941 when he had career highs in home runs (33) and runs batted in (122).

The Yankees released the slugger after the 1949 season. Keller played the next two seasons with the Detroit Tigers before coming back to the Yankees in 1952. Keller played two games in September and was released a second time in October.

Keller played in 11 seasons with the Yankees. He was a five-time All-Star and a three-time World Series champion.

Pitcher Brian Bruney (2009) and Aaron Judge are the only other two Yankees to wear #99.

Steve Balboni was the first Yankee to wear #66.

Aaron Judge
ARTURO PARDAVILA VIA WIKIMEDIA COMMONS

Balboni was a second-round pick of the Yankees in the 1978 MLB June Amateur Draft out of Eckerd College. The 6'3", 225-pound slugging first baseman did two stints with the Yankees but never lived up to his potential.

Playing at Columbus, the Yankees' Triple-A affiliate in the International League in 1981, Balboni slammed 33 home runs and drove in 98 runs. Balboni appeared in four games for the Yankees in 1981. Going into the 1982 season, Balboni was behind starting first baseman John Mayberry and a young Don Mattingly, who was on the rise.

In December 1983, the Yankees traded Balboni to the Kansas City Royals, where he won a World Series in 1985. In March 1989, Balboni was reacquired in a trade with the Seattle Mariners. He played two more seasons in New York before he was released in April 1991.

Catcher Gary Sánchez was the first Yankee to wear #73 when he debuted in 2015 and played in two major-league games. The native of the Dominican Republic signed with the Yankees as an international free agent in 2009 when he was 17 years old.

In 2016, Sánchez was recalled from the minors for one game in May, but he was called back up in August and burst on the scene with a bang. The 23-year-old finished the season with 20 home runs and 42 RBIs in 53 games. Sánchez slashed .390/.458/.832 with an OPS of 1.290 in August, including 11 home runs. His batting average slipped in the last portion of the season, but he still hit nine more home runs.

Sánchez became the first player in major-league history with at least 11 home runs and 31 hits in his first 23 career games. Sánchez won back-to-back American League Player of the Week awards in late August. In his 45th career game in late September, Sánchez hit two home runs to reach 19 for the season and set a record for the fastest player in the modern era to reach 19 home runs. Sánchez finished second to Detroit Tigers pitcher Michael Fulmer in the American League Rookie of the Year voting, despite playing fewer than 60 games.

Sánchez was an All-Star and a Silver Slugger Award winner in 2017 after he hit 33 home runs with a career-high 90 runs batted in.

The slugging catcher struggled in 2018 due to a groin injury that limited him to 89 games. Sánchez was placed on the disabled list in late July and did not return until September. He batted only .186 but still hit 18 home runs.

In 2019, Sánchez was an All-Star for the second time, and he finished with 34 home runs and 77 RBIs. In August, Sánchez hit his 100th career home run and set an American League record for the fastest player to 100 home runs.

Sánchez had his limitations defensively when he was first called up from the minors, but in his final two seasons, his offense started to regress and his defense didn't improve.

In the shortened 2020 season, Sánchez appeared in 49 games and hit .147 with 10 home runs and 24 runs batted in. By the end of the season, Sánchez was replaced by Kyle Higashioka as the starting catcher and that carried over into the playoffs.

Sánchez started the clinching Game 2 of the 2020 best-of-three Wild Card Series against the Cleveland Indians and had a three-run homer as the Yankees won, 10–9. In the American League Division Series against Tampa Bay, Sánchez was relegated to backup duty. In the fifth and deciding game, Sánchez entered as a defensive replacement but never came to bat as the Yankees lost, 2–1.

Sánchez's stock plummeted in 2021 as he slashed .204/.307/.423 with an OPS of .730. His defense continued to deteriorate as he had six errors and eight passed balls. Sánchez's arm, one of his few strengths defensively, also regressed as his caught stealing percentage dropped to a career low 17 percent.

In March 2022, the Yankees traded Sánchez and third baseman Gio Urshela to the Minnesota Twins in exchange for third baseman Josh Donaldson, shortstop Isiah Kiner-Falefa, and catcher Ben Rortvedt.

Right-handed pitcher Stan Bahnsen was the first Yankee to wear #60.

Bahnsen was a fourth-round pick of the Yankees in the 1965 MLB June Amateur Draft from the University of Nebraska-Lincoln.

In 1966, Bahnsen threw a no-hitter for the Toledo Mud Hens, the Yankees' Triple-A affiliate in the International League. The 21-year-old was a September callup in 1966 and got a save in his first major-league game. Facing the Boston Red Sox at Fenway Park, Bahnsen tossed two perfect innings to preserve a 2–1 win. In his first major-league inning, Bahnsen struck out Boston's Joe Foy, Hall of Famer Carl Yastrzemski, and Tony Conigliaro.

Bahnsen did not make the team in 1967 and spent the entire year at Syracuse, the Yankees' Triple-A affiliate in the International League, but he had a breakout season in 1968 that ended with him becoming the fifth Yankee to be named the American League Rookie of the Year. Bahnsen made 34 starts and was 17-12 with a sparkling 2.05 ERA. After two relief appearances to start the season, Bahnsen started his first game on April 17 and beat the California Angels at Anaheim Stadium with 8⅓ innings of two-run ball. Bahnsen went on to win seven of his next nine decisions. The best outing of his rookie season came on August 1 at Fenway Park when he shutout the Boston Red Sox on three hits with no walks and 12 strikeouts.

Bahnsen could not follow up his outstanding rookie season as he went 9-16 in 1969. In 1970 and 1971, he won 14 games in each of those seasons.

Bahnsen played five seasons with the Yankees and was 55-52 overall with a 3.10 ERA. After the 1971 season, the Yankees traded Bahnsen to the Chicago White Sox for third baseman Rich McKinney.

The number 42 has been retired by the Yankees for Mariano Rivera and by baseball for the legendary Jackie Robinson. Long before that, pitcher Vic Raschi was the first Yankee to wear #42.

The 6'1", 200-pound right-hander was born in Springfield, Massachusetts. Raschi threw hard and became known as "The Springfield Rifle" for his live fastball. Raschi was a four-time All-Star and six-time World Series champion.

Raschi first wore the legendary number when the Yankees called him up for the first time in September 1946. In his first major-league start against the Philadelphia Athletics, Raschi gave up six runs but went nine innings in a 9–6 win. Six days after that, Raschi gave up a run in seven innings and was credited with a complete-game, 2–1 win when the game was called due to darkness.

Raschi was bitter that the Yankees sent him to the Portland Beavers, their Triple-A affiliate, to begin the 1947 season. He initially refused to report, but he went to Portland and started 11 games and posted an 8-2 record with nine complete games.

Raschi had just won his fourth in a row in San Diego when he was called up by the surging Yankees to pitch three days later. Raschi gave up three runs in 6⅓ innings pitched to beat the Chicago White Sox in the second game of a doubleheader as the Yankees won their 14th straight game.

Pitching on short rest for a second straight start, Raschi tossed a complete game to beat the Cleveland Indians 7–2 in the second game of a doubleheader. The win gave the Yankees a franchise record 19th consecutive win and established the Springfield Rifle as a consistent member of the starting rotation. Raschi did not start in the 1947 World Series against the Brooklyn Dodgers, but he pitched twice in relief.

Starting in 1948, Raschi became a consistent winner. From 1948 to 1953, he won 111 games, including three straight seasons of 20 or more wins.

Raschi was 21-10 in 1949, but his most important win came on the final day of the regular season. The Yankees were tied with Boston for first place with one game remaining between the rivals at Yankee Stadium. Raschi got the start and pitched a complete game to beat the Red Sox, 5–3, and give the Yankees the American League pennant.

In 1950, Raschi led the American League with a .724 winning percentage (21-8) and finished seventh in the American League MVP voting.

In February 1954, the Yankees traded Raschi to the St. Louis Cardinals. Raschi pitched in parts of 12 seasons for the Yankees and was 120-50 with a .706 winning percentage, good for fifth all time in Yankee history.

Raschi was a key member of the Yankee team that won an unprecedented five consecutive World Series championships from 1949 to 1953. Raschi made eight World Series starts in that span, posting a 5-3 record with a 2.14 ERA.

Who is the first Yankee to steal second, third, and home in the same inning?

On April 17, 1915, third baseman Fritz Maisel became the first Yankee to steal second, third, and home in the same inning.

The Yankees were playing the Philadelphia Athletics at Shibe Park and had an 8–1 lead in the top of the ninth, when Maisel reached first on a fielder's choice. With outfielder Hugh High at the plate, Maisel proceeded to steal second, third, and home, giving him a total of four stolen bases in the game.

Maisel was born in Catonsville, Maryland, and was known as the "Catonsville Flash," because of his speed. The 5'7", 170-pound Maisel played third base, second base, and center field and was a player who lacked power and relied on his running ability.

Maisel played five of his six major-league seasons with the Yankees. In 1914, he led the American League with 74 stolen bases. His best season was 1915 when he hit a career-high .281 with 149 base hits and 51 stolen bases.

The only other Yankee to steal second, third, and home in the same inning was outfielder Bob Meusel. On May 16, 1927, Meusel pulled off the rare feat in the third inning of the Yankees' game against the Detroit Tigers at Navin Field.

After Lou Gehrig's solo home run cut the Tigers lead to 2–1, Meusel singled and stole second. Tony Lazzeri walked and with Joe Dugan at the plate, Meusel stole third and home to tie the game.

Meusel's first season coincided with Babe Ruth's inaugural season with the Yankees in 1920. The two became friends despite conflicting personalities. Ruth liked to party while Meusel was a little more reserved.

Meusel played 10 of his 11 major-league seasons with the Yankees, winning three World Series championships. He finished his Yankee career with a .311 average, drove in 100 or more runs five times, and had 1,009 runs batted in. Meusel's best season was 1925 when he led the American League with a career-high 33 home runs to go along with 134 RBIs. Meusel was tied with Detroit's Harry Heilmann for the league lead in runs batted in.

Meusel was part of the famed Murderers' Row, the heart of the famed and powerful Yankee lineup that featured Hall of Famers Ruth, Lou Gehrig, and Tony Lazzeri, who all drove in 100 or more runs in 1927.

The San Jose, California, native did not put up big numbers in World Series play, but he did have some moments.

In Game 5 of the 1923 World Series against the New York Giants at Yankee Stadium, Meusel was 3-for-5 with three RBIs, including a two-run triple that gave the Yankees a 2–0 lead in the bottom of the first inning.

In Game 6 at the Polo Grounds, Meusel capped off a five-run, eighth-inning rally with a two-run single. The hit gave the Yankees the lead, and they went on to a 6–4 win to wrap up their first world championship.

In 1929, Meusel's numbers dropped off, and he was waived after the season.

Name the first Yankee to be hit by a pitch 20 times in one season.

In 1984, Yankees designated hitter Don Baylor became the first player in franchise history to be hit by a pitch 20 times in a single season.

Baylor stood on top of the plate and after getting hit by a pitch, he would merely shrug it off and head to first base. The fearsome right-handed hitter led the American League eight times in getting hit by a pitch. In 1984, Baylor led the Yankees and the major leagues by getting hit 23 times, a franchise record at the time. The next season, Baylor broke his own record by being hit by a pitch 24 times.

Baylor signed a four-year contract to join the Yankees for the 1983 season. In his first season, Baylor slashed .301/.361/.494 with an OPS of .856, along with 21 home runs and 85 RBIs.

The Yankees were in the race for the American League East Division title and Baylor was at his best down the stretch. In the final month, Baylor slashed .349/.400/.551 with a .951 OPS, and won the Silver Slugger Award as the designated hitter, but the Yankees came up short and finished third in the division.

In 1984 and 1985, Baylor hit 50 home runs with 180 runs batted in, but the Yankees failed to win the division and the slugger was feeling the heat from Yankee owner George Steinbrenner.

On March 28, 1986, the Yankees traded Baylor to the rival Boston Red Sox in exchange for left-handed-hitting designated hitter Mike Easler. In his three seasons with the Yankees, Baylor hit 71 home runs and had a slugging percentage of .472.

Who was the first Yankee pitcher to throw the final pitch in two World Series Game 7s?

Right-hander Ralph Terry is the first Yankee pitcher to throw the final pitch in two World Series Game 7s. Terry was the losing pitcher in Game 7 in 1960 and the winner in 1962.

Bill Mazeroski's home run off of Terry on the final pitch of Game 7 of the 1960 World Series loss to the underdog Pittsburgh Pirates was devastating for the Yankees right-hander and the team. Two years later, Terry redeemed himself.

In Game 7 of the 1962 World Series against the San Francisco Giants, Terry's final pitch resulted in a win and a memorable ending.

With the Yankees leading 1–0 in the ninth, a Willie Mays double gave the Giants runners on second and third with two out. The next batter was the Giants' fearsome left-handed hitter, Willie McCovey.

Yankee manager Ralph Houk had a decision to make. Do they walk McCovey to pitch to another dangerous hitter in Orlando Cepeda, a right-handed batter, or do they pitch to McCovey?

At a meeting on the mound, Terry told Houk he wanted to go after McCovey. The memory of Bill Mazeroski had to be on his mind after McCovey lined the first pitch deep down the right field line.

On the 0-1 pitch, McCovey hit a bullet line drive right at second baseman Bobby Richardson, who made the grab despite nearly being knocked down by the game-ending blow. This time, Terry was a winner with a four-hit shutout to lead the Yankees to their 20th World Series championship. Terry made three starts in the Series and finished 2-1 with a 1.80 ERA and was named the Series' Most Valuable Player.

Terry signed with the Yankees in 1953 as a 17-year-old and made his major-league debut in August 1956. Terry was 13-4 at the Yankees' Triple-A affiliate in Denver and earned a win in his first major-league game against the Boston Red Sox at Fenway Park.

The 21-year-old earned a spot on the Yankees pitching staff to start the 1957 season. In early June, Terry pitched a complete-game, three-hit shutout against the Baltimore Orioles. Later that month, he was traded to the Kansas City Athletics as part of a seven-player deal that also included Billy Martin leaving the Yankees. After spending parts of three seasons in Kansas City, Terry was traded back to the Yankees in May 1959.

After posting a 16-3 record in 1961, Terry had his best season in 1962. The Oklahoma native was 23-12 with a 3.19 ERA. Terry made 39 starts, led the American League with 298⅔ innings pitched, and was named to both 1962 All-Star Games.

During the season, Houk would use Terry as a closer. After pitching five innings on July 13 in a loss to the Los Angeles Angels, Terry pitched in relief two days later and got the save in an 8–6, 10-inning win in Kansas City. Two days after that, Terry shutout the Boston Red Sox at Fenway Park with a complete-game four-hitter in a 1–0 win.

Terry won 24 games over the next two seasons with the Yankees. In 1963, he tied for the American League lead with 18 complete games.

Terry was injured to begin the 1964 season and missed the first month. After a rough outing against the Red Sox in June, Terry was relegated to bullpen duty. In August, Terry returned to the starting rotation but he wasn't pitching well and ended up back in the bullpen at the end of the season.

After the 1964 season, Terry was traded to Cleveland as the player to be named later to complete the deal for reliever Pedro Ramos.

The Yankees have had four managers inducted into the Baseball Hall of Fame. Who was the first Yankee manager to be inducted?

In 1957, Joe McCarthy became the first Yankee manager to be inducted into Baseball's Hall of Fame.

McCarthy is considered by many to be one of the greatest managers in the history of baseball. During his 16-year tenure with the Yankees, McCarthy won seven World Series championships and eight American League pennants.

The 5'8" McCarthy was a tough, no-nonsense manager who piloted some of the greatest players in baseball history. Among the players who wore the uniform under him were Babe Ruth, Lou Gehrig, and Joe DiMaggio. McCarthy was nicknamed "Marse Joe," short for "Master Joe," for the strict way he ran his ballclubs.

McCarthy treated all players alike, except when it came to the tempestuous Ruth. The strict skipper basically let Ruth do what he wanted as long he continued to produce. McCarthy realized it would be futile if he quarreled with his star player and better for the team if he just let Ruth be his outgoing self.

Before he came to the Yankees, McCarthy managed the Chicago Cubs for five seasons including 1929 when he won the National League pennant. The Cubs lost the World Series to the Philadelphia Athletics in five games and McCarthy took much of the blame.

Cubs owner P. K. Wrigley lost faith in McCarthy. After the Cubs finished second in 1930, McCarthy did not have his contract renewed. McCarthy reportedly turned down a two-year deal from the Boston Red Sox to become the Yankee manager.

The Yankees won 94 games in 1931, McCarthy's first season, but they finished 13½ games behind the first-place Philadelphia Athletics. The Yankees turned the tables on the A's in 1932 as they won 107 games and won the pennant by 13 games over Philadelphia. By winning the

American League pennant, McCarthy became the first manager to win a pennant in both leagues.

The Yankees beat the Chicago Cubs, McCarthy's former team, in the 1932 World Series with a four-game sweep. It was McCarthy's first World Series championship. He would later refer to it as his "greatest thrill," because it was his first and it came against the Cubs.

The Yankees missed the World Series for three straight seasons from 1933 to 1935, but that drought preceded a run that put McCarthy's Yankees in the upper echelon of greatest teams ever. From 1936 to 1939, McCarthy's Yankees won an unprecedented four straight World Series championships.

After only winning 88 games in 1940, McCarthy won three consecutive American League pennants from 1941 to 1943. The Yankees won the World Series in 1941 and 1943, which was McCarthy's last championship.

A health issue forced McCarthy to retire in May 1946, but he finished his Yankee career with a franchise record 1,460 wins.

Miller Huggins was inducted in 1964. Huggins won three World Series. Casey Stengel, who tied McCarthy with seven World Series titles, was inducted in 1966. Joe Torre, who won four World Series championships from 1996 to 2000, was inducted in 2014.

Since the designated hitter rule debuted in the American League in 1973, very few Yankee pitchers have come to bat. Who was the first Yankee pitcher to be listed in the starting lineup as the designated hitter?

On June 11, 1988, at Yankee Stadium, right-hander Rick Rhoden became the first Yankee pitcher and the first in baseball history to start a game as the designated hitter since the inception of the rule in 1973.

Rhoden was a very good hitting pitcher who hit nine career home runs while he was pitching in the National League. Yankee manager Billy Martin decided to roll the dice by using the right-handed-hitting Rhoden against the Orioles starting pitcher, left-hander Jeff Ballard.

Rhoden batted seventh and made two plate appearances against the Baltimore Orioles. In the bottom of the third, Rhoden batted against Ballard and grounded out to third.

Rhoden came up with runners on first and third and one out in the bottom of the fourth and drove in a run with a sacrifice fly to left field to give the Yankees a 3–0 lead. José Cruz pinch-hit for Rhoden when his spot came up in the bottom of the fifth inning.

Rhoden was a former first-round pick (20th overall) of the Los Angeles Dodgers in the 1971 MLB June Amateur Draft. The Yankees acquired Rhoden from the Pittsburgh Pirates after the 1986 season along with pitchers Pat Clements and Cecilio Guante in exchange for pitchers Doug Drabek, Brian Fisher, and Logan Easley. Being a 10-year veteran, Rhoden had veto power over the deal, but the Yankees reworked his contract and he agreed to come to New York.

The Boynton Beach, Florida, native had a very good first season in New York in 1987. Rhoden led the team with 16 wins and a 3.86 ERA. Rhoden made 29 starts with two complete games. He went seven or more innings 10 times during the season and was especially good at Yankee Stadium, going 10-3 with a 3.29 ERA.

Rhoden was the Opening Day starter in 1988, and he pitched his best game during his two-year Yankee tenure. The 35-year-old tossed a three-hit, complete-game shutout of the Minnesota Twins at Yankee Stadium.

Rhoden finished the 1988 season with a 12-12 record and a 4.29 ERA in 30 starts. After the season, the Yankees traded Rhoden to the Houston Astros.

Who was the first Yankee to steal 80 bases in a single season?

Hall of Famer Rickey Henderson was the first Yankee to have 80 stolen bases in a single season.

In his first season with the Yankees in 1985, Henderson led the American League with 80 steals while being caught only 10 times, an 89 percent success rate.

The Yankees acquired Henderson in December 1984 as part of a blockbuster, seven-player deal. The talented outfielder was not just a speed merchant. Henderson is considered by many to be the greatest leadoff hitter in baseball history, and he spent parts of five seasons with the Yankees.

In 1985, Henderson was the catalyst atop a potent Yankee lineup that featured American League MVP Don Mattingly, Hall of Famer

Dave Winfield, Ken Griffey Sr., Don Baylor, and Willie Randolph. The Yankees led the major leagues with 839 runs scored, with Henderson scoring a major-league-leading 146 runs. Henderson, who was an All-Star and Silver Slugger Award winner, slashed .324/.419/.516 with an OPS of .934 and finished third in the voting (to his teammate Mattingly) for the AL MVP award. Henderson also hit 24 home runs and became the first Yankee and first major leaguer to hit over 20 homers and steal 80 bases in the same season.

Henderson led the AL in runs (130) and stolen bases (87) for a second consecutive season in 1986, but the 1987 season would be filled with controversy.

Henderson reportedly injured his hamstring in late May and the severity of the injury became an issue. A few days after suffering the initial injury, Henderson reinjured the hamstring and missed 25 days. After his return in late June, Henderson injured himself once again in late July. He wouldn't return until September 1.

Yankee manager Lou Piniella did not believe Henderson was hurt badly enough that he missed so much time and ended up playing only 95 games. Piniella was fired after the 1987 season and replaced by Billy Martin, who was rehired for a fifth time. Henderson enjoyed playing for Martin, who was also his manager in Oakland in the early 1980s. In his first two seasons with the Yankees, Henderson was the starting center fielder. Martin returned him to his more familiar spot in left field in 1988, and he returned to form as he scored 118 runs and broke his own Yankee record with 93 stolen bases.

Martin was fired after the 1988 season and replaced by Dallas Green. Henderson got off to a slow start and in June 1989, he was traded back to the Oakland Athletics.

During his five-year tenure with the Yankees, Henderson had 326 stolen bases, which was a franchise record until it was broken by Derek Jeter in May 2011.

The New York Yankees (nee New York Highlanders) franchise history began in 1913. Who was the first winning pitcher in Yankees' franchise history?

On April 15, 1913, the New York Yankees beat the Boston Red Sox 3–2 at Fenway Park for the team's first ever win. Right-hander Ray Keating, a Bridgeport, Connecticut, native, was the first winning pitcher in franchise history.

Keating went the distance, giving up two unearned runs on eight hits with no walks and five strikeouts in the Yankees' third game of the season. Keating was the winning pitcher in the first three wins in franchise history as they started the season with a 3-15 record.

Keating played semipro ball in Bridgeport, and pitched for Niagara University before the Yankees purchased his contract from the minor-league Lawrence Barristers of the New England League during the 1912 season. Keating was a September callup and the 18-year-old made five starts and was 0-3.

In 1913, Keating made 21 starts and was 6-12 with a respectable 3.21 ERA for a Yankee team that finished 37 games under .500.

In late April, he pitched a complete-game, three-hit shutout against a Philadelphia Athletics lineup that featured Hall of Famers Eddie Col-

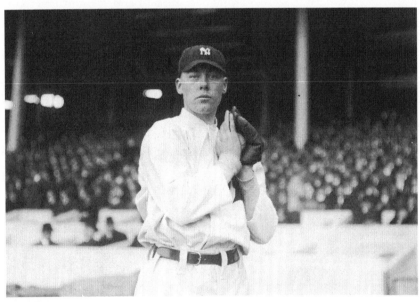

Ray Keating
LIBRARY OF CONGRESS

lins and Frank "Home Run" Baker. Later in the season, Keating twirled a shutout against Hall of Famer Ty Cobb and the Detroit Tigers.

In 1914, Keating set career highs in games started (25), wins (8), and innings pitched (210). He also learned how to scuff the ball with emery paper, something that caught Collins's attention when the teams met later that season.

According to an article in the *New Castle Herald*, dated September 14, 1914, Collins struck out in the first inning and then issued a complaint to umpire Tommy Connolly. At the end of the half inning, Connolly asked for Keating's glove and found emery paper in the hollowed-out portion. The glove was confiscated and Athletics manager Connie Mack played the game under protest, but Keating went the distance in a 2–1 win.

A few days later, American League president Ban Johnson ordered all managers to stop their pitchers from using the "emery ball." Johnson said any player found with emery paper would automatically be suspended for 30 days and fined $100.

Keating went 5-6 with a 3.07 ERA in 1916, but after the season his contract was sold to Toledo of the American Association where he pitched the 1917 season.

The Yankees reacquired Keating in July 1918, and he pitched in 15 games before he was sold to the Boston Braves before the 1919 season.

Who was the first Yankee to have 170 singles in a season?

In 1989, second baseman Steve Sax became the first Yankee to have 170 singles in a single season. Sax finished with 171, breaking the previous all-time franchise record of 167 that was set by the New York Highlanders' "Wee" Willie Keeler in 1906.

The former National League Rookie of the Year in 1982, Sax spent the first eight seasons of his career with the Los Angeles Dodgers, where he was a three-time All-Star. He was a free agent after the 1988 season. After talks with the Dodgers stalled, Sax decided to sign with the Yankees, who had opted to move on from fan favorite Willie Randolph.

Sax had a fantastic first season with the Yankees in 1989. The second baseman led the team in batting average (.315), hits (205), runs (88), and stolen bases (43) and was an All-Star for the fourth time, first as a Yankee. Unfortunately, the team won only 74 games and had an in-season managerial change as Dallas Green was fired and replaced by Bucky Dent.

Sax played only two more seasons with the Yankees. In 1990, he made the All-Star team, but his numbers dropped off from the previous season.

Sax slashed .304/.345/.414 with an OPS of .759 in 1991, his final season in New York. The Yankees won 71 games and decided to go with promising young second baseman Pat Kelly in 1992.

Sax was traded to the Chicago White Sox for three right-handed pitchers, Domingo Jean, Mélido Pérez, and Bob Wickman. Jean's major-league career consisted of 10 major-league games, all for the Yankees during the 1993 season. Pérez was a promising young right-hander who had spent the previous four seasons with the White Sox.

The Yankees were well aware of what Pérez could do. During the 1990 season, Pérez threw a rain-shortened, six-inning no-hitter against the Yankees at Yankee Stadium. The game originally counted as a no-hitter, but Major League Baseball later ruled that no-hitters had to be, at a minimum, nine innings so it was removed from the record books.

In 1992, Pérez was anointed the ace of the Yankee staff and tied a career-high of 13 wins with a 2.87 ERA. The Dominican-born pitcher played in three more seasons with the Yankees, but his career ended after he tore an elbow ligament during the 1995 season.

Wickman became a reliable middle reliever with the Yankees from 1992 until August 1996, when he was traded to the Milwaukee Brewers as part of a six-player deal.

In the inaugural baseball Amateur Draft in 1965, the Yankees had the 19th overall pick. Who did the Yankees select as their first ever Amateur Draft pick?

The Yankees selected pitcher Bill Burbach, a 6'4" right-hander out of Wahlert High School in Dubuque, Iowa. Unfortunately, Burbach never lived up to the status of being a first-round pick as his career lasted only three seasons.

Burbach made his major-league debut in 1969 and was the fourth starter in the Yankees' rotation. He appeared in 31 games, 24 starts, and was 6-8 with a 3.65 ERA.

Burbach made his debut on April 11 against the Detroit Tigers at Tiger Stadium and gave up one earned run in six innings while getting a no decision in the Yankees' 9–4 win. In his second career start on April 20, Burbach tossed the only shutout of his career as he blanked the Tigers on five hits at Yankee Stadium. The 21-year-old had his ups and downs in his first season and ended up in the bullpen for the last five weeks.

Over the next two seasons, Burbach would only appear in a total of six games. In 1970, he spent most of the season in the minors and pitched in only four games for the Yankees. The next season, Burbach made two relief appearances in April. He was in the minors when he was traded in May to the Baltimore Orioles for pitcher Jim Hardin, who lasted half a season.

Two years later, the Yankees held their first ever, first overall pick in the 1967 Amateur Draft. The Yankees selected Ron Blomberg, a three-sport star from Atlanta. Being of the Jewish faith and coming to New York City which had a very large Jewish population, Blomberg seemed like a perfect match for the Yankees.

Blomberg spent his first three professional seasons in the minors and was a September callup in 1969. In 1970, Blomberg was promoted to Syracuse, the Yankees' Triple-A affiliate, but injuries limited him to half the season. Blomberg spent the first few months of the 1971 season with Syracuse and was batting .326 with six home runs and 20 runs batted in when he was recalled in June to replace injured outfielder Roy White.

On June 25, the Yankees hosted the Washington Senators and Blomberg started in right field. The left-handed slugger took advantage of the right field dimensions at Yankee Stadium and hit his first major-league home run, deep into the right field stands, off of Washington Senators pitcher Pete Broberg.

Despite playing only 64 games in 1971, Blomberg put up some impressive numbers. He slashed .322/.363/.477 with an OPS of .840 with seven home runs and 31 runs batted in. In 1972, the Yankees moved

Blomberg to first base where he platooned with Felipe Alou. Blomberg's batting average dropped off to .269, but he had a career-high 14 home runs along with 49 runs batted in.

Blomberg made history in 1973 when the American League adopted the designated hitter. The Yankees were scheduled to play the Red Sox at Fenway Park in the season opener and because of the 1:30 p.m. start time, that game would feature the first at-bat by a designated hitter in baseball history. Blomberg was batting sixth as the Yankees' first designated hitter, while the Red Sox had Hall of Famer Orlando Cepeda as their DH, batting fifth.

Blomberg came to bat in the top of the first. With two out and the bases loaded. Blomberg walked to force in a run and record the first RBI by a DH in baseball history. Cepeda was 0-for-6 in the game, so Blomberg had the first hit by a (major-league) designated hitter when he singled in the third inning. After the game, Blomberg's bat and jersey were sent to the Baseball Hall of Fame in Cooperstown.

In the first half of the season, Blomberg played mostly at first base, but he was the designated hitter against right-handed pitchers for almost all of the second half. He had his best overall season in 1973. Blomberg slashed .329/.395/.498 with an OPS of .893 and a career-high 57 runs batted in.

In 1974, the Yankees were playing the first of two seasons at Shea Stadium, while Yankee Stadium was being renovated, so Blomberg would not have the advantage of the short right field dimensions at the Bronx ballpark. Blomberg batted .311 with 10 home runs and 48 RBIs in 1974, but injuries began to curtail his career.

In May 1975, Blomberg suffered a shoulder injury that kept him out for six weeks. He returned in June but tore a muscle in his right shoulder in July and was done for the year after playing in only 34 games. It was a precursor to the end of Blomberg's career.

In the final exhibition game of the 1976 season, Blomberg hurt his shoulder once again. He underwent surgery and appeared in only one more game for the Yankees in September.

Blomberg recovered to join the Yankees in spring training in 1977, but he missed the entire regular season after tearing cartilage and breaking his kneecap during an exhibition game. The Yankees won the World Series and Blomberg was voted a full share of the World Series pot.

After the season, Blomberg became a free agent and signed with the Chicago White Sox where he played his final major-league season in 1978.

Over the years, the Yankees have had some memorable first-round picks. In 1968, one year after selecting Blomberg, the Yankees took a catcher from Kent State University named Thurman Munson.

In 1991, the Yankees had the number one overall pick in the draft and they chose Brien Taylor, a highly touted left-handed pitcher out of East Carteret High School in North Carolina. Unfortunately, Taylor injured his shoulder during an altercation in December 1993. The young pitcher was never the same and never threw a pitch in the major leagues.

The following year, the Yankees had the sixth overall pick and selected shortstop Derek Jeter out of Kalamazoo Central High School in Kalamazoo, Michigan.

Who was the first Yankee designated hitter to hit a home run?

Third baseman/outfielder Jim Ray Hart was the first Yankee designated hitter to hit a home run.

On May 18, 1973, Hart was in the lineup as the designated hitter when he hit a solo home run off of Milwaukee Brewers pitcher Skip Lockwood in the sixth inning at Yankee Stadium. Hart thus became the first Yankee DH to hit a home run.

The DH rule began in the 1973 season, but it took 34 games for a Yankee starting DH to hit a homer. Ron Blomberg made history as the first ever designated hitter to come to bat, but he did not hit a home run as a DH until July 11.

After playing parts of 11 seasons with the San Francisco Giants where he was an All-Star and finished second in the National League Rookie of the Year voting in 1964, Hart's contract was sold to the Yankees in April 1973.

Hart was not a good defensive player, so the Yankees felt he would thrive as the right-handed portion of a DH platoon with Blomberg. The right-handed-hitting slugger got off to a fast start with the Yankees. In his first five games, Hart was 10-for-26 (.385) with five runs batted in.

Hart appeared in 114 games with the Yankees in 1973, but did not play one game in the field. He hit .254 with 13 home runs and 52 RBIs.

In 1974, Hart started the season 1-for-19 (.053) and was sent to Triple-A Syracuse. The Yankees released him in July.

On May 12, 1973, the Yankees hosted the Baltimore Orioles at Yankee Stadium. In the seventh inning, Celerino Sánchez pinch-hit for Blomberg, who entered the game as a pinch-hitter for Hart, the starting DH. That home run is in the record books as a pinch-hit home run, not one that was technically hit by a designated hitter. Sánchez homered off of Orioles pitcher Mickey Scott and stayed in the game as the DH, but that would be the only major-league home run of his career.

Sánchez had a very modest career that lasted two seasons and 105 games. The Yankees acquired the 28-year-old third baseman out of the Mexican League in a trade with the Mexico City Tigers. Sánchez was an outstanding defensive third baseman who didn't hit with power but could drive in some runs.

Sánchez began the 1972 season with Syracuse, the Yankees' Triple-A affiliate, and was slashing .327/.358/.491 with an OPS of .849 and 28 RBIs in 43 games.

The Yankees penciled in Rich McKinney as their third baseman for the 1972 season. McKinney was acquired from the Chicago White Sox during the offseason in a controversial trade that sent pitcher Stan Bahnsen, former American League Rookie of the Year, to Chicago. McKinney was disappointing at the plate and in the field as evidenced by a record-tying four-error game against the Boston Red Sox at Fenway Park in late April. The Yankees decided to flip the two players. McKinney was sent to Syracuse and Sánchez was promoted in June.

In his first of two major-league seasons, Sánchez was an upgrade defensively. In 71 games, he hit .248 but his OBP was .292 and he slugged .304 with no home runs and 21 runs batted in. Sánchez played 34 games in his final season of 1973.

McKinney was recalled in September and played six more games for the Yankees. In December 1972, McKinney was traded to the Oakland Athletics as the player to be named later from an earlier deal that brought outfielder Matty Alou and pitcher Rob Gardner to the Yankees.

The Yankees' franchise history has featured many home-run feats. Who was the first Yankee to hit a home run in eight straight games?

During the 1987 season, first baseman Don Mattingly became the first Yankee to hit a home run in eight straight games.

Mattingly's streak set an American League record and tied a major-league record. Dale Long of the Pittsburgh Pirates set the mark in 1956, and it was later tied by Seattle's Ken Griffey Jr. in 1993.

On July 8, 1987, Mattingly hit two home runs against the Minnesota Twins at Yankee Stadium to begin the streak. The Yankee first baseman tied the American League record of six straight games with a home run on July 16, when he hit a grand slam home run off of Texas Rangers' knuckleball pitcher Charlie Hough at Arlington Stadium and added a two-run shot for a total of seven runs batted in. The next night, Mattingly set a new American League record when he hit a solo home run off of Rangers' left-handed pitcher Paul Kilgus to extend his streak to seven straight games.

The streak was garnering a lot of attention from around the baseball world, but Mattingly was not one to wilt under the pressure. On July 18, Mattingly tied the major-league record when he hit a solo home run off of Rangers pitcher José Guzmán in the fourth inning.

Mattingly went for the record the next night, but came up short. He had two hits, but none that left the ballpark. During the eight-game streak, Mattingly hit 10 home runs, including two grand slams, drove in 21 runs, and batted .459 with an eye-opening slugging percentage of 1.324.

Mattingly is widely considered the second-best first baseman in Yankee history behind Lou Gehrig. He's the only Yankee player to have his number retired that did not appear in a World Series.

The Evansville, Indiana, native played all 14 of his major-league seasons with the Yankees. Mattingly won a batting title in 1984. He was a six-time All-Star, nine-time Gold Glove Award winner, three-time Silver Slugger Award winner, and was the American League MVP in 1985.

Mattingly was a three-sport star (baseball, football, and basketball) at Reitz Memorial High School in Evansville. Most clubs thought he would go to college, so he dropped to the 19th round when the Yankees selected him in the 1979 MLB June Amateur Draft.

From the moment Mattingly made his professional debut as an 18-year-old at Oneonta of the New York–Penn League, it was clear that he was a very good hitter. Mattingly played 53 games at Oneonta and batted .349 with 31 RBIs.

In 1980, Mattingly moved up to A ball where he put up some impressive numbers at Greensboro. Mattingly led the league with a .358 average. His .422 OBP and .498 slugging percentage gave him an OPS of .920 with nine home runs and 105 runs batted in.

It was a steady progression for Mattingly through the Yankees' minor-league system. In 1981, he played for the Double-A Nashville team and then was promoted to the Triple-A affiliate in Columbus for the 1982 season. After batting .315 with 10 home runs and 75 RBIs, Mattingly was called up to the Yankees in September.

Mattingly made his major-league debut at Yankee Stadium on September 8, 1982, as a defensive replacement. Mattingly's first hit came three weeks later when he singled off Boston Red Sox pitcher Steve Crawford in the bottom of the 11th inning of a 3–2 loss at Yankee Stadium. Mattingly was 2-for-12 in his first taste of big-league pitching.

Mattingly began the 1983 season at Columbus. After 43 games, he was hitting .340 with eight home runs and 37 RBIs. On June 12, veteran Bobby Murcer announced his retirement and Mattingly was promoted to take his spot on the roster.

Mattingly played more games in the outfield than he did at first base in 1983, but he was at first when Dave Righetti tossed a no-hitter on July 4 on Yankee owner George Steinbrenner's birthday.

On June 2, Mattingly went deep against Boston Red Sox left-handed pitcher John Tudor at Fenway Park for his first career home run. In August, Mattingly slashed .356/.406/.563 with an OPS of .970, but he struggled in the final month.

On July 24, 1983, the Yankees and Kansas City Royals played what came to be known as the "Pine Tar Game." George Brett's two-run, two-out go-ahead home run in the ninth inning was negated by the umpires, who called him out for using an illegal bat. According to the rule book, the amount of pine tar (used to improve the grip) on the bat could not exceed 18 inches from its end. American League president Lee MacPhail later ruled that the home run would count and that the game would be resumed from that point and completed on August 18.

Mattingly had entered the game as a pinch-hitter in the seventh and stayed at first base. When the game resumed in August, Mattingly, a left-handed thrower, was at second base. In a 1986 game in Seattle, Mattingly played five innings at third base and handled six chances flawlessly, including starting a 5-4-3 double play.

In 1984, Yankee manager Yogi Berra named Mattingly as his starting first baseman and he responded with a breakout season. At the All-Star break, Mattingly was hitting .330 with 12 home runs and 53 runs batted in and was named to the All-Star team for the first time.

The Yankees were not in contention for the American League's East Division title in 1984 as they trailed the front-running Detroit Tigers by 20 games in July, so the focus shifted to the remarkable season that Mattingly was putting together. Similar to 1961, when Yankee teammates Roger Maris and Mickey Mantle were vying to break Babe Ruth's single-season home-run record, Mattingly and teammate Dave Winfield were vying for the American League batting title in 1984.

Entering September, Mattingly was batting .352 and Winfield was at .351. With a week left in the season, Mattingly was leading the league with a .344 average, while Winfield was at .341.

The race for the batting title came down to the final day of the season. Winfield had pulled ahead by two percentage points (.341 to .339), but he had one hit in the final game to finish at .340. Mattingly had four hits and won the batting championship with a .343 average.

Mattingly led off the bottom of the eighth with his fourth hit but was forced at second by Winfield in his final at-bat. Both players were given an ovation as they left the field together.

Mattingly's greatest season was 1985 when he was named the American League's Most Valuable Player. The Yankees had acquired Hall of Famer Rickey Henderson during the offseason to set the table for the Yankee lineup in 1985, and Mattingly capitalized on his presence by producing a career-high 145 runs batted in. Henderson scored a league-leading 146 runs with 55 of those coming as a result of hits by Mattingly.

The Yankee first baseman led the league in RBIs, doubles (48), and total bases with 370. Mattingly also won his first Gold Glove Award and first Silver Slugger Award in 1985. The Yankees won 97 games but finished two games behind the Toronto Blue Jays in the AL East, as Mattingly came up short in his quest to play in the postseason.

Mattingly was in contention for a second straight MVP award in 1986. The left-handed-hitting first baseman hit a career high .352, second to Boston's Wade Boggs (.357) for the batting title. Mattingly also led the league with a career-high 238 hits, a career-high .573 slugging percentage, and a career-high OPS of .967, while capturing his second Gold Glove and Silver Slugger awards.

Mattingly continued to be one of the most productive players in baseball in 1987. Despite missing 21 games due to a back issue, he hit .327 with 30 home runs and 115 RBIs and finished seventh in the MVP voting.

Late in the 1987 season, Mattingly set a major-league record by hitting his sixth grand slam of the season. The record-setting blow came on September 29 at Yankee Stadium against the Boston Red Sox. In the bottom of the third, Mattingly came up with the bases full against Red Sox left-hander Bruce Hurst. On a 1-2 pitch, Mattingly unloaded on a hanging breaking ball and drove it into the upper deck in right field for a grand slam to break the record of five in one season that was previously held by Chicago Cubs Hall of Famer Ernie Banks (1955) and Baltimore Orioles first baseman Jim Gentile (1961). (Cleveland Indians DH Travis Hafner tied the record in 2006.)

The back problem that cost Mattingly 21 games in 1987 was the beginning of a chronic problem that would continue to plague the Yankee first baseman for the remainder of his career. Mattingly's power numbers began to drop off in 1988 with 18 home runs but in 1989, he had his final season of 20-plus home runs (23) and 100-plus runs batted in (113).

Mattingly got off to a very slow start in 1990. Going into June, the Yankee first baseman had only five home runs and 24 runs batted in. Mattingly's skills had begun to wane due to his chronic back problem.

In early July, Mattingly went on the disabled list with back spasms and stiffness. He returned on July 14 but went back on the DL on July

Don Mattingly
WIKIMEDIA COMMONS

26. Mattingly was activated in mid-September but did not hit another home run and finished the season with his lowest power numbers since he became a regular player in 1984.

After an offseason of rigorous treatment for his back, Mattingly was named the captain of the Yankees in March 1991, but his numbers were still below the standards that he set in the 1980s. In the first half of the 1991 season, Mattingly was batting over .300, but he had only six home runs and 34 runs batted in. Mattingly ended up playing in 152 games in 1991 and finished with a .288 batting average and nine home runs with 68 runs batted in.

In 1992 and 1993, Mattingly combined for 31 home runs and had 86 RBIs in each of those two seasons, but as had been the case since he debuted in 1982, the Yankees were not in the postseason.

The Yankees won 12 more games in 1993 than they did in 1992, but 1994 was probably Mattingly's most frustrating season. The Yankees were a first-place team and looked like they would finally give Mattingly his chance to play in the postseason. Mattingly was 33 years old in 1994, but he was still productive, although not to the levels that he produced earlier in his career.

On August 11, the Yankees lost to the Toronto Blue Jays in extra innings, but they were 70-43 and in first place in the AL East with a 6½-game lead over second-place Baltimore. But a labor issue would wreck the season. The players went on strike on August 12 and the season, along with the World Series, was canceled and Mattingly was denied entry into the postseason once again.

The 1995 season would see baseball expand into three divisions in each league and mark the debut of the wild card. The second-place team with the best record from the three divisions would make the playoffs as the wild card team. The season was only 144 games because the strike from the previous season was not settled until early April 1995, so it was not feasible to play a full 162-game season.

An eight-game losing streak in late August left the Yankees at 53-58. They were 15½ games behind the front-running Boston Red Sox, but they were only 5½ games behind the Texas Rangers in the AL wild card race. From that point on, the Yankees went on a tear and Mattingly was right in the middle of their late-season surge.

Over the final 33 games, the Yankees went 26-7. Mattingly played the final 28 games of the regular season and slashed .321/.359/.472 with an OPS of .831 as the Yankees went 22-6 in those games.

The Yankees merely needed to beat the Toronto Blue Jays in Toronto on the final day of the regular season and they would end a 14-year playoff drought and get Mattingly into the postseason for the first time in his career. It appeared Mattingly, who was revered by teammates and opponents, was the inspirational force that helped the Yankees make this remarkable run.

The Yankees beat the Blue Jays 6–1 as Mattingly had two hits, including a solo home run. When the final out was recorded, Mattingly took a few steps toward the pitcher's mound and got on one knee and pounded the turf as if to say, "finally."

The Yankees played the AL West Division–winning Seattle Mariners in the best of five American League Division Series with the first two games scheduled for Yankee Stadium.

A crowd of over 57,000 was on hand to see their beloved first baseman play in his first postseason game. During the pregame player introductions, Mattingly received a thunderous standing ovation. There was another standing ovation when Mattingly came to bat in the bottom of the second as he flied out to right.

Mattingly gave the crowd what they came to see when he snapped a 2–2 tie in the sixth inning with an RBI single for his first postseason hit, scoring Bernie Williams with the go-ahead run. He added a double in the eighth as the Yankees beat Seattle 9–4 to take Game 1.

Mattingly gave the fans even more reason to roar in Game 2. The Yanks trailed the Mariners 2–1 in the bottom of the sixth inning, but Rubén Sierra led off the inning with a home run off of Mariners pitcher Andy Benes to tie the game at 2.

Mattingly was next and on a 1-0 pitch, he drove a ball into the right-center field bleachers to give the Yankees a 3–2 lead. The Stadium exploded and fans began throwing things on the field, so Mariners manager Lou Piniella temporarily took his team off the field.

The Yankees went on to beat Seattle 7–5 in 15 innings on Jim Leyritz's walkoff two-run home run. Mattingly was 3-for-6 with an RBI in the game as the Yankees seemed primed to move on to their first appearance in the American League Championship Series since 1981.

Unfortunately, the Yankees lost all three games in Seattle, including a heartbreaking 6–5 loss in 11 innings in Game 5. When Seattle's Ken Griffey Jr. slid across the plate with the game-winning run in the bottom of the 11th inning, it marked the end of Mattingly's career.

Despite the loss, Mattingly acquitted himself very well in his only postseason appearance. In five games, Mattingly led the team with 10 hits and slashed .417/.440/.708 with an OPS of 1.148 with a home run and six runs batted in.

After the season, Mattingly did not formally retire but said he would sit out the 1996 season. The Yankees moved on and acquired first baseman Tino Martinez in a trade with Seattle as it was apparent that Mattingly was not going to play again.

Mattingly announced his retirement in January 1997. In August, the Yankees held Don Mattingly Day and retired his #23.

Who was the first Yankee pitcher to throw a complete-game shutout in an American League Championship Series game?

Roger Clemens tossed a complete-game, one-hit shutout against the Seattle Mariners in Game 4 of the 2000 American League Championship Series. Clemens became the first Yankee to toss a complete-game shutout in an ALCS game, but he nearly entered the record books with one of the great performances in postseason history.

On October 14, 2000, Clemens pitched the most dominant game of his Yankee tenure at Safeco Field in Seattle as the Yankees beat the Mariners, 5–0. Clemens gave up one hit with an ALCS record 15 strikeouts to become the first Yankee pitcher to toss a complete-game shutout in an American League Championship Series game.

The seven-time Cy Young Award winner was in complete command as he no-hit the Mariners through the first six innings. Clemens opened the game with back-to-back strikeouts and then walked Alex Rodriguez with two out, but Hall of Famer Edgar Martínez fouled out to end the inning.

Clemens rolled from there as he set down 16 hitters in a row. Derek Jeter hit a three-run home run in the fifth to give Clemens some runs to work with.

Seattle's Al Martin led off the bottom of the seventh with the first and only hit off of Clemens, a line drive double down the right field line. The ball glanced off the glove of first baseman Tino Martinez, who made a valiant, leaping attempt to snare the hit.

Clemens bore down and struck out Rodriguez and Martínez before he walked Mariners first baseman John Olerud on a 3-2 pitch. With runners on first and second and the tying run at the plate, Clemens painted a 3-2 fastball on the outside corner to get Mike Cameron looking and end the Mariners only threat of the game.

Yankees left fielder David Justice hit a two-run home run to make it 5–0, and Clemens finished it off by retiring the final six Seattle hitters, four by strikeout, in the final two innings. In the Seattle ninth, Clemens struck out Martin for the second out and his 15th strikeout, and then got Rodriguez on a groundout to end a memorable performance.

Yankee owner George Steinbrenner always had an affection for Clemens. He tried to acquire Clemens when he first became a free agent after the 1996 season, but the right-hander opted to sign with the Toronto Blue Jays. After Clemens won back-to-back Cy Young Awards in 1997 and 1998, Toronto traded him to the Yankees for pitchers David Wells and Graeme Lloyd and utility player Homer Bush.

In his first season with the Yankees, Clemens was 14-10 with a 4.60 ERA. In a little over 187 innings, Clemens had 163 strikeouts, which were pedestrian numbers for a pitcher of his caliber.

The Yankees were back in the playoffs and Clemens tossed seven shutout innings in the clinching Game 3 of the American League Division Series against the Texas Rangers at the Ballpark in Arlington.

Roger Clemens
KEITH ALLISON VIA WIKIMEDIA COMMONS

His next start was not so stellar.

Clemens matched up with Hall of Famer and Red Sox ace Pedro Martínez in Game 3 of the American League Championship Series at Fenway Park. Martínez was his dominant self, but Clemens was rocked for five runs in two innings in an embarrassing outing.

Clemens went back out for the third inning and gave up a lead-off single to Mike Stanley. Clemens threw one more pitch that Brian Daubach fouled off before Yankee manager Joe Torre came out to get his right-hander. Clemens left the field to the delight of the Red Sox faithful and was replaced by Hideki Irabu.

Daubach hit a two-run home run off of Irabu, and Clemens's line was done. The game got out of hand as the Red Sox won 13–1 to hand the Yankees one of their worst postseason losses in franchise history.

Clemens redeemed himself in the 1999 World Series against the Atlanta Braves. In the series-clinching Game 4 at Yankee Stadium, Clemens gave up a run in 7⅔ innings as the Yankees won their second consecutive World Series with a 4–1 win.

In 2000, Clemens was 13-8 with an ERA of 3.70, nearly a run better than his previous season with the Yankees. During the season, Clemens was involved in a controversial incident that set a tone for the rest of the season.

On July 8, the Yankees hosted the New York Mets at Yankee Stadium. In the top of the first, Clemens hit Mike Piazza in the helmet with a pitch that outraged the Mets. Piazza had enormous success in his career against Clemens, and the Mets felt the pitch was intentional.

Adding fuel to the fire was the fact that the teams would end up meeting in the 2000 World Series, with Clemens scheduled to start Game 2 at Yankee Stadium In their first meeting since the incident in July, Piazza broke his bat while hitting a foul ball. Part of the bat broke off and went in Clemens's direction. Clemens picked up the barrel of the bat and threw it toward the first base line while Piazza was running in that direction. The two stars began yelling at each other while both benches emptied. No one was ejected and Clemens went on to pitch eight shutout innings as the Yankees won Game 2.

Clemens set a major-league record when he began the 2001 season with a 20-1 record. Clemens lost his first decision of the season in late May and then rolled off 16 straight wins.

On September 5, Clemens beat the Toronto Blue Jays to go 19-1 but had to wait 13 days to make his next start due to the 9/11 attacks. On September 19, Clemens won his 20th for the first and only time as a Yankee when he bested the Chicago White Sox at Comiskey Park. Clemens finished the season 20-3 with a 3.51 ERA.

Clemens was at his best in the 2001 World Series loss to the Arizona Diamondbacks. With the Yankees trailing two games to none, Clemens started Game 3 at Yankee Stadium and gave up a run in seven innings to earn the win and get the Yankees back in the Series.

Clemens got the nod in Game 7 in Arizona and matched Curt Schilling's brilliance to give the Yankees a chance to win. Clemens gave up one run in 6⅓ innings pitched and left the game with the score tied 1–1, but Arizona eventually won Game 7 and the Series.

In 2003, Clemens closed in on 300 career wins. He recorded career win #299 on May 21 when he beat the Red Sox at Fenway Park. He had three starts to reach the coveted milestone but failed each time.

Finally, on Friday, June 13, Clemens beat the St. Louis Cardinals at Yankee Stadium to join the 300 Win Club. In the top of the second inning, Clemens struck out Cardinals shortstop Édgar Rentería swinging to become the third pitcher in history to reach 4,000 strikeouts (Nolan Ryan and Steve Carlton were the other two).

During the 2003 season, Clemens announced he would retire after the season. It appeared that Game 4 of the 2003 World Series against the Florida Marlins at Pro Player Stadium would be Clemens's final appearance, but he returned in 2004 to sign with the Houston Astros.

After three seasons in Houston, Clemens retired again but came out of retirement again in 2007 when he returned to the Yankees. The 44-year-old joined the team in June and went 6-6.

In what was his final appearance, Clemens started Game 3 of the American League Division Series against the Cleveland Indians and got a no decision when he gave up three runs in 2⅓ innings.

GLOSSARY OF MODERN STATISTICAL TERMS

OBP
On-Base Percentage

OPS
On-Base Percentage Plus Slugging Percentage

OPS+
On-Base Percentage Plus Slugging Percentage, normalized for park factors

Slash Line
Batting Average/On-Base Percentage/Slugging Percentage

WAR
Wins Above Replacement

REFERENCES

BOOKS AND PERIODICALS

2022 New York Yankees Official Media Guide and Record Book. New York: MLB Advanced Media, LP, 2022.

Appel, Marty. *Pinstripe Empire: The New York Yankees from Before the Babe to After the Boss*. New York: Bloomsbury, 2012.

Fischer, David. *The New York Yankees of the 1950s: Mantle, Stengel, Berra and a Decade of Dominance*. Guilford, CT: Lyons Press, 2019.

Pennington, Bill. *Chumps to Champs: How the Worst Teams in Yankees History Led to the '90s Dynasty*. New York: Mariner Books, 2019.

Pepitone, Joe, with Berry Stainback. *Joe, You Coulda Made Us Proud*. New York: Sports Publishing, 2015.

WEBSITES

baseball-almanac.com
baseballhall.org
baseball-reference.com
sabr.org
spotrac.com
yogiberramuseum.org

ACKNOWLEDGMENTS

I must start with my lovely wife, Kathy Block Karpin. I wouldn't be publishing any books if she weren't a big part of my life.

I would also like to thank my sons, Danny and Jake, and their wonderful wives, Emmy Karpin and Anita Pino, Carol and Barry Shore, Wendy Shore Rosano, Sharon Shore-Berrios, and Israel Berrios. I'm lucky to have such a great family.

Lastly, I would like to thank all my friends, from childhood friends, to all my softball friends, to the many friends that I've met along the way during my professional career.